5 Blueprint

The True
Costs of Road
Transport

5

Blueprint

The True Costs of Road Transport

David Maddison
David Pearce
Olof Johansson
Edward Calthrop
Todd Litman
Eric Verhoef

CENTRE FOR SOCIAL AND ECONOMIC RESEARCH ON THE GLOBAL ENVIRONMENT

C|S|E|R|G|E

Earthscan Publications Ltd, London

First published in the UK in 1996 by
Earthscan Publications Limited

Reprinted 1997, 1999

A catalogue record for this book is available from the British Library

ISBN: 1 85383 268 5

Typesetting, figures and page design by PCS Mapping & DTP,
Newcastle upon Tyne

Printed and bound by Clays Ltd, St Ives plc

For a full list of publications please contact:
Earthscan Publications Limited
120 Pentonville Road
London N1 9JN
Tel: (0171) 278 0433
Fax: (0171) 278 1142

Earthscan is an editorially independent subsidiary of Kogan Page Limited
and publishes in association with WWF-UK and the International Institute
for Environment and Development.

Contents

Part I The Theoretical Background

Part II The External Costs Of Road Transport
In The United Kingdom

Part III International Case Studies

Boxes

Notes On The Authors

David Maddison is Research Fellow in CSERGE at University College London, Gower St, London, WC1E 6BT, and the University of East Anglia, Norwich, NR4 7TJ.

Olof Johansson is a Research Fellow in the Department of Economics at the University of Götenborg, Viktoriagatan 30, Götenborg, Sweden.

David Pearce is Professor of Environmental Economics at University College London and Director of CSERGE at University College London, Gower St, London, WC1E 6BT, and the University of East Anglia, Norwich, NR4 7TJ.

Edward Calthrop is a consultant with Economics for the Environment Consultancy (EFTEC), 16 Percy St, London, W1P 9FD, UK.

Todd Litman is Director of the Victoria Transport Policy Institute, 1250 Rudlin St, Victoria, British Columbia, Canada, V8V 3R7.

Eric Verhoef is with the Department of Spatial Economics, Free University of Amsterdam, de Boelelaan 1105, 1091 HV Amsterdam, the Netherlands, and is also affiliated to the Tinbergen Institute.

Preface 1

This is the fifth volume in the 'Blueprint' series. It began with *Blueprint for a Green Economy* in 1989, which looked at the meaning of 'sustainable development' in the UK context; *Blueprint 2* (1991) dealt with the application of environmental economics to global environmental issues; *Blueprint 3* (1993) returned to the UK context and showed how sustainable development could be measured and what the issues of concern were in the UK; and *Blueprint 4* (1995) returned again to global and international issues to show how the clue to solving major environmental problems lies in the design of economic incentives.

Blueprint 5 is a departure since it is the first volume in the series to address a sectoral issue. We chose transport for reasons that will become more than evident as the catalogue of environmental costs is drawn up in each chapter of the book. It is also a departure in that my colleagues David Maddison and Olof Johansson took over the direction and format of the book. They also invited international scholars Todd Litman (who contributed Chapter 10) and Eric Verhoef (who contributed Chapter 11) to give a perspective from North America and from the Netherlands. They have done a magnificent job and my role in the book has been a suitably limited one.

I believe few issues are more important than addressing the social costs of road transport, and that is a message that would hold for urban areas of many developing countries, too. We have allowed a steady drift to the motor car to develop without a true understanding of what we have done and what it has cost us and our descendants. The first stage in combatting this irrationality is to show people just what these costs are. That is the main aim of *Blue 5*.

DWP, December, 1995

Preface 2

This book has its origins in a chapter written by two of the current authors (Pearce and Maddison) in *Blueprint 3: Measuring Sustainable Development* published in December 1993. We argued that:

> Transport is one sector of the economy in which almost everything has gone wrong; previous transport policy has resulted in too much pollution, too much congestion, too much investment in profitable roads, too little investment in public transport and planning decisions being taken on the basis of misleading price signals.

The chapter generated considerable interest mainly because of the high figures for the social costs of transport in the UK (£22.9bn–£25.7bn) which it suggested and partly because of the high profile that transport issues in general were receiving at that time. To the authors these figures indicated that there were many journeys for which the private benefits were outweighed by the wider costs to society. But these figures, as well as the methodology of the underlying study, were attacked by some as being wrong. Notable among our critics were, not unexpectedly, the Society of Motor Manufacturers and Traders and the motoring organisations. It was suggested that we had overestimated the external costs of transport and had not included some of the relevant benefits. It was further claimed that we had underestimated the amount of tax paid by road transport and that, when our estimates had been corrected, the apparent discrepancy between the costs and the benefits of road transport would disappear. Some claimed that the appropriate solution to the UK's transport problems was to construct more roads. Many other comments we found profoundly silly.

We believe that the methodology and assertions made in *Blueprint 3* were basically correct and note the fact that there are many other economists both in the UK and elsewhere applying essentially the same approach. In fact, we would now go so far as to say that the figures describing the environmental damage arising from road transport were in some respects serious underestimates. We do however recognise that the brevity of the *Blueprint 3* chapter was hardly commensurate with the extent of the subject matter. *Blueprint 5* therefore corrects the imbalance and is intended to propound our views on the UK's transport problems more fully, as well as answering our critics. In so doing we hope to provide some small contribution to the ongoing 'Great Transport Debate' in the UK initiated by the then Secretary of State for Transport Dr Brian Mawhinney. In the course of writing this book we have uncovered further information relating to the probable impacts of environmental pollution from road transport on the UK economy. Some of this information, for example the claim that pollution from road transport kills more people than die in traffic accidents, will doubtless prove to be controversial. We have not set out to be controversial: that is the way the numbers have developed.

DJM, OJ and DWP.
December, 1995.

Acknowledgements

A large number of people have contributed either directly or indirectly to the production of this book. The authors would like to thank Andrew Evans of the Centre for Transport Studies at University College London and David Banister from the Bartlett School, also at UCL, for their comments on early drafts of this text. The authors have also benefitted from conversations with, among others, Duncan Austin, Ken Button of Loughborough University, John Peirson and Roger Vickerman of the University of Kent at Canterbury, Piet Reitveld of the Free University of Amsterdam and Werner Rothengatter of the Institut für Wirtschaftspolitik und Wirtschaftsforschung at Karlsruhe University in Germany. None of the above is responsible for any errors or omissions. The authors have also had the benefit of viewing pre-publication material prepared by David Newbery of Cambridge University for which we are grateful. Edward Calthrop not only contributed a chapter on the external costs of air pollution but also proof read the manuscript and commented upon aspects of it.

Thanks are due to Joanne Aylmer (without whose services this book would never have been finished) and to Ulrika Johansson and Sue Pearce for their support. We would also like to thank our friends at Earthscan and especially Jonathan Sinclair Wilson for his continuing encouragement and guidance on the *Blueprint* series.

This book is dedicated to GAKM and TMM; and also to LM.

DJM, OJ and DWP
December, 1995.

PART I

The Theoretical Background

Chapter 1

Introduction

DIFFERENT PERSPECTIVES ON THE UK'S TRANSPORT PROBLEMS

For passenger traffic in the United Kingdom the last 30 years has been a period of phenomenal growth (Box 1.1). The number of households with access to one or more cars is now 67 per cent. At the same time growth in the relative share of private transport is matched by a correspondingly precipitous decline in public transport. Underlying these changes are the improvement in real incomes and a divergence in the real price of private and public transport. It is notable that over the last decade the real price of both rail fares and bus fares has increased much faster than the index of all motor vehicle cost components and that the real price of private motoring has actually fallen (Box 1.2)

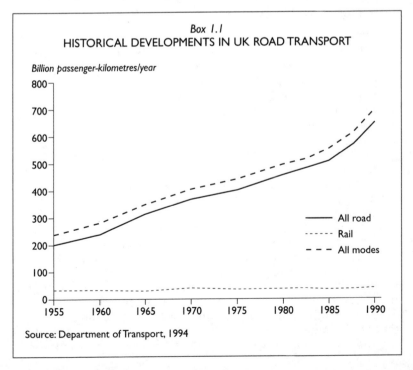

Box 1.1
HISTORICAL DEVELOPMENTS IN UK ROAD TRANSPORT

Billion passenger-kilometres/year

Source: Department of Transport, 1994

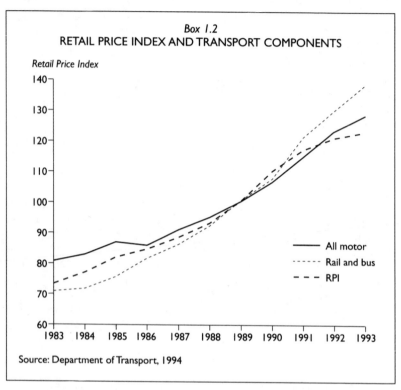

Box 1.2
RETAIL PRICE INDEX AND TRANSPORT COMPONENTS

Source: Department of Transport, 1994

The average distance that each of us travels by bicycle has declined markedly, as has the distance travelled on foot. The falls in cycling are particularly marked for children, a point to which we return in a subsequent chapter (Box 1.3). The trends in freight transport are more mixed, but once again the relative share and absolute volume of freight hauled by rail has fallen sharply compared to that hauled by road (Box 1.4)

In the view of many, this rapid increase in road transport stands squarely in the way of a growing desire for a cleaner, safer and quieter environment. Road transport has begun to erode the benefits that it once brought and now it is difficult to countenance the impact on the environment of the continuation of current trends. And yet, the National Road Traffic Forecasts made in 1989 suggest that the tremendous surge in vehicle kilometres will continue over the next 30 years, growing by between 61 and 98 per cent on 1993 levels (Department of Transport, 1994). There are genuine doubts as to whether the road network can actually accommodate this much traffic and, if it cannot, traffic growth will be left to find its own level. This will result in more congestion, and therefore longer journey times for all motorists, which in turn will dissuade people from making more trips, not least because of the sheer unpleasantness of

Box 1.3
CYCLE MILEAGE PER PERSON PER YEAR

Age and sex	1975/76	1991/93
Male 5–10	32	15
Female 5–10	18	9
Male 11–17	226	161
Female 11–17	56	36
All inc. adults	51	39

Source: National Travel Survey, 1994

driving. The speed of travel in London is no faster now than it was at the turn of the century, and much investment in road infrastructure appears to fill up as soon as it is opened.

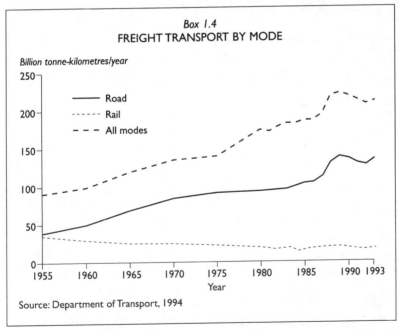

Box 1.4
FREIGHT TRANSPORT BY MODE

Billion tonne-kilometres/year

———— Road
------- Rail
– – – All modes

Source: Department of Transport, 1994

Those connected with the green movement claim that the general public is no longer prepared to tolerate the environmental degradation associated with road transport. Evidence for this comes in the form of the increasing number of people describing themselves as 'very worried' about transport-related problems, in response to a questionnaire regularly conducted by the UK Department of the Environment (Box 1.5). There have been attempts to prevent the construction of new roads, occasionally culminating in violent encounters between protestors and the police. There have been calls to close roads in the capital, either as a response to poor air quality, or because of the effects of the roads on the communities through which they pass. Whereas once such protests might have been dismissed as little more than a focus for those malcontented with the Government's policies in general, it is now apparent that concern about the environmental impact of road transport and road infrastructure cuts across social classes. This is particularly so in the case of ozone, which is blamed by many for the prevalence of asthmatic attacks, particularly among children. Many parents also feel obliged to constrain the activities of their children in order to safeguard them from road traffic. Thus, far from promoting personal freedom, private transport may have had the opposite effect, requiring the restriction of personal movement. Industrial action taken by those who work on London Underground and the railways has coincided with atmospheric conditions over the UK that exacerbate pollution problems. The summer of 1995 witnessed bright sunshine and still air, giving conditions ideal for the formation of ground-level ozone. The record-breaking hot weather has also givern warning as to the possible onset of the so-called 'Greenhouse Effect', caused in part by escalating carbon emissions from cars. Some environmentalists also argue that the growth aspirations of developing countries, or those of future generations, cannot be accommodated without a curtailment of certain activities in the developed world.

Box 1.5
GROWING PUBLIC CONCERN AT THE IMPACT OF ROAD TRANSPORT

Issue	Percentage of those interviewed 'very worried' by issue		
	1986	*1989*	*1993*
Traffic exhaust fumes and urban smog	23	33	40
Traffic congestion	–	–	35
Noise	10	13	16
Losing Green Belt land	26	27	35

Source: Department of the Environment, 1995

These observations have led to calls for strict regulations governing the construction of new vehicles, such as minimum standards for fuel efficiency, and a freezing of all new road building. Car pooling has been advocated by some, along with the creation of special roads along which only cars with multiple occupants can travel. What is required apparently is an 'integrated transport policy' which can be interpreted as greater investment in public transport and the subsidisation of more environmentally friendly modes of transit. Other interpretations might involve more stringent planning controls over the siting of out-of-town shopping complexes, and greater coordination between the timetabling of different services. Many commentators are in favour of closing roads at times of air pollution 'emergencies'. And if there is uncertainty about the extent to which individuals are willing to make the required changes, then, according to some in the environmental movement, there needs to be an effort to change the mindset of the general public. Motoring should be viewed as an anti-social activity. Society, it is said, needs to have as its goal a 'sustainable transport system' with a return to mass public transit and the use of walking and cycling for short journeys with beneficial effects on the nation's health.

Predictably, these views have met stout resistance from certain quarters. The 'roads lobby' is apt to stress arguments relating to personal freedom and the right of individuals to be mobile if they so wish. And the fantastic growth in road transport over the last 30 years is taken as an overwhelming endorsement of that view. The roads network certainly has provided people with considerable choice over where to live in relation to their work and an ability to pursue a wide range of social activity. Road infrastructure may have brought prosperity to peripheral regions and permits people to exercise choice. Private transport brings privacy, flexibility and security. It enables people to engage in sporting and leisure activities in the countryside. Many in the roads lobby are genuinely appalled that the aforementioned benefits are not accorded the same priority as the disbenefits from private transport. They feel that the environmental debate is taking place in a vacuum and the benefits of private transport are being taken for granted.

The roads lobby is also able to point to a palpable lack of alternative means of transport for the majority of people. The general pattern is that car ownership is much higher in rural than in urban areas and statistics like this form the backbone of arguments regarding the supposed adverse distributional incidence of environmental taxes on motoring. People in peripheral areas have no choice but to use the car and any attempt to increase fuel taxes will have little effect on traffic volumes. Because of the lifestyles which people lead and the dispersion of the places that we like to visit, access to a car has become 'essential'. The Royal Commission on Environmental Pollution (1994) details the major changes in the way people shop and the rise of out-of-town shopping complexes. A particularly telling statistic is that in 1980 only 5 per cent of retail sales were made in out-of-town locations but by 1992 this had risen to 37 per cent.

Furthermore, the evidence linking carbon emissions to climate change and ozone concentrations to asthmatic attacks is far from conclusive and what is required, some argue, is more research rather than rash and probably unnecessary intervention. In any case, it is claimed that many of the environmental problems posed by road transport are capable of being solved by technological means, and hence there is no need either for taxes on polluting activities or on policies aimed at reducing the demand for travel. Moreover, the road transport lobby is frequently able to muster considerable support for local bypass schemes taking traffic and its noise and fumes away from town centres. In the view of road builders, the construction of new roads can relieve both environmental pressures and also contribute to economic growth, by providing the transport infrastructure required for a competitive economy. Proposals to freeze all road-building projects are viewed with horror. Indeed, to those involved in the business of equipping and supplying road transport, attempts to reduce mobility are a direct threat to their livelihood. The supply of road transport obviously absorbs the output of a considerable number of other industries such as vehicle manufacturing, filling stations, vehicle repair and maintenance. The impact on employment is typically offered as a reason for avoiding policies which might lead to the contraction of the road transport sector.

Finally the roads lobby is able to present balance sheets detailing the annual expenditure on roads combined with the costs of air pollution and other effects of road transport borne by society. These costs are compared with the taxation paid by road users, and illustrate that the taxes paid by motorists exceed the expenditure on roads and the environmental effects felt by non-road users. This enables road lobbyists to claim that any measures involving increases in the tax burden on road users would be unfair.

Others, some outside of the road transport lobby, view mass private transport as a transitory phase. Mackintosh (1994) argues persuasively that information technology (IT) will begin to exert a profound influence over patterns of transport usage. He considers transport to be about shifting goods, persons and intangibles such as information. He argues that the physical delivery of intangible entertainment and information will be superseded by electronic delivery systems along the information superhighways. He continues:

> The transport of people will also be affected by the near universal availability of high definition full colour low cost video and telephony and video conferencing. Man's need to observe body language and to engage in social contact will be met partially by these new IT tools thus reducing significantly the need for meetings, especially for business purposes. At the same time, easy to use tele-everything will reduce the desire and need for local and domestic travel....Only in the transport of goods (such as food, fuels and materials) is the IT revolution likely to be modest. (Mackintosh, 1994)

One might expect the Government to have taken on the role of coercion and to have constrained the rise in road transport. By and large, however, this has happened only to a limited extent. The Government has rather attempted to pass back the responsibility for the control of environmental pollution from road transport back to the road users themselves. A striking example of this is the attempt of the Government to encourage road users to leave their cars at home on high pollution days. But the Government's actions are fashioned by a fear of alienating particular groups of supporters. Moreover, the Government is operating under budgetary and ideological constraints which limit its behaviour with regard to transport policy. Private transport embodies major themes of the current administration: individuality and freedom of choice. The need to curtail that choice is for some within the administration a matter of regret. There is a presumption against the use of any new tax instrument, even one which is offset by an equivalent reduction elsewhere. In other areas of transport policy such as the construction of new roads and the operation of the railways, the Government is attempting to reduce the involvement of the state. And, finally, the administration's at times strained relationship with the European Union has had a defining influence over the nature of the policies adopted to meet the Government's commitments towards the Framework Convention on Climate Change, leading directly to repercussions for road transport policy in the UK.

TOWARDS AN ECONOMIC ANALYSIS OF ROAD TRANSPORT

The preceding paragraphs have attempted to characterise the typical positions of the main protagonists in the 'Great Transport Debate', and give a flavour of their often emotive arguments. But listening to these arguments does not get us very far even in deciding whether a transport problem exists, let alone in what direction the appropriate policy response may lie. Throughout this book, therefore, we dispassionately analyse the problems of road transport using economics. Economics has a great power to focus attention on the important aspects of the road transport problem, and in doing so demonstrates why some of the arguments touched upon above are correct while others are bogus or misplaced. Economics is an aid to understanding and clarifying the choices which confront society with regard to transport policy.

As an example of the insights afforded by economics, consider the rise of the environmental movement against road transport not as an autonomous development but in terms of changes in the supply and demand for 'environmental quality'. Largely because of increasing amounts of road transport, and the infrastructure required to convey it, the supply of environmental amenities (unspoilt landscapes, quiet areas, areas of special scientific interest and built heritage) has been decreasing. Those sites which remain become more valuable because of their relative scarcity. The other explanation as to why the people are becoming more concerned is to be found in the 'Kuznets Curve' effect and the demand for environmental quality. The Kuznets Curve illustrates how demand for the environment increases with income. Whereas initially people prefer consumer goods and greater material standards of living, eventually people desire greater environmental quality. The fact that in many cross-country studies various indices of environmental quality are seen first to deteriorate and then to improve with income per capita is consistent with the operation of a Kuznets Curve effect. But traditional markets for environmental quality do not exist and so these preferences take the only form that they can – as a demand for regulations. That is what is observed today in Britain and other countries: higher incomes lead people to become more strenuous in their demand for regulations to enhance environmental quality.

Economics is also able to pinpoint the flaw in the road lobbyists' argument that the terrific growth in road transport 'proves' that individuals do not want to see limitations placed on their mobility. The answer is well explained by Hardin's (1968) now famous allegory 'The Tragedy of the Commons'. In that article, Hardin describes a situation in which each member of a community is allowed open access to a common resource (which could be road space), but, in using the resource, dissipates the available benefits. Some form of restraint would improve the well-being of the community as a whole, but individual restraint is not compatible with rational self-interest, at least not while any other member of the community reserves the right to use the resource (ie drive on it) as much as they choose. To attain the maximum benefit from the resource requires government intervention. Thus the massive growth in road transport does not endorse the desirability of mass private transport but merely reminds us that in many instances self-restraint is not compatible with self-interest. The massive use of the road network is emphatically not a vote for the status quo.

As for the argument that the dispersion of the places that we like to visit has rendered mass private transport essential, it appears more accurate to say that the cost of transport has actually facilitated these developments. Ultimately the viability of these developments relies upon cheap private transport. Part of the solution to the transport problems of the UK involves drawing closer together the places that we like to visit. This is indeed likely to take decades and it is not obvious how subsidised public transport, as suggested by some in the environmental movement will help achieve this contraction. Indeed, there is a long-established view that the relative price of transport shapes the cities in which we live. It may be difficult for people to imagine their life without access to a car, given the fact that so many supermarkets are now out of town. These out-of-town developments are clearly disadvantageous to those who do not have access to a car (mainly the old, the infirm and the poor).

No doubt the growth in road transport reflects the considerable benefits which it makes available. But it is becoming increasingly apparent that the success of private transport is also to some extent due to the fact that it succeeds in 'externalising' a range of impacts, ie shifting many of the costs for which it is responsible on to other people without the motorist being charged for those costs. Costs in economic language comprise losses of well-being or 'welfare'. That this process of shifting costs to others has been allowed to continue for so long is mainly a function of the physical difficulty of confronting road users at all times and on all occasions with the true cost of their activities (but it is also something of a tribute to the success of the roads lobby and their populist arguments influencing successive Governments). The basic problem of road transport is that there are currently many journeys undertaken where the costs to society outweigh the benefits to the individual. It is these journeys which must be curtailed while at the same time giving other road users appropriate incentives to reduce the environmental impact of their journeys. Economists are generally of the opinion that any policy to tackle these problems must involve confronting the motorist with the true cost of his or her journey – hence the title of the book. Only by these means will society be able to derive the utmost benefit from its road network or rely upon price signals for the purposes of planning investment projects. It is indeed the Government's own objective:

> ...to ensure that users pay the full social and environmental cost of their transport decisions, so improving the overall efficiency of those decisions for the economy as a whole and bringing environmental benefits (UK Department of the Environment, 1994).

This book advocates using 'market based instruments' as a means of ensuring that environmental costs are taken into account in private decision making. Once the relative advantages of these instruments are understood, many of the alternative policy recommendations made by both the environmentalists and the roads lobby begin to sound like expensive ways of achieving given environmental goals and more like an attempt to engage in what is often referred to as 'regulatory capture' – an attempt to influence policy to the advantage of the membership of particular organisations. This, for example, can help to explain why road lobbyists very often appear to rely upon technological solutions to environmental problems rather than a direct curtailment of demand. But before confronting road users with the true costs of their activities we first have to work out what these costs are.

There have actually been many attempts to quantify the external costs of road transport, presumably with the intention of influencing transport policy. These have not had the impact that the researchers working on these projects have intended. One reason for this is that researchers have, often without appreciating it, been involved in exercises of a radically different nature and ended up confusing equity and efficiency issues. Furthermore, there is a feeling among policy makers that the monetary values which emerge from valuation exercises are too imprecise and unreliable to be built into financial decision making or cost–benefit analyses alongside other more concrete figures relating to construction costs, time and fuel savings and the like.

These prices on environmental amenities are derived by examining the rate at which people are prepared to trade off greater environmental quality against wealth via hypothetical questionnaire techniques or techniques of 'revealed preference'. Valuing all commodities in terms of a common denominator (money) enables different physical effects to be aggregated together and directly compared with the economic sacrifice required to maintain or improve environmental quality. Monetisation of the demand for environmental quality forms the basis for calculus designed to answer questions regarding the efficient allocation of resources in the economy between road transport, abatement measures and other less environmentally damaging activities. It is indeed true that the environmental impacts of road transport are difficult to place money values on; and that when lists are compiled of alternative estimates of the same external effects the variation in the figures can seem extreme. It is important to realise though, that the various techniques available for measuring these effects often measure different approximations of the true measures of social well-being and examine only a subset of the total benefits related to an environmental amenity, or measure them for different populations. Moreover, some authors insist on using entirely inappropriate techniques. Once these estimates have been expunged, the divergences are reduced and the case for including these measures alongside conventionally included money measures is considerably strengthened. And to omit such effects altogether from transport policy is to continue with policy as it is today with all its obvious deficiencies.

But using prices to achieve environmental goals within the road transport sector often results in unintended transfers of money and welfare between different groups in society. In reality most of the arguments concerning environmental policy are about the incidence of environmental taxes and the preservation of the existing distribution of welfare. It is for these reasons that Governments, often confronted by a well-organised road transport lobby, have shrunk from the task of initiating such changes as are necessary. Clearly there is no point in advocating a set of policies which are not politically supportable. But are the distributional impacts of environmental taxes from road transport what they are commonly supposed to be? Or do arguments about the regressive impacts of environmental taxes focus on only a subset of the overall effects, or hypothesise that the measures are imposed in a rather unrealistic way, such as supposing that the revenue raised by environmental taxes will not be returned in the form of higher government spending or lower taxes elsewhere? And in any case, should these arguments be allowed to stand given that there are less distorting instruments much better suited to achieving goals of distributional equity?

Setting prices on environmental pollution from road transport is, we believe, an integral and essential part of transport policy. Nevertheless transport systems are often characterised by other market failures relating to economies of scale and the exercise of market power. These effects are important not only in their own right, but also because they can exacerbate or suppress environmental problems. These other causes of market failure have not been addressed in this book except where they impinge directly upon environmental policy. The interested reader can consult Barde and Button (1990) or Button (1993). We do not think that the explicit treatment of such issues would significantly change the policy conclusions which emerge in this book.

This book is primarily concerned with the efficient use of the existing road network. This involves asking whether, and to what extent, the Government has succeeded in meeting its stated aim of ensuring that the users of the road network pay the full social costs of their journeys and, if not, how these costs can best be brought into the decision-making processes of the individual. It is not concerned with the external effects relating to the construction of roads, although these may well be profound. Nor does it seek to quantify the environmental effects of those industries that support road transport by means of a 'cradle to grave analysis' (life cycle analysis) although it is possible that these, too, might be significant especially in the case of oil extraction and refining, steel and electricity production and the disposal of old cars. Finally, the book has nothing to say on the issue which dominated most of the 1970s: the 'impending depletion' of scarce oil and mineral reserves. These issues have been totally overshadowed by the emerging environmental problems posed by road transport, to which this book is devoted.

THE ORGANISATION OF THIS BOOK

Chapter 2 considers the theoretical basis for the argument that road transport has become excessive and that the evolving modal split does not reflect the relative costs and benefits associated with each mode, but instead reflects regulatory failure. The concept of external effects is introduced and their occurrence explained in terms of absent property rights. It is shown that an activity which enjoys considerable 'internal' benefits can at the same time suffer from sizeable external costs and that these two costs do not offset one another. Arguments are rehearsed in favour of using 'economic' instruments rather than 'command and control' standards and regulations to deal with external effects in an efficient manner. The comparative dearth of economic instruments is also explained in terms of anxieties regarding their distributional impact. The need to place money values on environmental degradation is explained, as are the techniques regularly used for this purpose.

The remaining chapters examine the external costs of road transport in the UK context. A number of authors (Bonnafous, 1994) have sought to classify the environmental impacts of road transport according to the geographical domain of their effects: global, regional, local and user-on-user effects. We will adopt that typology in what follows. The chapters also attempt to give some indication of the likely directions of these physical impacts in the instance where no additional policy measures are undertaken beyond those which are already announced. The point is made that those modes of transport contributing most to environmental degradation are precisely those which have been growing fastest over the last 30 years. Immediately, therefore, much could be done to mitigate environmental degradation merely by changing the desired mode of transport.

Globally, the concern over road transport is in respect of its contribution to the enhanced greenhouse effect in the form of carbon dioxide (CO_2) emissions. Currently, only 8 per cent of the world's population owns a car but in the absence of concerted action there seems no reason to believe that the developing countries will not evolve a pattern of ownership and usage similar to that in the developed world. The environmental consequences of such a scenario are potentially alarming (Hughes, 1992). Following the June 1992 United Nations Conference on Environment and Development (UNCED) conference in Rio, it is now widely understood that developing countries cannot follow the same pattern of growth as that taken by the developed world because of physical constraints of the planet and its climate. The view of the developing countries is that the developed world needs to rein in its emissions in order to make room for the growth aspirations of the former. The ability to treat the global atmosphere as a free waste repository has effectively ended and the UK, along with other industrialised countries, is now under an obligation to return its carbon emissions to 1990 levels by the year 2000. Vehicle emissions account for about one-fifth of the UK's carbon emissions, and it is apparent that those modes of transport showing the greatest year-on-year growth rates are the more carbon-intensive ones. Greenhouse gas emissions from UK road transport form the basis of the discussion in chapter 3. The chapter describes the enhanced greenhouse effect and how prices for unit emissions of greenhouse gases may be derived from the available information; and the relationship between a number of linked concepts. These prices are then used to derive damage estimates for greenhouse gas emissions from road transport. The policy measures employed by the Government to secure savings in carbon emissions from the road transport sector are presented, and we argue that the appropriate policy to deal with carbon emissions is an economy-wide tax on carbon emissions and not to set reduction targets on a sectoral basis.

Most other environmental problems, however, are much more localised in their effects, such as urban air quality and noise pollution. Most recently a report published by the Association of London Government, and prepared by the Institute of Public Health (1995), documents a deterioration in London's air quality in 1994 relative to 1993 despite the increasing use of catalytic converters in cars. Guidelines for nitrogen dioxide, ozone and sulphur dioxide were regularly breached at a number of sites in the South East. The report warned that, without action to curb road traffic, air quality standards would not be met.

Automobile emissions are largely responsible for low-level ozone pollution in cities caused by the action of sunlight on oxides of nitrogen (NO_x) and volatile organic compounds (VOCs). Once formed, ozone persists for several days and can be transported over considerable distances. As such it constitutes a transboundary pollution problem. Depending upon the direction of airflow a substantial proportion of ozone present during a pollution episode may be a result of vehicle emissions on the continent and vice versa. NO_x also contributes to acid rain, causing acidification of soil and fresh water as well as damage to buildings and other man-made constructions. Both ozone and NO_x are capable of causing damage to crops although these have not been quantified in the case of the UK.

Inevitably, however, most interest has focused upon the impact of these emissions upon human health. The impact of road transport on air quality is the subject of chapter 4. The chapter commences by outlining a methodology for calculating the health impacts of a variety of air pollutants. Recent work by American epidemiologists has focused on the health impacts of particulate matter of less than 10 microns in diameter (PM_{10}). On the basis of various studies, it has been argued that, given the levels of PM_{10} typically found in urban areas, it is possible that 10,000 people in the United Kingdom are dying annually from the inhalation of these particles (Bown, 1994). These calculations have been refined somewhat in chapter 4 without significantly altering the conclusions.

Meanwhile, diesel has been advertised by its manufacturers as a 'green' fuel largely on the basis of lower CO and CO_2 emissions.

Other emissions from diesel cars may be higher and this raises the question of the relative merits of the various fuels available and whether these are reflected in the duties paid on fuel. The environmental costs associated with each of the main fuels is another topic that is dealt with in chapter 4. It is argued that the majority of people who are killed as a result of road transport die not as a consequence of traffic accidents but from adverse air quality. This claim, however, is subject to numerous caveats including the uncertainty surrounding the evidence itself, the identity of those at risk and the inadequate measurement of air pollution around the country.

There is no long-term consistent index of noise nuisance for the UK, but it seems improbable that such an index would have registered any improvement. UK noise levels have only been measured since 1985 and these figures give some indication of the relative contribution of road transport to noise nuisance in the UK, if not to the underlying trends. It appears that road transport is the main source of noise nuisance in the UK by some considerable margin and there are few locations that are not now afflicted by traffic noise. Chapter 5 looks at noise nuisance, beginning with issues of measurement and the differing concepts of noise. The chapter then moves to consider the evidence on the extent to which populations are willing to pay to avoid noise nuisance, the shortcomings of the various techniques employed, and the extent to which they succeed in measuring noise in all contexts rather than just in the context of the home. The available evidence is then synthesised and, in conjunction with information relating to the number of homes exposed to particular noise levels, is used to illustrate a sizeable premium on the elimination of noise nuisance from road transport.

Turning now to consider user-on-user effects, despite considerable investments in road infrastructure, average travel speeds in London (and presumably other major cities in the United Kingdom) are now falling, after having been stable over most of the century. Congestion costs are the subject of chapter 6. The chapter discusses the existence of congestion costs and argues forcefully that these are 'external costs' and therefore have a rightful place alongside other environmental costs of road transport. The chapter briefly looks at the circumstances under which it may be desirable to expand the road network to deal with traffic congestion and demonstrates why the road planning system, as it is currently conceived, is capable of making economically irrational decisions by neglecting the phenomenon of 'generated traffic'. The theoretical solution to the problem of traffic congestion is shown to involve taxing road users in accordance with the time delays imposed on others. The implementation of such a policy requires such advanced technological systems that simpler alternatives have to be chosen. The public hostility to road pricing is explained. The chapter then considers the task of measuring the economic costs of congestion and which out of a number of related concepts is the relevant measure of congestion costs for the purposes of this exercise.

Road accidents appear to be one of the relatively few measures of the impacts of road transport which has been steadily improving over time and, moreover, it is a measure in which the United Kingdom compares favourably with other countries. There are, however, considerable difficulties (which are outlined in chapter 7) in deciding whether accident costs are really a matter for Government intervention at all. A model is developed in which it is shown that the need for Government intervention rests on an uncertain empirical relationship. Settling the empirical dispute over this relationship deserves high priority because of the effect which it would have on the amount of traffic that would optimally be allowed on the road. Techniques are used to illustrate the means used to place money values on lives lost, and why these techniques are superior to methods used in other countries and, until recently, the methods used in the UK. The point is made that using a low value for lives lost in cost–benefit appraisals appears to produce a bias in favour of schemes which save time rather than schemes which save lives. But a measure based on accidents provides an incomplete picture in that it does not examine the change in behaviour of pedestrians and cyclists as they try to adapt themselves to the growing volume of road traffic. These adaptations are not without cost and there is evidence of varying types that these changes are of consequence.

Chapter 8 summarises the arguments, aggregates the external costs and compares them with the taxes currently paid by road transport. These estimates are then compared to those of the authors' earlier work, the work of others, as well as to estimates and associated policy measures from the recent Royal Commission Report on Environmental Pollution. It is demonstrated that many road users do not pay the full social costs associated with their journeys and that there is accordingly considerable economic inefficiency in the road transport sector. Higher taxes are required on polluting activities in order to dissuade socially inefficient journeys and there needs to be a switch away from taxes on ownership to taxes on pollution.

Chapters 9, 10 and 11 take the methodology developed in the previous section and apply it to three different places: Sweden, North America and the Netherlands. The authors of these three chapters also attempt to give some sense of the means by which these countries have attempted to incorporate environmental concerns into transport policy.

In chapter 9 Olof Johansson considers the environmental impacts of road transport in Sweden and the attempts of the Swedish authorities to deal with these problems. A considerable amount of information is offered regarding the ability of catalytic converters to reduce air pollution under a variety of conditions relating to the distance of the journey and the outside temperature. Sweden as a nation has had some experience of the kind of measures which many would wish to see enacted in the United Kingdom, such as the fitting of odometers to heavy goods vehicles, tax differentiation for vehicles with different environmental characteristics and an economy-wide carbon tax. Yet despite these and other measures Johansson argues that there remains a degree of inefficiency within the Swedish road transport sector.

In chapter 10 Todd Litman considers the case of North America, which represents an excellent contrast to Sweden. Litman argues that although the costs of owning a car are high, fuel and parking costs are low resulting in gross inefficiencies in the road transport sector of North America. An interesting feature of Litman's chapter is that he draws attention to the widespread provision of free parking in North America which he argues represents a significant subsidy to driving. Non-drivers receive no comparable subsidy. Motor vehicles are also shown to be major contributors to air pollution (at least in the US) and Litman argues that there are limitations to the technological controls that can be exercised over vehicle emissions especially in so far as one of the major pollutants, particulate matter, may result from tyres and brake linings as well as dust stirred up by the motion of the vehicle. Since ownership costs are high, but operating costs are very low, average vehicle costs decline with increased use so drivers have an incentive to maximise their driving in order to 'get their money's worth'. This encourages environmental degradation and the development of patterns of land use that are unsuitable for any other mode. The situation in North America clearly has many parallels with that experienced in the UK.

Finally, in chapter 11, Erik Verhoef looks at the environmental impact of road transport in the Netherlands. Verhoef commences by defining 'externalities' and explaining why there are no external benefits in the case of road transport but only external costs. He demonstrates that the tension that often exists between equity and efficiency considerations leads to rather unfocused discussions about the policy implications of research findings. Verhoef then moves to discussing the alternative techniques for placing monetary values on the environmental damage done by road transport as well as various short-cut approaches and their deficiencies. Verhoef argues that while there may be an approximate balance between the taxes paid and the external costs of road transport in the Netherlands, the taxes paid need to be shifted away from ownership and on to the use of road vehicles.

Supplementary is an annexe which contains details of all available estimates of the costs of transport from around the world.

Chapter 2

External Costs and Economic Efficiency

INTRODUCTION

This chapter seeks to explain the existence of market failure in the case of road transport and to justify the need for government intervention. In so doing it introduces a lot of economic terminology. Understanding this terminology is essential for what follows. There are many currently engaged in the transport debate who are inclined to use economic arguments to support their point of view as to which direction policy should take. But economics is a rigorous subject and some words and phrases in everyday parlance have completely different meanings in economics. It is important to be clear about what these meanings are in order to avoid confusion and the drawing of erroneous policy conclusions which are not supported by economic theory. A prime example of this occurring is the assertion that congestion costs are 'internal costs' rather than external and that, for the purposes of determining the appropriate level of taxes on road transport, they can be ruled out of court. A second example is the view that 'because road transport has so many external benefits these must balance the environmental costs'. This chapter explains why both of these commonly heard statements are plain wrong.

The chapter also attempts to explain why it makes sense to tax road transport beyond the level of total damage costs which it imposes on society and even beyond the level of the taxes required to 'internalise the externalities'. Moreover, it shows why car tax and Value Added Tax (VAT) on fuel cannot be offset against the external costs of road transport despite the attempt of many in the road transport lobby to do just that. The chapter also deals with economists' preference for what are called 'market based instruments' as a means of dealing with the pollution and congestion problems posed by road transport and reveals why such instruments have not been embraced by policy makers to the extent that economists had hoped for. The chapter describes the need to place money values on environmental amenities as a first step to confronting road users with the true cost of driving and gives a typology of the different techniques of monetary evaluation available for that purpose.

OPEN ACCESS RESOURCES AND THE MEANING OF 'EXTERNALITY'

Economists are predominantly interested in the economic benefits arising from activities such as motoring. The economic benefits over and above the costs of an activity are known as the 'economic surplus'. An efficient allocation of resources occurs when this economic surplus is maximised. This can be illustrated by a supply and demand curve as shown in Box 2.1. Suppose that the demand curve represents the additional benefits derived from the last kilometre travelled (the demand curve is for this reason also known as the 'marginal' benefit curve). The demand curve slopes downward, incorporating the assumption that as more trips are undertaken the value of additional trips starts to decline. The economic costs of an activity like motoring are represented by the supply curve. This curve shows the additional (or marginal) costs associated with the last kilometre travelled. The area bounded by the demand and supply curve is the economic surplus from the activity. The surplus is clearly maximised at the point where the demand and supply curve intersect. At that point the benefits to society derived from the last unit of travel equal the additional costs incurred.

A problem arises however, whenever the costs associated with an activity are not entirely borne by individuals involved. In the case of motoring these extra costs might include things like the costs associated with air and noise pollution which the individual road user will not take into account in deciding how many journeys to make, either because they are unaware of them, or because they are unwilling to do so. The existence of such costs can be represented by distinguishing the marginal private costs of the activity from the (higher) marginal social costs of an activity. In the absence of any intervention the resultant level of the activity will be where the private marginal cost curve and the demand curve intersect. It is apparent from the diagram that this no longer represents the social optimum. The costs to society from the last kilometre driven exceed the benefits derived from it. The vertical difference between the social costs and private costs is referred to as the 'marginal external cost' or just the 'externality'. The loss which this externality imposes on society can be represented by the triangle BGC in Box 2.1. It is also clear from the diagram that an economic activity like road transport can have associated with it a large economic surplus whilst at the same time imposing considerable external costs on the rest of society. These costs and benefits do not offset one another, but rather the implication is that the (undoubtedly substantial) economic benefits from road transport could be increased even further by restricting the activity. This can be achieved by levying a tax on the activity equal to the marginal external cost, which economists usually refer to as a Pigouvian tax after the economist Pigou. Levying this

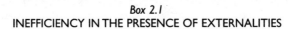

Box 2.1
INEFFICIENCY IN THE PRESENCE OF EXTERNALITIES

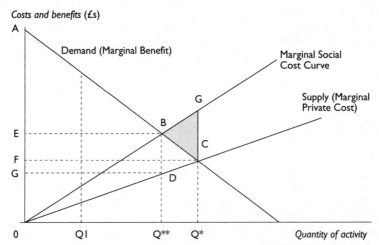

An efficient allocation of resources requires economic surplus to be maximised. Economic surplus is the difference between economic benefit of an activity and its cost. If Q1 road trips are currently made by a person, an additional trip would increase his or her economic surplus. This is because at Q1 trips, marginal benefit is greater than the marginal cost. The person will keep undertaking another trip until the marginal benefit from the trip equals the cost, which in this case is with Q* trips. At this point, economic surplus for the individual and society are simultaneously maximised. This is shown in the diagram as area 0CA0. If all people keep undertaking trips until marginal benefit equals marginal cost, then all individuals maximise consumer surplus, and hence society has maximised surplus.

Economic surplus for society is not maximised, however, when the costs that the person faces in deciding whether to make another trip, are not the same as the costs imposed on society. This case is shown by the marginal social cost curve. Economic surplus for society in this case is maximised at Q** trips, less than the private optimum Q*. Economic surplus is maximised at area 0BA0, which can be shown to be greater than the private surplus 0AC0 at Q* with a social loss of 0CG0. For each additional trip taken after Q** trips, the cost to society is greater than the benefit of the trip to the driver. The loss to society equals the shaded area BGC.

Note that a tax equal to BD per trip will ensure that the incentives faced by the individual generate the same equilibrium number of trips as that which maximises social economic surplus.

tax secures the 'internalisation' of the externality and results in a welfare gain equal to the triangle BGC. In other words, road users are confronted by the true cost of their decision to drive. Note that the tax revenue raised by the optimal tax may be greatly in excess of the external damages caused in an effort to induce economic efficiency. This is because the appropriate charge is the marginal and not the average external cost, which is lower. The tax revenue is not of itself an economic cost but merely represents a transfer to the rest of society.

But road users already pay considerable tax revenues. To what extent do these succeed in internalising the external costs of road transport? Throughout the remaining chapters of this book we compare the tax revenue raised from road transport with estimates of the aggregate marginal external costs. Should the latter exceed the former then there is an inefficiently high level of road transport and road transport or its external effects should be reduced. Even if the two sums exactly balanced or taxes exceeded the marginal external costs there would still be an interest in determining whether each individual road user pays the appropriate charge, or whether some pay too much and others too little. This is a much more complicated question and in many ways a more important one.

In the presence of external effects then, there is a 'market failure' in the sense that social well-being could be improved by less road transport. Road users drive until they are indifferent about the last kilometre. The net private benefit of the last kilometre is zero. It seems therefore likely that those who suffer from the external effects of the road transport would be willing, at least at the margin, to pay more than the road users need to be compensated in order to get them to reduce the amount of motoring currently undertaken. There is a scope for bargains between victims of air pollution and the road users who generate it. Yet such deals evidently do not occur very much in practice. We have never heard of any individual or group entering into a private contract with a set of road users, paying them to reduce the number of trips they undertake. But what is to stop such private contracts being reached? One immediate problem is ill-defined property rights over whether road users have the right to pollute or society has the right to enjoy clean air. Property rights would have to be made clear before a contract could even be arranged. Apart from taxation, therefore, one other possible solution to the problem of the externality is to create property rights for the resource where none existed before. Economists refer to this as the 'Coasian' solution to common property disputes, after its originator Ronald Coase. The Coase theorem states that so long as there is cost-less bargaining between the generator of the pollution (here the motorist) and the victim, an efficient outcome will emerge provided that one or other party holds the relevant property right to the environmental amenity. The important question is to what extent can a clear definition of property rights result in an efficient outcome in the case of road transport?

In fact, while analytically correct, the Coase theorem does not really apply to the major pollution problems generated by road transport. Partly this may be because of high costs involved in setting up an agreement known as 'transaction costs' and the sheer number of people to be involved in bargaining. In many cases the long-term nature of pollution problems (for example, climate change) means that those who cause the pollution are dead before the damage shows up. People living at different points in time obviously cannot make contracts with one another. Furthermore, some important environmental amenities like air quality have the property of what economists refer to as 'public goods', meaning that the benefits of reduced pollution are not specific to the individuals who contribute to their up-keep. Everyone attempts to 'free ride' on everyone else's decision to purchase a reduction in the ambient level of pollution. This leads to a situation of under-provision where no one wants to voluntarily contribute to clean-up costs even though everyone values clean air. In practice, therefore, environmental taxes or some other form of Government regulations are required to tackle transport-related problems rather than relying on the market, aided by a clear definition of property rights, to sort it all out. Even so, there is one area in which the creation of property rights has been mooted as providing a solution to a rather pressing transport problem. This is the problem of traffic congestion, which we deal with in a later chapter.

Presumably noone would wish to deny that road transport inflicts external costs on society. But are there external benefits from road transport, too? Although we have focused on the case of external costs associated with an activity, it is also possible to conceive of an activity possessing external benefits, which means that the benefits to society exceed the benefits to the individual decision makers. The classic example of external benefits in economics is the owner of an apiary whose bees pollinate a nearby orchard. External benefits would imply an inefficiently low level of an activity and the need to expand the activity by means of a subsidy, in the above example a subsidy paid to honey production. Critically, it is often suggested that road transport possesses external benefits and that these offset for the external costs of road transport. It might seem on the face of it rather easy to think of a whole range of additional benefits which road transport confers on non-users. After all, has not road transport contributed greatly to economic growth over the past 50 years? Does not road transport make available a diverse range of goods at affordable prices? Has it not contributed significantly to the development of peripheral regions and does it not employ many individuals in the transport system? These observations are all true. But the important question is whether these undeniable benefits are external to the road users or not. To put it another way, if there were no external costs to worry about, would there be a reason to subsidise private transport to compensate for the supposed presence of these alleged external benefits?

We suspect there is a tendency to confuse the benefits arising from the provision of infrastructure with the benefits of road transport itself. The provision of infrastructure results in a reduction in both private and social costs of transport. These benefits are in common parlance 'external' to the transport sector in that they are an element determined from outside. But they do not of themselves justify the excessive use of the said infrastructure by the transport services sector. What about other producers who make use of goods transported by road and the consumers in the shops who benefit from lower prices and fresh produce? Surely these individuals enjoy external benefits from road transport? Consumers do indeed derive considerable benefits from low-cost road transportation. But the lower delivery prices which are handed on to other producers and finally to consumers in the shops are pecuniary benefits and simply the realisation of the economic surplus. They are not external benefits since they are exclusive to those who purchase the goods concerned and pay for the cost of delivery at each stage of the production process. In fact, the only external benefits that we can think of are benefits to individuals who enjoy 'car-spotting'! This activity constitutes an external benefit since, unlike consumers of delivered commodities, these benefits are the direct result of road transport activities determined by others who do not take the delight of car-spotters into account when deciding how far to drive. The reader who has reached this point and is still not convinced that there are no external benefits from road transport should ask themselves this question: Will I benefit if my neighbours drive more than they do already?

The dominance of external costs over external benefits is not unusual. Private agents always have an incentive to seek out external benefits which their activities create and to internalise them. Button (1993) provides a nice example of this: at one time British Rail sold platform tickets to train-spotters (the practice was, however, eventually discontinued presumably because of high transaction costs). But the example illustrates well the incentives of private agents whose activity generates external benefits. Obviously no such private incentives operate in the case of external costs. There are no significant external benefits arising from the usage of the road transport network and those who reach the contrary conclusion do so on the basis of faulty reasoning (see Rothengatter, 1994). The supposed 'external benefits' of road transport actually refer either to the economic surplus generated or to the road infrastructure itself and not to its use.

Nevertheless, the 'road lobby' is frequently apt to point out that road users already pay more in tax than they receive back by way of expenditure on road construction and maintenance. The implication seems to be that motorists are paying more than enough tax already. But as we have already seen, what matters from the perspective of economic efficiency is whether individual road users pay the full marginal costs of their journey. The argument that motorists pay more than they receive back by way of expenditure on infrastructure should be seen for what it is: an argument about the distribution of welfare (ie that those who use the roads should be made to pay for them) and nothing to do with economic efficiency. Thus it is possible to distinguish two different types of accounting exercise which have commonly been pursued in the literature.

The first type calculates the average external costs of road transport not borne by the road users themselves (ie excluding congestion costs) and compares this with the taxes paid by road users to the rest of society net of any expenditure on new road infrastructure. This may be referred to as 'unpaid bill to society' approach. The argument is presumably that from an equity perspective the two should balance. Now, there is nothing wrong with undertaking such an exercise (although we doubt that it is possible to draw a clear distinction between 'road users' and 'non road users') provided that it is realised that striking such a balance will not result in an economically efficient allocation of resources. In other words, there may be many journeys undertaken where the private benefits are more than outweighed by the wider costs to society. Moreover, we will soon ask whether taxing road users might actually improve the distribution of welfare from an egalitarian perspective and even if it does not, whether there are less distorting means of achieving a desired distribution of welfare than tolerating the current inefficiencies in the road transport sector.

The second type of exercise (and the one which was alluded to earlier) is to compare the marginal external cost with the taxes paid by road transport. A balance between the two would ensure that there were no journeys undertaken where the costs to society outweigh the private benefits (although there may, as we have already mentioned, be reason to allocate these costs differently among different classes of road users). Such a situation may indeed involve a transfer of resources away from road users in general and the purchase of the output of various supportive sectors (which is precisely what most motoring organisations seek to avoid). But these redistributions may be compensated for elsewhere in the fiscal system.

When undertaking either type of exercise one encounters the question: what taxes can be allowed to offset the marginal external costs of road transport? Road users pay a variety of taxes including, primarily, Vehicle Excise Duty (VED), fuel duty, car sales tax and Value Added Tax (VAT). There is a view which states that if motorists are to make a large payment to reflect the presence of external effects of their journeys, then they should be exempted from making any further contribution to tax revenues because of that fact. In other words, taxes such as VAT aimed predominantly at raising revenue rather than fulfilling any other purpose ought to be allowed to offset the marginal external costs of road transport. This is a claim which deserves close examination because of the effect that it would have on defining the economically efficient level of road transport.

Environmental taxes are seen to improve economic efficiency by bridging the gap between social and private costs whereas most revenue-raising taxes result in a deadweight burden to society which rises with the square of the tax rate (this is known as Harberger's Law, after the economist Harberger). This deadweight burden is illustrated in Box 2.2. The deadweight burden of revenue-raising taxes exerts a drag on the economy which Governments have traditionally sought to minimise. The necessary condition for minimising the deadweight cost of raising a given amount of tax revenue is that the cost of the last pound raised be equal across all taxed goods and activities. Unless this condition were met it would be possible to raise the same amount of revenue at less cost simply by increasing

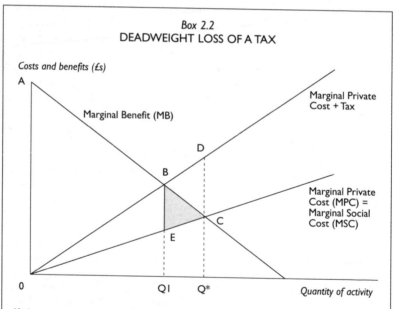

Box 2.2
DEADWEIGHT LOSS OF A TAX

If there is no divergence between marginal private and marginal social costs, then a tax reduces the amount of economic surplus that could be gained from an activity. Typically a tax is placed on the good in question, which raises the marginal private costs (MPC) faced by the individual consumer. Economic surplus falls from 0CA0 by an amount BCE. BCE is referred to as the 'deadweight loss of the tax'.

This situation can be compared with that in Box 2.1 of a tax on pollution. If marginal social and marginal private costs are the same, as in this box, then a tax causes loss in economic surplus. If the costs diverge, then a tax can increase economic surplus.

the tax on some goods and reducing it on others. It makes sense to push taxes on road transport beyond what can be justified on purely environmental grounds. Exempting road transport from taxes intended for purely revenue-raising purposes increases unnecessarily the overall cost of distortionary taxes elsewhere in the economy. For this reason economists exclude purely revenue-raising taxes from calculations pertaining to the efficient level of road transport (Pearce 1993; Newbery, 1995).

THE ROLE OF ECONOMIC INSTRUMENTS IN SECURING ECONOMIC EFFICIENCY

Hitherto it has been assumed that the only means of reducing the level of an external cost is to reduce the level of the activity causing it. Generally, however, this is not the case and hardly ever the case in pollution generated by road transport. There are numerous opportunities for both the road user to undertake abatement activity (such as the fitting of catalytic converters to reduce air pollution or driving a less powerful car) as well as for the victims to undertake defensive measures (such as double glazing to reduce noise nuisance or staying indoors on days of high air pollution). It is thus quite wrong to talk as some have done of 'the need to make motoring expensive'. There is no obvious need to do so and the authors of this book would be strongly opposed to any restrictions, for example, placed on vehicle ownership. Rather, we would argue that there is a need to make polluting expensive. Statements hinting at the need to 'punish' motorists are likely to be perceived by the collective of road users and motoring organisations as a direct assault on personal liberty. Indeed, it is also:

> ...a fundamental part of the Government's approach that people's aspirations to own and use a car should not be artificially constrained (statement by the Minister of Transport, 1989).

But if some are capable of suggesting that only a reduction in the amount of motoring or a stabilisation in the levels of car ownership will suffice, others are equally capable of implying that technical means alone are capable of obtaining the required reduction in the environmental impact of transport. The fact of the matter is that at the margin some reduction in the level of the activity will always be preferable to total reliance upon technological measures. Verhoef (1994) formally demonstrates this proposition. How can this least cost combination of responses (reducing the need to travel, reducing the amount of pollution per journey, mitigating the effects, etc) possibly be elicited, given that the Government cannot observe the individual costs involved? The answer is to use 'economic instruments'.

Economists are typically in favour of the use of 'economic' or 'market based' instruments as a means of procuring economic efficiency. It is well worthwhile rehearsing the arguments in favour of market based instruments as well as their practical limitations. Why are market based instruments the 'least cost' means of achieving environmental improvements? The advantage of market based instruments lies in their ability to equalise the marginal costs of abatement across different agents. This occurs because economic instruments involve a uniform tax on the polluting activity and all generators pollute up to the point where their marginal costs of abatement equal the tax. Hence the marginal costs of abatement are equalised across all polluters which is a necessary condition of least cost compliance. Simply speaking, private self interest implies that the cutbacks in pollution are made where it is cheapest to do so. Placing a tax on pollution also affects locational choices, the level of activity, the demand for goods which embody a large element of transportation services. These prices serve as proper signals upon which to base investment decisions whether in terms of physical capital or in terms of investments in knowledge. Since these investment decisions include road and rail infrastructure as well as private property and other forms of capital it is important to get these right. Thus a whole hierarchy of decisions is affected by the imposition of an environmental tax. The second advantage of market based instruments lies in the dynamic efficiency of such an arrangement. The tax encourages innovation and rewards the development of measures which can cut pollution at low cost. The relative advantages of economic instruments are widely endorsed by, among others, the UK Government and the Organisation for Economic Cooperation and Development (OECD).

The ability of individuals to reduce pollution by means other than reducing the level of the activity causing it is best captured within a second diagram contained in Box 2.3. This diagram depicts the marginal costs of abatement and the marginal damage curve. These curves both embody the range of adjustments which both the polluters and the victims can make. Thus the marginal costs of abatement curve will represent the least cost combination of changes in the amount of abatement, the level of activity, locational choice decisions, etc, while the marginal damage function reflects the ability of individuals to undertake defensive activity such as double glazing, deciding to stay indoors on high pollution days, etc. The optimal position is not to eliminate all pollution but rather to equate the marginal cost of abatement with the marginal damage. At that point the cost of getting rid of the last unit of pollution is just equal to the additional damage which it causes. In the absence of any policies at all the extent of the policy failure is given by the triangle. This is the difference between the optimal policy and no policy. The tax revenue generated by the optimal tax is given by the rectangle. A very common misconception is to regard the tax paid as an indica-

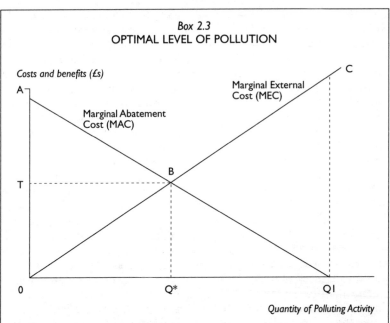

Box 2.3
OPTIMAL LEVEL OF POLLUTION

If motorists can pollute the environment without paying for it, they will demand trips up until the point that there is no more marginal benefit from the trip at all. This corresponds to point QI where QIC marginal external cost is imposed. The cost to motorists of abating pollution by reducing the number of trips taken is shown by the Marginal Abatement Curve. At point QI marginal external cost imposed by taking the trip is greater than the marginal abatement cost from staying at home. Economic surplus is gained by not taking the trip. The same process can be applied to all trips up until Q* number of trips. At this point it becomes more costly for the motorist to give up the trip than any benefit derived by people of reduced pollution.

tion of the real resource costs of achieving a given improvement. In fact the economic costs of producing a given reduction in the level of a pollutant are the area under the marginal costs of abatement schedule rather than the rectangle. The rectangle represents a transfer payment and not a resource cost. This payment can be returned although not in a way which alters the incentives to any of the polluters or the victims.

The importance of property rights as a fundamental cause of external effects prompted the concept of the tradeable discharge permit. These permits allow the owner to emit a given quantity of pollution over a certain time period. Individuals who do not hold permits are not allowed to pollute. By regulating the overall quantity of permits the government is able to place an upper limit on the emissions of a pollutant. The tradeability of the permits ensures that they always end up in the hands of those who value them most highly. Accordingly, permits share with taxes the 'least cost' property. In some ways permits are more flexible than environmental taxes since by altering the prior distribution of permits, policy makers can influence the distributional incidence of these measures without affecting the efficiency properties of the scheme.

In contrast to market based measures like permits and taxes, standards and regulatory measures risk imposing very high costs on some individuals and it is unlikely that the resulting control costs are minimised. Moreover, setting standards of whatever description does not encourage the search for more economical means of control. But some regulatory measures have an advantage over market based instruments in cases where it is difficult to observe the polluting activity or where the cost of monitoring the pollution levels for which any individual is responsible is high. With imperfect monitoring ability it is difficult to make any general statement about the relative merits of standards against market based instruments. It is also clear that the damage done by a particular level of emissions is dependent upon a variety of other factors which vary over the spatial and temporal ranges. These need to be accommodated for by charging different tax rates. The fact that pollution levels vary makes implementation of any scheme administratively difficult. Often, then, the charge will fail to reflect the marginal damage occurring in the particular instance.

Finally, it has been suggested that moral suasion provides a solution to the problem of environmental pollution. For example, the UK Government's practice is currently to ask motorists to leave their vehicles at home on high pollution days. The evidence is that moral suasion of any description simply doesn't work and nor should it when one considers the 'Tragedy of the Commons' allegory described in the introduction. There is no rationality in self-restraint while others retain the right to drive as much as they like.

EQUITY AND EFFICIENCY

Despite the considerable advantages favouring the use of market based instruments, the Government has so far been very reluctant to adopt them. The only example of the Government using a market based instrument to tackle a pollution problem is the price differential between leaded and unleaded fuel. Part of the reason for this has already been explained in terms of the inability of policy makers to observe the polluting activities of individuals at low monitoring cost. Clearly the Government can only charge for what it observes. But this does not fully explain the almost total absence of market based instruments to deal with environmental problems. The allegedly capricious distributional effects of environmental taxes are central to understanding why it is that Governments have been so reluctant to follow the advice of economists. Internalising externalities may have profound distributional consequences in terms of the monetary transfers referred to earlier. Internalising external costs improves economic efficiency but at the same time it redistributes welfare between different groups. These groups can be differentiated in terms of their income, geographical area or even, in the case of stock pollutants, by the time at which they exist.

This redistribution of welfare is often depicted as undesirable. In many situations it seems that those who are likely to be disadvantaged by a particular measure form a distinct and well-organised group. The benefits of environmental policies by contrast tend to be much more widely spread. Populistic arguments are developed by the former to create anxieties in the minds of policy makers. The standard paradigm is the case of 'the poor commuter who has to drive 100km a day for his journey to work and cannot afford higher road charges because he has a large family to feed on a meagre income'. It is thus frequently argued that the underpricing of transport is justified on grounds of equity. But it is easy to show that on average the emotive argument described above cannot be correct. The higher income classes run up a higher mileage and spend more on road transport. Thus when pressure groups complain about the 'unfair' distributional impacts of higher transport taxes they are often trying to preserve their own high income positions. Furthermore, the idea that we cannot do anything about environmental pollution from road transport because of an overriding need to preserve the current distribution of welfare is most peculiar. The point is not that distributional effects are unimportant, but that there may be many less distorting means of producing the desired distribution of welfare than through environmental policy. That this is so is often overlooked. It is partly for this reason that we have focused on estimating the correct level of taxes to induce economic efficiency in the road transport sector, and not to measure the 'unpaid bill' that motorists impose on the rest of society.

A further point to bear in mind is that, although it might not seem like it, most of the arguments concerning the distributional incidence of taxation on road transport are very partial in nature and might more properly be regarded as analyses of the distribution of the financial costs associated with particular measures. A complete picture of the distributional impact of financial measures impinging on road transport requires understanding the distribution of the environmental benefits which accrue and the distribution of the proceeds of any new tax. Yet these two elements are typically ignored because it is 'impossible' to put money values on intangible environmental improvements at all, much less know how different groups value environmental benefits; and because it is possible to make a great many assumptions concerning exactly how the revenue might be returned to society, each of which might produce a different distributional outcome. All this makes it very difficult to say whether an environmental tax per se is regressive or has an adverse effect on macroeconomic indicators without stating the policy context within which such changes are made and which taxes are to be lowered. Stand alone statements such as 'a tax on carbon emissions is regressive' simply don't make sense to an economist unless qualified by some statement such as 'as long as we assume that the revenues are returned in this manner'. This immediately prompts the question as to whether the revenues from a carbon tax can be recycled in a different way which would avoid the regressive impact. Any presentation therefore rests on assumptions made about the means by which the tax revenue is recycled. Because of the axiomatic nature of these assumptions to the results, the nature of the assumptions ought to be explicit. But often they are not.

As a standard benchmark we often find that revenue is assumed not to be redistributed but instead 'kept' by the Government. Sometimes this is taken as more than a benchmark and as a literal interpretation of what would happen if the Government started to charge road users for the environmental degradation they cause. The Government, it is said, cannot be trusted with environmental tax revenues. How sensible is this as a working assumption? The introduction of any new tax can be 'non-neutral', 'fiscally neutral' or 'revenue neutral'. These refer to changes in which the net borrowing position of the Government is altered, the Government spends all the extra revenue received, and changes whereby the Government reduces other taxes by an equivalent amount. Since taxes on pollution and congestion are intended to divert expenditures away from motoring and into abatement activity rather than exercising a degree of control over the macroeconomy or providing revenues for unspecified public works, one would assume that the most appropriate policy context would be that any new taxes are offset by tax cuts elsewhere in the system. Indeed, it is possible to make any environmental tax reform look bad by assuming it to be non-neutral. Increasing tax revenues typically causes a multiple contraction of the economy with adverse effects on employment and output. But it should be clear that these outcomes are due to the policy context and not to the tax measures themselves. As an example, consider the often made claim that increasing taxes on road transport will cause unemployment. If increases in taxes on road transport are not offset by tax reductions elsewhere there will indeed be a multiple contraction of economic activity. But it is clear that this is due to the non-neutral nature of the hypothesised tax change. The proper context is one where the Government reduces taxes elsewhere in the economy in order to avoid a multiple contraction of the economy. If the Government finds it desirable to reduce the budget deficit by putting up taxes, the changes ought to be compared relative to other taxes being increased to achieve the same reduction in the budget deficit thereby making the non-neutral nature of the change explicit.

This example should warn the reader to treat claims about the adverse effects of tax changes on road transport circumspectly. The difficulty of using partial economic analyses to reach decisions about the overall economic impact of environmental measures should be obvious. Many road users are just as concerned about the impact of road transport on the environment as the rest of society and there is evidence that they themselves may be among the most susceptible to adverse air quality. At the present time there is no evidence regarding the full distributional impact of environmental taxes to be had.

In similar vein, it is often argued that environmental taxes on transport would have much greater public acceptability if the (often substantial) revenues from environmental taxes were earmarked for projects falling within the transport sector, such as the subsidisation of public transport or the construction of more transport infrastructure. We imagine that, if this is true, it must be because in the questionnaires people are asked to respond to they are confronted by two choices: either the tax revenues are kept by the Government or they are returned in the form of greater spending on public transport. It would be interesting to see whether the preference for hypothecation remains if people were offered a third choice involving equivalent cuts in other taxes. Standard public finance theory states that taxes should be raised in the least cost manner and public funds spent where their returns are highest. The purpose of environmental taxes is not obviously to raise funds for public works. While hypothecation might be possible to some small extent due to the fungibility of tax revenues, carried out to any significant extent it could prove to be extremely wasteful. Any attempt at hypothecation of tax revenues would be fiercely (and no doubt successfully) resisted by the UK Treasury. It is wrong to think that the route to enacting measures to reduce the environmental impact of road transport lies in hypothecation.

TECHNIQUES FOR VALUING ENVIRONMENTAL DEGRADATION

In order to pursue the kind of strategy advocated here whereby road users are to be charged for the environmental degradation they cause, there is a need to place money values upon environmental amenities. This is so that the trade-offs between material goods and consumption versus greater environmental quality can be calculated in terms of a common denominator. There are a variety of techniques commonly used to monetise changes in environmental quality and the simpler of these are described below. These methodologies have found natural application in measuring the environmental impact of road transport and reappear throughout the remainder of the book. But before we introduce them, it seems appropriate to explain the different sources of value that people derive from improvements in environmental quality. The reason is that several of the techniques are capable of measuring only a subset of the overall benefits. The best introductory reference to these methodologies is Pearce and Markandya (1989).

Environmental Economics has provided a taxonomy of the different sources of value derived from environmental resources. The Total Economic Value (TEV) of an asset is the sum of the User Value, the Indirect Value, the Option Value and the Existence Value. The User Value is the direct and private benefit which people obtain from an environmental amenity. Indirect Values are ecological values which arise because of the functions which certain ecosystems perform (eg a particular habitat supports particular species of animals). Option Values are more complicated. Due to uncertainty regarding the future, people may be willing to pay certain kinds of insurance premiums in order to see environmental assets preserved even when it is suspected that no use can be found for them. The payment is made to retain the option as to their use. Existence Values include benefits obtained from sympathy for animals, gifts to other people or later generations and intrinsic values.

The most basic method for eliciting people's preferences for environmental amenities and other non-marketed goods is the hypothetical markets (stated preference) approach. There are several related approaches of which the main is the Contingent Valuation Method (CVM). The CVM method relies upon survey data to reveal the Willingness To Pay (WTP) for a hypothetical change in the quantity of some environmental amenity. The typical CVM study generally comprises three elements: a description of the scenario in which the respondent is to imagine himself placed; questions from which values are to be inferred (eg how much are you willing to pay for the preservation of this landscape?); and questions relating to the respondent himself. The strength of the CVM approach is that not only is it applicable in all contexts, but also WTP responses may include non-user values from different sources.

A variety of elicitation techniques have been employed in CVM studies such as open-ended formats (ie what is the maximum amount that you are willing to pay to secure this improvement?), dichotomous choice (ie will you pay amount X for this improvement?) and iterative bidding in which the respondent is given escalating bids until they eventually refuse to pay any more. Each of these approaches has deficiencies. The open-ended format is difficult for people to respond to, while the dichotomous choice requires large samples to work satisfactorily. Iterative bidding can suffer from an anchoring effect whereby respondents take cues about how much they 'ought' to offer. Varying the format of the questionnaire often affects the results obtained substantially.

One might suppose that a strategic bias problem occurs in CVM studies. If respondents realise that the results of this survey will be used to determine the extent of government expenditure they have an incentive to overstate their WTP. If on the other hand they realise that their response will determine their individual contribution they will understate their WTP for a public good. There are ways of testing for the presence of this effect. There are also likely to be information effects present. This means that respondents' replies are contingent upon what they perceive to be the effects of a particular pollutant rather than what the real effects may be. Providing information may substantially amend the bids received. Bias arises where the WTP depends upon the instrument of payment and whether the respondent is reminded about the existence of close substitute goods. Some respondents are apt to make protest bids of zero simply because they object to the nature of the valuation experiment. Clearly some means has to be found of discriminating between these people and people who do not value the environmental good in question or are unable to pay for it. Debriefing is normally used for this purpose. A particularly intractable problem is the issue of 'embedding'. This occurs when respondents have difficulty in separating component values from more broadly defined goods. Thus when respondents are asked for their willingness to pay to reduce noise levels from road traffic by 20 per cent, they may give responses which are based on the assumption that road traffic (and all its other external effects) is to be reduced by 20 per cent. The scope for double counting is obvious.

WTP responses are usually regressed by the socio-economic characteristics of the respondents in order to demonstrate that these responses are not just random impulses, and also to provide a basis for aggregating the responses to cover the entire population. The remaining techniques are all based on the revelation of preferences through behaviour rather than relying on hypothetical experiments and this is their relative strength compared to the hypothetical markets approach. On the other hand it is typically argued that these techniques only reveal the use value of an environmental amenity and therefore provide an incomplete statement of what a particular amenity is worth.

Possibly the most useful of the revealed preference techniques is known as the Hedonic House Price technique. The argument here is that the closer a property is to valuable environmental amenities (eg parks) and the lower pollution variables are (eg less noise) the more valuable the property will become. These amenities will be reflected in the sale price or rental cost of the house. Damages suffered away from the home or damages not perceived by the residents are not valued so that the information provided by such studies will never be more than partial. The technique involves running a statistical regression with price as the dependent variable and numerous housing, locational and environmental variables as explanatory variables.

level of an environmental amenity is to confront individuals who are alike in all respects with different prices for obtaining extra amounts of the environmental amenities and to observe the amounts which they choose to consume. This requires data from geographically or temporally separate markets and has not been seen as a priority, if judged by the number of studies that seem content to calculate marginal willingness to pay and then to proceed no further. Economists are also able to calculate attitudes to risk and other phenomena from hedonic wage studies. The rationale for wage–risk studies is that some jobs are more hazardous than others and differences in wage rates have to compensate for this.

Even though entry to certain environmental amenities such as a national park is free, every user of these amenities pays a price in terms of his or her travel costs to that site. This is referred to in the literature as the Travel Cost Method (TCM) and it permits the analyst to estimate the 'user value' of the amenity (although again, not any other sources of value that the site may have). The basic TCM works by estimating the travel costs to the site from certain zones and the number of visits per capita which arise from each of the zones (Box 2.5). A distance–decay function is estimated and the economic surplus gained by people living in each zone can be

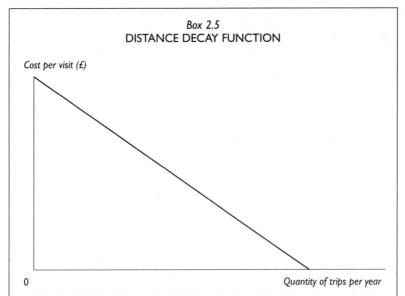

Box 2.5
DISTANCE DECAY FUNCTION

Cost per visit (£)

0   Quantity of trips per year

The Travel Cost Method attempts to construct a demand curve for an environmental amenity by examining how the number of visits to a site varies with the cost of travelling to see the site. As distance from site increases so does the cost involved in getting to the site.

calculated. The underlying assumption of the technique then is that visitors respond in the same way to an increase in travel costs as they would to an increase in the admission price. Notice that unlike the hedonic approach it is the site itself which is valued and not particular aspects of it.

The main problems with the TCM are to be found in the valuation of time and in whether the full costs of the travel (eg fuel, wear and tear of the vehicle) are properly perceived by the visitors. In TCM studies the cost of time spent travelling is typically assumed to be some fraction of the average wage. But the values used typically refer to the value of saving a few minutes spent commuting rather than of several hours spent travelling to a recreational site. The value of the time spent at the recreational site also needs to be valued and these are difficult in the extreme.

Finally, Household Production Function (HPF) methods work in situations where either an environmental amenity is complementary to, or a substitute for, a range of marketed goods. An example might be medicine and air pollution in the preservation of health. By examining the consumption patterns for like individuals living in areas characterised by different levels of the environmental amenity, it is possible to obtain an idea of the value of changes in the level of environmental amenities to the consumer and how these values might vary with his or her income level. But the HPF method relies upon the assumption of prior restrictions on individual preferences, which amounts to saying that changes in the levels of environmental amenities are fully reflected in differing consumption patterns. In fact, it is quite possible to conceive of environmental amenities which, although of high value to individuals, would not be reflected in changes in consumer purchases. In these circumstances the method fails entirely. The method also requires extremely detailed data on the consumption patterns of individuals and the level of the environmental disamenity to which they are exposed and these data are seldom available.

PART II

The External Costs of Road Transport in the United Kingdom

◆

Chapter 3

Road Transport And The Enhanced Greenhouse Effect

INTRODUCTION

The environmental problems posed by road transport and discussed in this part of the book are organised in terms of the geographical domain of their effect. The only global effect of road transport resides in its contribution to the so-called enhanced greenhouse effect resulting in possible changes in the earth's climate. Although the UK's contribution to the total emissions is small, the UK, along with all other developed countries, has committed itself to restraining future emissions and road transport is one sector which contributes significantly to overall emissions.

The first section summarises the science underlying the enhanced greenhouse effect and the potentially disruptive effects of rapid climate change. The second section considers the protocols restricting the ability of countries to emit gases contributing to the enhanced greenhouse effect, the measures that the UK has employed to meet its international obligations and their likely distributive consequences. The next section discusses the appropriate charge to place on greenhouse gas (GHG) emissions from road transport and the alternative suggestions that have been made in this respect. The complex empirical models required to calculate what is arguably the appropriate charge for greenhouse gas emission are explained. Money values are then attached to emissions from the UK road transport sector to arrive at an estimate of the marginal external cost of these emissions. The concluding section considers the economic advantages of using a carbon tax to cut carbon emissions relative to alternative measures.

WHAT IS THE ENHANCED GREENHOUSE EFFECT?

Depending on planetary albedo, a certain fraction of the incoming shortwave solar radiation is reflected straight back in the direction of space. The remainder is absorbed by the surface of the planet warming the air that comes into contact with it. Part of this energy also evaporates water carrying latent heat up into the atmosphere. Any remaining energy is reflected back into space in the form of longwave radiation. But GHGs are partially opaque to this outgoing radiation and absorb its energy. This serves to raise the temperature of the planet until equilibrium in the form of the earth's radiation balance is restored. Without the blanketing provided by the greenhouse effect the mean surface temperature of the planet would be approximately 33°C cooler than at present.

Anthropogenic emissions of these GHGs have been increasing rapidly since the time of the industrial revolution. The relatively long atmospheric lifetime of some of these gases has resulted in an accumulation in the atmosphere with the possibility of a sustained increase in the amount of energy incident at the earth's surface (radiative forcing). The enhanced greenhouse effect (the term 'enhanced' is usually dropped) is the most compelling explanation of the recent rise in global temperatures. But the greenhouse effect is not the only explanation for changes in the earth's climate and nor is it a simple process to argue from increased GHG concentrations to global temperature rises due to the presence of a variety of both positive and negative feedbacks.

By far the most important GHG is carbon dioxide (CO_2) which arises predominantly from the burning of fossil fuel, although methane (CH_4), nitrous oxides (N_2O), chlorofluourocarbons (CFCs) and a large number of other gases are also important. Various fossil fuels are implicated to a differing degree in the production of carbon dioxide emissions, with coal the dirtiest fuel when measured on a carbon per unit of energy basis, and gas the cleanest. The residence of CO_2 in the atmosphere is governed by the carbon cycle and about 15 per cent of the carbon dioxide emitted will be retained in the atmosphere indefinitely. The current expectation among scientists is that a doubling of the concentration of carbon dioxide in the atmosphere is likely to lead in the long run to a 2.5°C rise in average global temperature and a change in patterns of precipitation (Intergovern-mental Panel on Climate Change (IPCC), 1992). Elevated global temperatures impact upon the exchanges occurring within the hydrological cycle. Net flows from freshwater lakes, glaciers, ice caps, man-made reservoirs or groundwater into the oceans plus the thermal expansion of the various layers of the oceans will cause the sea level to rise.

For the purposes of developing policy measures, the instantaneous and long-term global warming potential (GWP) of each gas needs to be considered. The instantaneous impact of a gas is defined as the product of its increase in atmospheric concentration multiplied by the increase in radiative forcing per unit of concentration. The GWP is the instantaneous impact of the gases integrated over their lifetime residency in the atmosphere (or other suitably long period of time) taking into account the decay and transformation processes. GWPs are always expressed relative to that of carbon dioxide which is given a GWP of unity. Used in conjunction with information relating to comparative abatement costs it permits the development of an efficient abatement strategy. The properties of the key GHGs are described in Box 3.1.

Box 3.1
PROPERTIES OF KEY GHGS

Greenhouse gas lifetime	1991 concentrations (ppmv)	Annual increase (percentage)	Direct GWP	Lifetime
Carbon dioxide	355	0.5	1	120
Methane	1.72	0.6–0.75	11	10.5
Nitrous oxide	0.31	0.2–0.3	270	132
CFC-11	$2.55*10^{-4}$	4.0	3,400	55
CFC-12	$4.53*10^{-4}$	4.0	7,100	116

Source: Department of the Environment, 1992
Note: These are integrated over 100 years.

THE FRAMEWORK CONVENTION ON CLIMATE CHANGE AND THE UK CONTEXT

An appreciation of the potentially disruptive effects of rapid climate change has led to an international policy response in the form of the Framework Convention on Climate Change (FCCC). The FCCC was created at the United Nations Conference On Environment and Development (UNCED) held in Rio in June 1992. It has been signed by 168 countries and having achieved its fiftieth ratification came into force in March 1994. Its ultimate goal is:

...the stabilisation of GHG concentrations in the atmosphere at a level which will prevent dangerous anthropogenic interference with the climate. Such a level should be achieved within a time frame sufficient to allow ecosystems to adapt naturally to climate change, to ensure that food production is not threatened and to enable economic development to proceed in a sustainable manner.

While all signatories are to prepare national inventories of GHG emissions and sinks, the Convention states that the climate system is to be protected with regard to the differentiated capabilities of states. Accordingly, developed countries are required to provide to the Conference of the Parties, within six months of the date of the convention coming into force, details of measures to individually or jointly reduce GHG emissions back to 1990 levels by the year 2000. A certain degree of flexibility was afforded to the economies in transition in respect of meeting the target. Developed country parties (excluding the transition economies) are further required to provide financial resources to meet the '...agreed full incremental costs...' of implementing a range of measures in developing country parties (UNCED, 1992).

The UK Government ratified the Convention on Climate Change in December 1993 and in January 1994 produced the UK's first report to the Conference of the Parties to the Convention as required under article 12 of the Convention. This report included inventories of the main GHG emissions and detailed measures aimed at returning the emissions of each GHG to 1990 levels:

> ...the UK accepts...the commitment to take measures aimed at returning emissions of Greenhouse Gases to 1990 levels by the year 2000. The UK has prepared...measures designed to achieve this commitment for each of the main greenhouse gases... (HMSO 1994; section 1.2).

UK emissions represent approximately 2.2 per cent of global emissions and despite any impression to the contrary, UK emissions of carbon have actually fallen from a high point of 181mtC (million metric tonnes of carbon) in 1970 to 151mtC in 1993. The fall in emissions appears to have been the result of a decline in emissions from the industrial sector, although domestic emissions and emissions from power stations have also been declining. These reductions, however, have been partially offset by a very rapid rise in emissions from road transport which over the same period rose by nearly 88 per cent and now account for 20 per cent of all emissions by source. In the UK road transport is thus the only growing source of CO_2 emissions. The Government initially forecast that by the year 2000, in the absence of any policy changes, UK emissions would turn up once more and reach 170mtC, although due to various uncertainties this was set to range from between 157 and 179mtC. In early 1995, however, the Government produced revised year 2000 forecasts of the UK's emissions of carbon which showed that the UK was set to undershoot the target by a considerable margin (between 6 and 13mtC). With hindsight then, no measures were necessary in order to comply with the Rio targets!

In contrast to carbon, methane emissions have declined only modestly since 1970. The single most important source of methane emissions in the UK is the deep mining of coal. Emissions from this source mirror the general decline in the coal industry over the same period and have now been halved. Unfortunately, the decline in emissions from this source has been balanced by increases in emissions from landfill sites and leakages of gas. A data series for nitrous oxides is not currently available and the emission sources themselves are still uncertain but almost all of the 78,000 tonnes are accounted for either by industrial emissions or by emissions from the soil. The contribution of road transport to overall emissions of both methane and nitrous oxide is relatively small (Box 3.2).

Nonetheless, as part of its overall effort to help meet the UK's obligations to the FCCC the Government adopted a range of mea-

Box 3.2
UK EMISSIONS OF KEY GHGS BY SOURCE (1993)

Greenhouse gas	Total emissions, tonnes	Road transport, tonnes	Percentage road transport
Carbon dioxide[1]	151,000,000	30,000,000	20.0
Methane	4,173,000	11,000	0.3
Nitrous oxide	78,000	3,000	0.4

Source: Department of the Environment, 1995
1 Measured in terms of carbon

Box 3.3
UK AVERAGE BUDGET SHARES FOR DOMESTIC FUEL AND MOTOR
FUEL EXPENDITURE BY INCOME DECILE GROUPS

Income group	Domestic fuel	Motor fuel
1 (lowest)	15.5	0.5
2	11.6	1.2
3	9.1	2.1
4	7.2	2.7
5	6.3	3.5
6	5.7	3.7
7	5.1	3.9
8	4.7	3.8
9	4.2	3.9
10 (highest)	3.9	3.3
All	7.3	2.9

Source: Smith, 1992

sures designed to assist in achieving (what was then perceived to be) the required reduction of 10mtC to return emissions to their 1990 levels by the year 2000. As part of these measures the then Chancellor Norman Lamont increased the duty on road fuel by 10 per cent in his March 1993 budget and made a commitment to raise duties by an average of 3 per cent annually in real terms in future budgets. This was expected to produce savings of 1.5mtC by the year 2000 (HMSO, 1994) and to raise £1.02bn additional revenue in 1995–96. In the November 1993 budget Chancellor Kenneth Clarke raised the duty on a gallon of petrol again and vowed to increase the duty on road fuel by at least 5 per cent annually in real terms. Using a model of the demand for road transport fuel, Virley (1993) has independently estimated the impact of fuel price increases on carbon emissions. Virley's model confirms that strict adherence to the minimum commitments made by Chancellor Lamont would reduce carbon emissions by 1.5mtC by the year 2000 with an uncertainty range of 0.6–2.2mtC. This should be compared to a baseline in which carbon emissions from road transport grow from 29.9mtC in 1990 to 36.5mtC by 2000.

One immediate objection to these increases in fuel duty was that they were 'regressive', placing a disproportionate burden on the poor. But as Box 3.3 makes clear, fuel taxes are in fact highly progressive in nature if the proceeds are refunded on a per capita basis for the brute reason that poor people generally do not own cars. In this respect raising fuel duty has a clear advantage over taxes on domestic fuel whose regressive nature has long been established. On the debit side the regional incidence of road fuel tax increases suggested other concerns, with a disproportionate burden of the tax falling upon isolated rural communities (Box 3.4).

Box 3.4
INTER-AREAL DIFFERENCES IN SPENDING ON PETROL

Administrative area	Petrol spending (£s per week)
London	7.49
Other metropolitan	6.37
Rural high density	7.65
Rural medium density	9.46
Rural low density	9.09

Source: Johnson et al, 1990

INTEGRATED ASSESSMENT MODELS AND THE SHADOW PRICE OF GREENHOUSE GASES

We now turn our attention to the difficult question of what it is appropriate to charge road users for their contribution to the enhanced greenhouse effect. Various authors have dealt with this question in a variety of ways. At one extreme it may be argued that because the UK's target is now likely to be met anyway, GHG emissions from the road transport sector ought not to be included in any estimate of the external costs of transport in the UK. However, even if the UK succeeds in meeting its targets, this is of little relevance to global atmospheric concentrations because the UK is such an insignificant contributor to the overall problem. It is emphatically not the case that if the UK succeeds in meeting its targets the value of the damage done by the remaining UK emissions is zero. Alternatively, for want of anything better, others have used the carbon taxes which have been proposed, or in some cases actually enacted by Governments, as a measure of the shadow value of carbon. Such procedures are likely to result in different shadow prices for GHGs being used in different studies, which is odd since the only certain fact about climate change is that a tonne of carbon does the same damage wherever it is released. Moreover, many countries such as the UK do not have an explicit tax on carbon. Many propose a 'carbon budget' approach in which a (pre) historical analogue is sought for threatened rapid changes in climate (eg Krause et al, 1989). This is taken as the maximum permissible rate of change and annual carbon budgets are set to ensure that this rate of change is not exceeded. With annual limits placed on carbon emissions the appropriate shadow price of GHG emissions from the road transport sector is the opportunity cost of making the required cutbacks elsewhere. In our view, however, this begs the question of why the observed maximum rate of change should be in any way relevant.

Given the available alternatives, our preference is to use as shadow prices for carbon those tax rates necessary to procure the 'optimal' cutback in emissions. Unfortunately, deciding what constitutes the optimal emissions strategy turns out to be rather involved, requiring an empirically based 'Integrated Assessment' (IA) model of climate change. IA models attempt to condense a diverse body of information relating to economic growth assumptions, carbon emissions forecasts, abatement cost estimates and global warming damage functions and incorporate them into a single model. The simplest of these models takes baseline economic output and GHG emissions as given. Given baseline emissions an IA model then computes forecasts of atmospheric concentrations of carbon dioxide dependent upon a model of the carbon cycle. Average global temperatures slowly adjust to elevated carbon dioxide concentrations. This rise in temperature is taken as an index of global environmental change which is assumed to cause economic damage. Such losses are quantified in terms of a 'damage function'. The damage function is basically a relationship between global temperature rise and economic damage in terms of percentage loss of gross national product (GNP). Tentative estimates of the money value of the damages done by GHG emissions have been made by Fankhauser (1995). Current enumeration of the impacts of climate change suggests that a 2.5°C rise in temperature would reduce global GNP by approximately 1.5 per cent. The warming process in these models can be delayed by reducing emissions from the baseline, which incurs a cost or alternatively emissions can be offset by terrestrial sink enhancement (planting forests to absorb carbon from the atmosphere).

Usually by means of iterative computer search, an IA model can be used to locate an abatement strategy for each time period in which the marginal cost to society of removing the last tonne of carbon is exactly equal to the marginal benefit in terms of climate change-related damage which is thereby avoided. It is this abatement strategy which is referred to as the 'optimal control'. Associated with the optimal control are a set of shadow prices for a unit emission of GHGs. These are dollar estimates of the present value marginal damage caused by the last unit of emission. Since they are evaluated along the optimal control they can also be interpreted as the optimal tax rate on GHG emissions. These tax rates are arguably the most appropriate measures of the harm arising from a unit emission of carbon into the atmosphere and have been widely endorsed as such.

An alternative assumption is that GHG emissions continue to rise without any checks whatsoever due to an inability on the part of governments to agree on the allocation of responsibility for controlling emissions. This is known as the 'Business As Usual' (BAU) assumption. In this scenario, abatement in an IA model is constrained to be zero in all time periods. Without any controls GHGs accumulate in the atmosphere more rapidly. With a higher stock of GHG emissions in the atmosphere the marginal impact of any additional emissions is likely to be increased. The difference between the marginal damage estimates evaluated along the optimal control and the marginal damage estimates evaluated along BAU is displayed in Box 3.5. These estimates are also a plausible candidate for the appropriate charge with which to confront road users.

The shadow price estimates for GHGs to be used in this study are taken from Maddison (1993) who calculates both the marginal damage evaluated along the optimal control and the marginal damage estimate evaluated along BAU. These are seen not to differ much reflecting the (contentious) finding that the optimal strategy appears to involve cutting carbon emissions by a remarkably small amount. These shadow prices are used to estimate the environmental impact of road transport in respect of its contribution to future climate change (Box 3.7). The estimates of the marginal damage caused by the various GHGs are not in proportion to their GWPs. The reason is that the economic damage depends upon when the impact is. We need to take into account the changing stocks of GHGs as well as the fact that the impact takes place further into the future, and should therefore be discounted. The final point is that over time, as stocks of GHGs accumulate in the atmosphere the cost of additional emissions will rise under both the optimal policy and the business as usual scenario. Thus the relative importance of GHG emissions, although small at the moment compared to the other external effects of road transport, will grow sharply over time as comparison of the shadow values of emissions in 1993 and 2025 demonstrates.

The value of the contribution of UK road transport to the enhanced greenhouse effect are given in Box 3.7. These estimates are based on the shadow prices evaluated along the optimal control rather than BAU. These estimates suggest that the present value damage of GHG emissions from the UK road transport sector are £0.1 bn annually.

ALTERNATIVE MEANS TO CUT CARBON EMISSIONS

The Royal Commission On Environmental Pollution (1994) has advised that the transport sector be given a specific target of reducing carbon dioxide emissions to 80 per cent of their 1990 levels. The Royal Commission seeks to justify this target by reference to the multitude of other external effects associated with road transport. The road transport sector has also been singled out for special treatment by others on the grounds that it is the only growing source of carbon emissions in the UK. The suggested means of reducing carbon emissions from road transport include increasing fuel taxes and setting minimum standards for vehicle design. Increasing fuel taxes certainly would, on the basis of historical evidence, reduce carbon emissions. Moreover, Wooton and Poulton (1993) consider there to be a potential to improve vehicle fuel efficiency by up to 30 per cent in the short term and by up to 50 per cent in the long term by means of engine re-design, transmission optimisation, weight reduction and reduction in drag.

But it seems to us that neither the fact that there are a multitude of other environmental effects associated with road transport nor the fact that it is the only growing source of emissions justify singling out road transport for special attention. For one thing fuel duty is a highly imperfect means of tackling more general problems (as later chapters will demonstrate) and there are much better alternatives. Secondly, if one seeks to minimise the costs of hitting a carbon constraint, ideally one would wish to equalise the marginal costs of abating carbon emissions throughout the economy rather than setting specific targets for particular sectors. This can only be achieved by a carbon tax. A carbon tax is a tax specifically on the carbon content of fuels and thus encourages substitution from high carbon fuels to low carbon fuels and away from energy in general. It also causes shifts in consumption by increasing the cost of carbon-intensive commodities relative to low carbon-intensive commodities. A carbon tax will provide the additional financial incentives for motorists to consider the use of renewable energy.

One response to a carbon tax might be a turn to electric-powered vehicles. The desirability of such developments, however, seems to depend on the means used to generate the electricity. Supplies from conventional power stations might mean that carbon emissions per kilometre are greater than those of conventionally powered vehicles. A more promising strategy might involve a switch to natural gas which contains considerably less carbon. Leakages of gas from extraction and distribution systems are likely to reduce these gains from gas-powered vehicles. In some countries, such as Brazil, alcohol-based fuels are widely used. The impact of such a change in terms of carbon emissions depends upon the manner in which the alcohol is manufactured. Although there is no net emission of carbon associated with ethanol derived from biomass, it is likely that large-scale biomass production would itself have environmental consequences.

Chapter 4

The Economic Costs of Air Pollution

INTRODUCTION

Concern over the quality of air we breathe, particularly in urban areas, and its effect on human health, has been increasing. A recent study confirms that there are 'serious grounds for concern about London's air quality', with numerous transgressions of European guidelines, and a series of high pollution episodes throughout the year (South East Institute of Public Health, 1995). Ambient concentrations of pollutants increased at most London monitoring sites between 1993 and 1994. The government has placed great faith in catalytic converters, which have been fitted to all new cars from 1993, to reduce urban air pollution. To date, at least in London, the evidence suggests that this measure alone will not be sufficient to reduce air pollution levels.

This chapter attempts to answer the following question: what are the external costs of air pollution imposed by road transport on society? More specifically, we estimate the external costs imposed on the UK economy in 1993. This chapter presents an overview of the work, and a more detailed exposition can be found in Calthrop (1995). The next section sets out a basic methodology for tackling the problem. Drawing heavily on the human health or 'epidemiology' literature, the effects of the differing cocktail of pollutants emerging from vehicle exhaust pipes on human health can be traced. This section is followed by a discussion of the general methodology used and points to concerns over use of this technique. All the available evidence for the key parts of the calculation are then discussed, and total external costs are estimated. Although some uncertainty should be attached to the magnitude of the estimates, we have found that very significant costs are being imposed on society from road vehicle exhaust emissions.

Once the total external cost from various pollutants has been determined, the damage per litre of fuel sold can be calculated. One question which has caused a great deal of controversy in recent times is the relative environmental benefits of using petrol or diesel fuel in cars. Although diesel manufacturers typically argue that diesel is a 'greener' fuel than petrol, each fuel emits a different cocktail of pollutants, and one cannot readily compare them. We suggest that by using our approach, in which money is the common measuring rod used to examine relative impact, a direct comparison can be made. We have also been able to estimate the external cost of a litre used by different modes of transport, which also produces interesting results. The final part of the chapter assesses possible policy responses and argues for more research into the effects of poor air quality.

This chapter examines only the impact of vehicle fuel consumption on levels of local air pollution. The cost of global atmospheric damage has already been discussed in chapter 3. Our calculations do not include pollution from fuel extraction and processing, nor vehicle manufacturing. Although this type of 'life-cycle analysis' has been undertaken in the literature (Eyre et al, 1995), it appears unlikely to change the magnitude of results presented below.

It is also worth noting that this chapter only explores the effect of air pollution on human health. As such it represents an underestimation of the true impact of air pollution given its role in damaging buildings, soiling clothes, reducing visibility, causing damages to forests and crops, creating unpleasant odours and so forth. It also does not evaluate the effects of the full range of pollutants emitted from exhausts: several potential cancer-causing substances, or 'carcinogens', including 1,3 butadiene, and aldehydes cannot be effectively evaluated at the moment. The 'true' external cost of air pollution from vehicles could be much higher than suggested.

CALCULATING THE EXTERNAL COST OF AIR POLLUTION FROM TRANSPORT

Three basic fuel types are currently used in the UK: leaded petrol (or 'gasoline' in USA terminology), unleaded petrol and diesel. This section presents a methodology for estimating the external costs from the use of these fuels in road vehicles. The following model, taken from Ostro (1994), has been adopted. It involves two stages: firstly, identifying the effect of the pollutants from fuels on human health; and, secondly, placing a money value on those changes in health.

The combustion of fuel within a motor vehicle engine results in a range of pollutants being emitted from the exhaust pipe. It is these pollutants that subsequently cause damage to human health. Emissions of these pollutants form concentrations in the local atmosphere. Calculating the damage done to human health by these emissions requires identifying the amount of the ambient concentration of pollution that has been generated by exhaust pipe emissions, the number of people exposed to these concentrations, and the effect of a unit of pollution on any exposed person. This can be expressed as:

$$\Delta H_{ij} = b_{ij} * POP_j * \Delta A_{jt}$$

where:

Δ = 'change in';
H_i = health impact i per year;
j = a particular pollutant j emitted from exhaust pipes;
t = transport fuel type – diesel, petrol, or unleaded;
b_{ij} = slope of 'Dose-Response function' of health effect i per year with respect to pollutant j;
POP = population exposed to pollutant j; and
A_{jt} = ambient concentration of pollutant j in 1993 attributable to emissions of specific fuel types.

This identifies the damage done from one particular pollutant emitted from a vehicle in terms of a single health impact. Hence it may describe the effect of small particles on lung disease cases. Scientists are able to produce 'dose–response functions' which tell us the impact on the health of a population of a certain dose of pollution. The slope of the function describes the change in human health, or 'response', we would expect from a unit change in pollution 'dose'. The second stage of the technique requires placing an economic value on the change in health impact. This can be expressed as:

$$P_i^* \Delta H_{ij} = P_i^* b_{ij}^* POP_j^* \Delta A_{jt}$$

where:
P_i = a 'price' or economic value for the change in health impact i.

The derivation and application of these 'prices', or 'willingness to pay' estimates as they shall later be called, is discussed below. However, the second equation identifies the economic impact of a particular pollutant on a single health impact. This is what we referred to earlier as the 'external cost' of the pollutant. The process is then repeated with respect to all the health impacts of any pollutant, and across all the pollutants emitted from a type of fuel. These costs can then be summed together, to form a total external cost.

Estimates of these total costs from each fuel are presented below. These costs can then be divided by the number of litres of fuel sold, and an average external cost per litre is derived. It is assumed that doubling the amount of pollution will double the impact on human health: ie there is a linear relationship. Hence each new litre sold (or 'marginal' litre) will inflict, on average, the same amount of damage. This result means that our average cost per litre is also the marginal cost per litre.

Diesel and petrol engines produce very different 'cocktails' of pollutants, and each pollutant has a different impact on human health. Some pollutants do damage directly (primary pollutants) when emitted into the atmosphere, such as benzene or lead, while others do damage both directly and in some secondary form (secondary pollutants). Tropospheric ozone (O_3) and small particulate matter (PM_{10}) are the main secondary pollutants considered below.

Nitrogen oxides (NO_x), sulphur dioxide (SO_2) and volatile organic compounds (VOCs) are all implicated in PM_{10} formation, while both NO_x and VOCs react together to produce tropospheric ozone. The pollutants examined in this paper are presented in Box 4.1. This list should not be interpreted as exhaustive: other pollutants are emitted from road transport, some of which are suspected of causing cancer, such as 1,3 butadiene. Some hydrocarbons are also not examined: formaldehyde is a common aldehyde, which is classed as a 'probable' carcinogen in the USA. The main source of butadiene is motor vehicle exhausts, and it is a very significant contributor to formaldehyde emissions. Although significant progress has been made on the monitoring of these pollutants, the epidemiological work is not yet sufficiently advanced to provide robust dose–response functions. This suggests that the calculations undertaken below could be a serious underestimation of the true impact on human health of exhaust emissions.

Box 4.1
IMPACT OF THE POLLUTANTS INCLUDED IN THE MODEL

	Direct impact on human mortality	Direct impact on human morbidity	Indirect impact on human mortality	via..	Indirect impact on human morbidity	via..
PM_{10}	✔	✔				
SO_x	✔	✔	✔	PM_{10}	✔	PM_{10}
NO_x		✔	✔	PM_{10} and ozone	✔	PM_{10} and ozone
VOCs			✔	PM_{10} and ozone	✔	PM_{10} and ozone
Lead	✔	✔				
Benzene	✔	✔				

To recapitulate, the estimation technique requires four key components:

1. b_{ij} the slope of the dose–response function for each pollutant;
2. ΔA_j the quantity of current ambient concentrations attributable to current emissions of pollutant j from road vehicles;
3. POP_j the population exposed to concentrations of pollutant j
4. P_i a willingness to pay measure for the economic value of a change in health status.

In practice none of these components are known with certainty. However we believe that sufficient robust work has been done to provide useful estimates, and that these are likely to be of the correct orders of magnitude. We recognise the need for far greater refinement of the figures presented.

GENERAL METHODOLOGICAL CONCERNS

It is useful to comment in a little more depth on some of the issues raised by adopting this technique.

The Dose–Response Functions

Ultimately, the question of whether air pollution from motor vehicles causes a deterioration of human health must be explained by scientific theory. However, consistent significant statistical relationships between high levels of a particular pollutant and excess mortality, or other health impacts, found under a variety of circumstances is taken as a plausible basis for causality, given the uncertainty inherent in research of human biology. Where the biological pathway through which the pollutant effects human mortality and morbidity is unresolved, consistent epidemiological studies discovering significant relationships is typically taken as 'proof' of causality. An ability to replicate findings of these statistical relationships on different populations and different time periods is clearly of central importance. Ideally, therefore, epidemiological studies should be conducted across a range of sample populations or cities, with varying levels of other explanatory variables, and a variety of ambient levels of the pollutant in question.

Socio-economic characteristics of a population such as smoking and diet may well interact with pollution variables as a cause of excess mortality. Correspondingly, most of the work in epidemiology has taken the form of time series analyses where data is drawn from a particular locality over a period of time and an attempt is made to correlate mortality or morbidity statistics with contemporaneous levels of one or more air pollutants. Weather may be correlated to both mortality and ambient pollutant levels and needs to be controlled for. There are also concerns regarding the stability of statistical relationships estimated over periods during disease epidemics. The advantage of time series studies relative to cross sectional studies, conducted over several populations at a single point in time, is that because the socio-economic characteristics of the population are fixed these characteristics need not be explicitly modelled. Small and Kazimi (1995), however, raises a legitimate concern over the use of time series studies: '...we believe the time series evidence is less appropriate because one cannot separate the long term causal effects of interest from the short term timing of the cause of the fatal illness.'

Joel Schwartz, a leading US epidemiologist, has commented that it is likely that some of the high doses of pollutants on particular days may cause the deaths of many people already weakened by diseases either related or unrelated to air pollution. If this were the case, it begs the question of whether the external cost of a pollutant that kills the already weak is less than one that kills fit and healthy people. This phenomenon is described, somewhat sardonically, as the 'harvesting effect'. Unusually low mortality following a high pollution incident would be consistent with the existence of a harvesting effect. The harvesting effect basically refers to the lagged impact of pollution variables and the difference between the instantaneous and long-run impact of poor air quality.

Other broader concerns about the robustness of the results include what statisticians refer to as multi-collinearity between explanatory variables. If all air pollutants are included in the regression the risk of wrongly attributing excess mortality to a harmless substance is clearly reduced. However, given the nature of the data-generating processes it is often the case that levels of many pollutants tend to move together rather than independently. This near-linear association between the explanatory variables may result in difficulties in estimating the coefficients with precision. In effect it becomes difficult for the technique to attribute the cause of excess mortality to one pollutant rather than another. Although in repeated sampling the estimates are not systematically biased by this, the standard errors (a measure of the precision of the estimates) are wide. The only solution to the problem of multi-collinearity is to obtain more data in which the near-linear relationship between the variables is absent. This typically requires combining time series data from multiple sites into 'panel data'. Panel data techniques lend themselves especially well to this sort of analysis although their application to date appears to be scarce.

With individually insignificant coefficients on the pollution variables the temptation is to drop some of the pollution variables in order to get a 'significant' result. But if a study omits an important explanatory variable the regression coefficient on the other pollutant variables will become biased since they pick up the correlation of the omitted variable. The upshot of this is that it is possible to explain essentially the same deaths by systematically regressing the mortality data against each of the different pollution variables in turn. The potential for exaggerating the impact of poor air quality on health should be apparent. Balanced against this is the fact that broadly the same relationships appear to hold over very many different cities despite what must be very different relative levels of the various pollutants. This militates against omitted variables being such a significant problem. Long-term illnesses are completely ignored by such analyses anyway, so it is impossible to conclude that the deaths from pollution have been systematically overestimated.

Several reported studies involve measuring the effect of very high doses of the pollutant, usually in the context of occupational exposure. To extrapolate the results to much lower doses, to which the general population are typically exposed requires that the dose–response function is linear, and therefore halving the dose of the pollutant will halve the health response. It is also assumed that there is no threshold level of the pollutant below which no health damage is done. In fact there is no obvious reason why the dose–response functions should take any prescribed form. The former administrator of the United States Environmental Protection Agency (USEPA) has stated that, 'In a heterogenous population it is unlikely that, for any pollutant, there will be a single scientifically defensible threshold applicable to all people. Instead there will be a series of thresholds for different sensitive populations and a threshold of zero for some people' (quoted in Ostro, 1994). Few if any of the estimated dose–response functions have attempted to fit different functional forms to the data or to demonstrate the adequacy of the functional forms that are used.

A lot of epidemiological literature raises the problem of transferring the results of one country to another. Significant work has been done in the USA and without transferring these results to the UK context nothing can be said concerning the health impacts of air pollution: UK-based epidemiology is currently inadequate for our purposes. To extrapolate the coefficients to the UK assumes a similar distribution of baseline factors throughout the population which are not controlled for, such as health status, and exposure, including time spent outside. Little work seems to have been done on examining exactly how people become exposed to air pollution, and the type of activity that may lead to one person receiving a higher dose than another. This may include, for instance, the relative exposure faced by people who exercise along a busy main road, or between those inside a car and those on the pavement. There are also likely to be differences in results from different countries from differing regulations governing the siting of the air pollution monitors themselves. Until such time as adequate epidemiological research emerges from the UK, assuming similar baseline factors between the USA and the UK would seem reasonable. However, certain results are extrapolated from Greece, and other countries where arguably the distribution of baseline factors may be significantly different to the UK.

Although considerable work has been done in the USA there seems to be an urgent need for a large-scale panel data examination of UK air pollution and mortality and morbidity rates. Furthermore, much of the USA work evidently lacks the benefits of sophisticated statistical modelling.

Responsibility for Ambient Concentrations

The outlined model requires an estimate of the absolute change in ambient concentrations of pollution that would arise if there were no road vehicle use at all. To do this requires rather a lot of information, although three key issues stand out. Firstly, what are the 1993 ambient concentrations of each primary and secondary pollutant across the UK? Secondly, if we can gauge the responsibility of the road transport sector alone for primary emissions of pollutants in 1993, can this be used to attribute responsibility for ambient concentrations? Thirdly, even if we estimate the responsibility of the road transport sector as a whole, can we then break down responsibility for concentrations between different fuel types, based on their relative emissions?

Unravelling this chain of causality is rife with difficulty, but the first step is relatively simple. The Department of the Environment (DoE) provides data on monitored levels of pollutants at a range of UK sites (Digest of Environmental Protection and Water Statistics, DoE, 1995). Although concern has been raised in the literature about the techniques adopted to measure the pollutants, the number of monitoring sites, and their location relative to busy roads, it is acknowledged that general progress has been made in this area over the last few years (AEA Technology, 1995). The available data for 1993 concentrations of each primary and secondary pollutant associated with road transport have been employed. The ambient levels vary widely throughout the country and, rather than simply use a national average figure, our calculations have, where possible, used an average urban and average rural figure to facilitate more precise estimates. The greater the degree of geographical disaggregation the better, and as more widespread monitoring is employed, so the figures presented below can be refined. With the data presently available, it is necessary to assume that concentrations are constant across all urban and all rural areas.

In assigning responsibility for these concentrations, the first issue to be addressed is the relationship between current primary pollutant emissions and current ambient concentrations. Ambient concentrations may reflect both 'man-made' pollution and natural atmospheric processes. Likely anthropogenic responsibility factors have been at least partially addressed in the literature. This anthropogenic total can be refined in light of the fact that scientists have estimated the percentage responsibility of different sectors of the UK economy to total anthropogenic emissions (Box 4.2). Our calculations assign responsibility for ambient anthropogenic concentrations according to responsibility for emissions, and hence a proportional change in emissions would be assumed to generate an equal proportional change in anthropogenic concentrations. This is a simplification, but Ball et al (1991) suggest that the linear approach we have used is quite reasonable for primary pollutants. The ambient concentration of a primary pollutant will be proportional to emissions as long as it is removed from a given volume of air at a rate proportional to its concentration. This, Ball argues, is typically the case for primary pollutants.

The case is somewhat complicated for secondary pollutants. It may be the case that linearity applies to secondary pollutant formation, for proportionate increases in the primary pollutants concerned. If emissions of both NO_x and VOCs double to a given volume of air, the concentration of ozone will typically double. Small et al (1995) noted that secondary pollution formation appears more non-linear if it is measured by the extremes of concentrations such as peak daily ozone levels. It is also a concern that specific emissions of primary pollutants may form secondary pollutant concentrations at geographically quite different locations. This may have implications for both our breakdown of costs between urban and rural areas, and may even raise the possibility of needing to account for transboundary pollution to and from the continent. We have not done this.

Box 4.2
SOURCE CONTRIBUTION TO TOTAL 1991 UK EMISSIONS
(All figures in percentage terms)

Source:	Fuel type	NO_x	CO	VOCs	CO_2	SO_2	PM_{10}	BS^I
Cars	Petrol	29	80	22	12	<1	9	3
	Diesel	<1	<1	1	<1	<1	1	3
LGVs[2]	Petrol	2	6	2	1	<1	1	<1
	Diesel	<1	<1	1	<1	<1	1	3
HGVs[3]	Diesel	17	2	4	4	<1	12	28
Buses	Diesel	3	<1	1	1	<1	2	6
Motorcycles		<1	1	2	<1	<1	<1	<1
Evaporation		0	0	5	0	0	0	0
Total road vehicles		52	90	37	19	2	27	42
Domestic		3	5	2	15	4	47	36
Power stations		26	1	<1	33	71	7	5
Other, inc industry		19	4	60	33	23	19	83

Source: Table 5.1, Quality of Urban Air Review Group Report, 1993.
1 BS=Black Smoke
2 LGVs=Light Goods Vehicles
3 HGVs=Heavy Goods Vehicles

The sectoral responsibility figures we use are presented for the UK as a whole. However, in practice at any one monitoring station the types of pollution generating processes may vary widely. For instance, in a rural area a locally situated power station may be responsible for nearly all of the local concentrations of a particular pollutant. However, within central London, concentrations of the same pollutant may be formed almost wholly by traffic exhaust emissions. Eyre et al (1995) uses a regional scale air pollution model to calculate the dose per person from power stations. This corresponds to the dose that most rural dwellers would receive, as most power stations are situated in rural areas. In order to calculate the equivalent dose per person for urban areas, Eyre assumes that most urban dose comes from the transport sector, and uses a more realistic 'Gaussian plume model' to estimate ground-level concentrations. Eyre's work provides estimates that can be used to convert the effect in terms of dose per person of an emission of a pollutant in rural areas (typically high level source) to an equivalent dose from an urban (typically low level) source. Pearce and Crowards (1995) apply the Eyre ratios to the national responsibility figures presented in Box 4.3.

Box 4.3 EYRE URBAN–RURAL DOSE RATIOS			
Pollutant	Dose (in person $\mu g/m^3$)		
	Total dose–rural source	Total dose–urban source	Urban–rural dose ratio
PM_{10}	790	5090	6.4
SO_2	240	4540	19
NO_2	350	1600	4.6
CO	5400	9700	1.8
Benzene	790	6.4	6.4

Source: Eyre et al, 1995

This data enables us to broadly ascribe the responsibility of the road transport sector as a whole to urban and rural ambient concentrations of pollution. We are fully aware that this is an area which requires far greater refinement, but believe on the basis of the available evidence that our estimates are correct. One final step remains: to ascribe the total responsibility of road transport between each fuel type. It seems unlikely that these proportions will change much across the country, and hence the nationwide estimates are used.

Population At Risk

The model presented above requires evidence on the size of the population at risk from concentrations of pollution. This is taken to be everyone in the UK, although it is necessary to break this figure down between urban and rural populations. Essential population data has been taken from the 1991 census (Office of Population Censuses and Surveys, 1992). It is not very clear how many people live in 'urban' or 'rural' areas. We follow the Pearce and Crowards (1995) paper, and use an estimate of an urban population of 44%, which is probably a conservative estimate. Data on the total annual number of mortalities are taken from the same source.

Economic Values

The final general methodological concern involves the economic valuing of the change in health status. To some, this idea of placing a money value on premature mortality, or any change in health status, may appear ethically distasteful. Although we understand this concern, we believe this criticism is based on a fundamental misunderstanding. The central arguments in favour using this economic value or 'willingness-to-pay' (WTP) valuation has been made vociferously within the economics literature (Jones-Lee, 1993; Freeman, 1993), and the interested reader is well advised to follow up the references. It is not our intention to discuss the validity of the approach at this stage: the debate over the 'value of a statistical life' (VOSL) has been left to our discussion of the costs of accidents in chapter 7. However, at this stage suffice it to say that if people's preferences are a valid basis upon which to make judgements concerning changes in human 'well-being', then it follows that changes in human mortality and morbidity should be valued according to what individuals are willing to pay (or willing to accept as compensation to forgo the change in health status).

Everyday individual actions in which people trade money against a small reduction in personal safety can be used to estimate the value of a statistical life. This is not the same as valuing an actual life, and should not be interpreted as such. The available evidence suggests that the current VOSL is approximately £2 million (Pearce and Knight, 1992). But an interesting point arises concerning the relationship between VOSL and age. Schwartz and Dockery (1992) find that the risks of mortality from air pollution are greater for people over the age of 65. If the air pollution is primarily affecting elderly people, with only a short remaining life expectancy, then what can be said about willingness to pay of these people and society to avoid small changes in the risk they face? Similarly, some of the dose–response work specifically identifies the change in premature mortalities for children. Are changes in risk to children to be valued differently from those to adults?

Freeman (1993) reviews the evidence provided by so called 'Life-Cycle Models', and demonstrates that, because it is assumed that human well-being is dependent on lifetime consumption, when expected lifetime consumption falls so the amount people are willing to pay (WTP) to reduce risk will also fall. Some evidence on WTP and age comes from one study by Jones-Lee (1985), and Cropper and Sussman (1990) have normalised these values (Box 4.4). The study indicates that VOSL of the most at risk group is around £2 million, and that it takes an inverted U shape with respect to age, maximising at the age of 40. But the Jones-Lee result found a VOSL for 40-year-olds of around £3 million, rather than our figure of £2 million. Hence using our figure for 40-year-olds, VOSL for 60-year-olds may be about £1.5 million. However, Jones-Lee et al (1993) finds no variation in VOSL with age. Empirical work is still very limited in this field. There is also evidence to suggest that people may value risks faced in crossing the road (contemporaneous risk) differently to risks of developing disease in the future (latent risk). The VOSL literature has largely evolved in the context of contemporaneous risk. Perhaps people would be willing to pay more to avoid latent risk? It seems plausible that people are not indifferent to the types of risk they face. Another interesting point concerns the difference between voluntary risk and involuntary risk. Much of the literature reviewed in obtaining the £2 million figure reflects changes in risk voluntarily undertaken by people. It is not obvious people voluntarily accept the risk involved in inhaling air pollution.

Box 4.4
RELATIONSHIP BETWEEN VALUE OF A STATISTICAL LIFE AND AGE

Age	WTP–1993 £ million	WTP/WTP aged 40
18	2.03	0.67
20	2.34	0.77
30	2.72	0.89
40	3.04	1.00
50	2.41	0.79
60	2.13	0.70

Source: Cropper and Sussman, 1990
Note: Jones-Lee et al (1993) finds no variation in VOSL with age. The empirical evidence is still rather limited in this area, and we have employed a single VOSL in our calculations.

We have not differentiated VOSL between age-groups in our calculations, largely because so few of the dose–response functions impart any information on the age of the victims, and also because of the uncertainties within the economics literature we have discussed.

Air pollution also affects human morbidity. Our calculations, based on the epidemiology literature, provide us with an estimate of the change in the number of cases of human morbidity. These in turn can also be valued. To measure the cost of increasing the frequency of headaches, it is reasonable to determine how much people are willing to pay to reduce the frequency of headaches. These values can be established using willingness to pay (WTP) techniques such as the contingent valuation method (CVM). However, empirical results using these techniques are still scarce, and we use a combination of WTP approach work (where available) and cost-of-illness (COI) approach. The COI approach is not the theoretically correct measure of the benefits enjoyed by people for improving air quality, and in particular makes no allowance for reduction in human pain or suffering associated with reduced illness. Hence using these studies alone may understate the case for reducing air pollution. Box 4.5 presents the morbidity values we use, based on a review of the available literature.

Box 4.5
UNIT ECONOMIC VALUES FOR MORBIDITY EFFECTS

	Study type	Unit values £/1993[1]			Fully adjusted unit values[2]	Study
		Low	Central	Upper		
Respiratory hospital admissions	COI	4900	10,200	14,700	9,280	Krupnick and Cropper, 1986
Emergency room visits	COI	85	390	555	351	Rowe et al, 1986
Restricted activity days	WTP+COI	25	51	75	46	Loehman et al, 1979
Asthma	WTP	9	25	40	23	Krupnick, 1986; Rowe and Chestnut, 1988
Respiratory symptoms	WTP	4	7	10	7	Loehman et al, 1979
Chronic bronchitis	WTP		153,000		139,213	Viscusi et al, 1991, Krupnick and Cropper, 1991
Bronchitis in children	WTP		200		179	Krupnick and Cropper, 1989
Minor restricted activity days	WTP+COI		18		16	Loehman et al, 1979, Tolley et al, 1986
Hypertension	COI		220		197	Shin et al, 1982
Coronary heart disease	COI		57,520		52,340	USEPA, 1985
IQ points loss per child	COI		340		341	Shin et al, 1982

Source: adapted from Rowe et al, 1995
1 Values taken from Rowe et al (1995): converted 1992 dollars into 1993 pounds
2 GDP adjusted Unit Values = Unit Value*(GDP$_{UK}$/GDP$_{USA}$)$^{0.35}$ for central value only. Note this assumes that the marginal utility of income is 0.35, and follows the work of Krupnick et al (1993). This is equivalent to multiplying the previous column by 0.908.

The next section outlines the exact studies used to estimate the effect of air pollution on human health, and some of the issues raised with respect to ambient concentrations, the populations exposed, and responsibility factors. Where a particular dose–response coefficient has been used, an attempt has been made to examine the source study of the figure in light of the concerns outlined above.

SMALL PARTICULATE MATTER

Evidence of the relationship between particulate-based smog and daily mortality can be traced from the turn of the century. The most frequently cited case concerns London during the winter of 1952. A temperature inversion enveloped the Thames Valley, and wind speeds dropped below 2 knots for around 48 hours. As the concentration of particulate smog rose, within a day or so there was a trebling of the daily death rate. However, evidence emerging from the USA has focused attention on the effect of very small particulate matter; that of under 10 microns diameter (PM_{10}). This work has come to the fore in the last year with a claim by the *New Scientist* magazine that 10,000 people die prematurely each year in the UK from PM_{10} emissions largely from vehicle exhausts (Bown, 1994). The term PM_{10} comprises several types of particulate matter. Broadly there are two types: that which is emitted directly to the atmosphere and that which is formed indirectly as a secondary pollutant. Hence emissions of SO_2 and NO_2 can both oxidise in the atmosphere to form ammonium sulphate and nitrate: both small particulate matter. Small and Kazimi (1995) reports an American South Coast Air Quality Management District-SCAQMD (1994, Appendix I-D) study, in which it is found:

> direct particulate matter emissions from motor vehicles
> = 10.6% of PM_{10} concentrations
> secondary carbon from motor vehicle VOC emissions
> = 4.4% of PM_{10} concentrations
> ammonium nitrate from motor vehicle NO_x emissions
> = 10.5% of PM_{10} concentrations
> ammonium sulphate from motor vehicle SO_x emissions
> = 5.3% of PM_{10} concentrations.

Hence responsibility for a unit concentration of PM_{10} from road transport can be allocated as:

> direct emissions = (10.6/30.8) = 35%
> VOCs emissions = (4.4/30.8) = 14%
> NO_x emissions = (10.5/30.8) = 34%
> SO_x emissions = (5.3/30.8) = 17%

Box 4.6
SUMMARY OF MORTALITY STUDIES OF A $1\mu g/m^3$ CHANGE IN PM_{10}

Study, City/Region, Data	Events/person/$\mu g/m^3$		
	Upper Bound	Central Estimate	Lower Bound
Schwartz and Marcus, London UK, time-series 1958-1972 (adapted by Ostro)	$3.1*10^{-6}$	$3.0*10^{-6}$	$2.9*10^{-6}$
Plagiannakos and Parker, Ontario Canada, Time-series 1976-1982 (adapted by Ostro)	$1.6*10^{-5}$	$9.8*10^{-6}$	$4.9*10^{-6}$
Schwartz and Dockery, Steubenville Ohio, Time-series	$1.0*10^{-5}$	$6.0*10^{-6}$	$4.0*10^{-6}$
Schwartz, Birmingham AL, Time-series	$1.3*10^{-5}$	$1.1*10^{-5}$	$1.0*10^{-5}$
Dockery et al, St.Louis, Time-series	$2.3*10^{-5}$	$1.6*10^{-5}$	$1.4*10^{-5}$
Pope et al, Utah Valley, UT	$1.8*10^{-5}$	$1.6*10^{-5}$	$1.4*10^{-5}$
Schwartz and Dockery, Philadelphia PA, Time-series	$1.5*10^{-5}$	$1.3*10^{-5}$	$1.0*10^{-5}$
Fairley, Santa Clara County CA, Time-series 1980-86 (adapted by Ostro)	$1.6*10^{-5}$	$1.2*10^{-5}$	$7.0*10^{-6}$
Ozkaynak and Thurston, 100 met. areas in USA, cross-sectional 1980, (adapted by Ostro)	$2.2*10^{-5}$	$1.6*10^{-5}$	$1.0*10^{-5}$

Source: Ostro, 1994 and Rowe et al, 1995.

These factors are subsequently used in the calculations. There is no obvious reason why the USA estimates should accurately reflect the UK. Indeed differences in the climate, the relative proportion of diesel cars, and the volume of traffic, may alter the results. However, there seems no comparable UK figures available, and while we await the results of the forthcoming Quality of Urban Air Review Group report on these issues, we have assumed that the USA figures are broadly correct. Recent United States Environmental Protection Agency work, cited by Todd Litman (Litman, 1995a), suggests that a considerable quantity of PM_{10} may also be generated as a result of braking and the movement of the car. This is not accounted for in our work.

The remarkable feature of the work done to date on estimating the dose–response function of PM_{10} and human mortality is the consistency of different studies in different cities in the US. This is reassuring and is the benchmark for establishing causality in epidemiology. Box 4.6 presents the range of findings in recent studies of the effects of PM_{10} on premature mortality.

Dockery et al (1993), in a highly influential study, examined data on six communities in the USA from 1974 to 1989, and found a significant relationship between fine particulate levels and premature mortality, especially from lung cancer and cardiopulmonary disease. Schwartz (1994) calculates the average of the coefficients from several recent studies, although uses a technique referred to as 'meta-analysis' to weight the more accurate studies more highly. Ostro (1994) uses an unweighted average of six studies to examine the benefits of reducing air pollution in Jakarta. The coefficient used for the slope of the dose–response function is 0.096: a $10\mu g/m^3$ change in PM_{10} levels is associated with approximately a 1 per cent change in mortality. This is used as the basis for our calculations.

In addition to its effect on premature mortality rates, evidence links PM_{10} with human morbidity: increasing cases of chronic bronchitis, respiratory disease, asthma attacks, and consequential hospital visits and restricted activity. The epidemiological evidence is reviewed in both Ostro (1994) and Rowe et al (1995), and is presented as Box 4.7.

There has been no evidence to date of the presence of a threshold in either the mortality or morbidity relationships below which a dose of PM_{10} does not damage. The issue has been explicitly addressed in the literature. Schwartz finds no evidence of a threshold in the Philadelphia study. Desvouges et al (1993) review the literature and adopts the 'conservative assumption of no threshold'. The assumption of a linearity relationship between dose and response (so doubling PM_{10} doubles the cases of premature mortality) has also been reviewed, and to date no evidence can be found to suggest a relationship other than a linear one. Several studies have included sulphur dioxide and ozone as additional explanatory variables, and found them not significant in explaining changes in premature mortality. In the St Louis and Santa Clara County studies negligible levels of SO_2 exposure were found. The consistency of the results, with or without SO_2 or ozone, is reassuring.

The biological mechanism through which PM_{10} affects human mortality and morbidity has been an area of controversy. However, very recent evidence may suggest one. Work by Japanese scientists (Ohtoshi et al, 1994) has confirmed the biological effects of exposure to PM_{10}. Cultures of nasal 'epithelial' cells produced large quantities of so called 'inflammation mediators' when exposed to PM_{10}, and these mediators are implicated in the onset of bronchial asthma and allergic responses. Diesel emissions of PM_{10} were found to be partic-

Box 4.7
SUMMARY OF MORBIDITY STUDIES OF $1\,\mu g/m^3$ CHANGE IN PM_{10}

Morbidity effect/year	Events/person/$\mu g/m^3$		
	High	Central	Low
Chronic bronchitis in adults	9.3*10–6	6.1*10–5	3.0*10–5
Respiratory symptoms inc. coughs, chest discomfort, eye irritations	0.2555	0.1679	0.0803
Emergency room visits	3.54*10–4	2.373*10–4	1.17*10–4
Asthma attacks	0.1971	0.0584	0.3285
Restricted activity days	0.09125	0.0584	0.0292
Respiratory hospital admissions	1.75	1.204	6.57
Acute bronchitis in children	0.0024	0.0016	0.0008

Source: Ostro, 1994.

ularly potent. Seaton et al (1995) reports that small particulate matter may provoke aveolar inflammation which may exacerbate lung disease and possibly the coagulability of blood. This may affect cardiovascular disease.

Data on ambient urban PM_{10} levels is presented in the 1995 Digest of Environmental Protection and Water Statistics (Department of the Environment, 1995). An average figure of 28.11 $\mu g/m^3$ is assumed for urban regions, based on 1993 data. Estimated annual rural mean PM_{10} concentrations are estimated to be 15 $\mu g/m^3$, which according to estimates made by the National Environmental Technology Centre (NETCEN) may be an underestimation (AEA, 1995). The percentage of concentrations that are anthropogenic in origin is taken to be 75 per cent, although this too may be something of an underestimate.

Assigning responsibility for both urban and rural concentrations of PM_{10} between a variety of sources is particularly problematic. The Quality of Urban Air Review Group (QUARG) Second Report (1993) states that 27 per cent of national emissions in 1991 were from the road transport sector (Box 4.2). Domestic sources account for a staggering 47 per cent of emissions, a figure that does not seem to accord with intuition given the move away from solid fuel in most parts of the country. Some other sources, such as power stations, are rurally based and therefore unlikely to be as responsible for emissions within urban areas as a national figure suggests. In order to account for this effect, the Eyre conversion factors have been applied as follows:

road vehicles = 27% of emissions * 6.4 = 1.728
domestic = 47% of emissions * 1.0 = 0.470
other emissions = 25% of emissions * 1.0 = 0.250.

Domestic sources have been weighted at only 1.0 to reflect the fact that all solid fuel burning takes place in rural areas. Hence:

revised total = 2.458

Therefore in urban areas road transport is responsible for:

road vehicles = 1.728 / 2.458 = 70.3 % of PM_{10} concentrations

This is used as the 1993 urban percentage responsibility, and hence we assume that the percentages have not altered between 1991 and 1993.

SULPHUR DIOXIDE

Sulphur dioxide can affect human health through two main channels: firstly, directly as SO_2 concentrations, and secondly, through its oxidation in the atmosphere to form small particulate matter. This section reviews the evidence of its direct or primary role. Recent studies have demonstrated that changes in 24-hour exposure to SO_2 is associated with respiratory disease and risk of mortality (Box 4.8). Several studies have investigated the effect of SO_2 directly on mortality. A proportion of these studies include other pollutants as explanatory variables. Ostro (1994) reviews the epidemiological evidence to date and comments that, '...although many of the investigations also indicate that particulate matter or ozone was associated with these adverse health outcomes, several studies appear to show an effect of SO_2 alone'.

The premature mortality figures used by Ostro rely heavily on one study: Hatzakis et al (1986). This study uses alternate measures of SO_2 and smoke since 'their simultaneous use was considered inappropriate because of high correlation'. This raises doubts over the accuracy of the coefficient: in effectively dropping a variable, Hatzakis et al risk what statisticians refer to as 'omitted variable bias'. The respiratory problems generated by SO_2 include child coughs, and chest discomfort for adults. The dose–response functions are based on the work of Schwartz et al (1990). None of the studies reviewed by Ostro seem to have explicitly tested for the shape of the relationship between dose and response, or for the presence of a threshold. A recent study commented that while levels of 100 parts per billion (ppb) have been shown to cause adverse respiratory effects in susceptible humans, particularly in asthmatics, other people may be unaffected at levels as high as 1,000 ppb (POST, 1994).

It is also difficult to estimate the percentage of total concentration that can be ascribed to anthropogenic emission sources. One method employed here is to examine the difference between the average urban concentration and the most remote monitoring station; name-

Box 4.8
EFFECT OF A 1 µg/m³ CHANGE IN SULPHUR DIOXIDE
CONCENTRATION

| | Study, Data, City | Events/person/µg/m³ | | |
		Upper Bound	Central Estimate	Lower Bound
Mortality	Hatzakis et al, time-series 1972–82, Athens	$1.32*10^{-5}$	$5.23*10^{-6}$	$2.18*10^{-6}$
Respiratory symptoms/ 1,000 child/year	Schwartz et al, time-series, Harvard, MA	0.026	0.018	0.010
Chest discomfort/ adult/year	Schwartz et al, time-series, Los Angeles	0.015	0.010	0.005

Source: Ostro, 1994.

ly Straith Vaich in Scotland. Reinforced by other references in the literature, this method suggests that nearly all emissions are anthropogenic in nature.

Road transport was only responsible for 2 per cent of total emissions of SO_x in 1991(QUARG, 1993). Applying the same techniques outlined for PM_{10}, the Eyre responsibility factors can be applied to the sources of emissions.

road transport	= 2% * 19	= 0.38
power stations	= 71% * 1	= 0.71
domestic	= 4% * 8	= 0.32
others	= 22% * 1	= 0.22
revised total		= 1.63

Hence:

road transport = 0.38/1.63 = 23% responsible for SO_2 emissions in urban areas.

NITROGEN OXIDES

Nitrogen and oxygen can combine to produce a variety of compounds. The significant ones for our work are nitrogen dioxide (NO_2), nitric oxide (NO) and nitrous oxide (N_2O), although nitrous oxide was dealt with in the previous chapter. Nitric oxide and nitrogen dioxide are jointly termed NO_x, and affect human mortality and morbidity through three separate channels: as NO_2 directly, as ammonium nitrate (a component of PM_{10}) and finally, through a secondary reaction with VOCs resulting in the formation of ozone. Ostro reports that the effects of ambient outdoor NO_2 on either children or adults are difficult to identify, despite having a significant effect at high doses indoors and on animals in laboratory experiments. One study (Schwartz and Zeger, 1990) has found a significant relationship between NO_x and increased phlegm production, which we have adopted. It is a concern to again find ourselves reliant on a single USA study, and we repeat our earlier call for a UK study examining all pollutants across several years. To calculate the percentage responsibility of road transport in urban areas, we have employed the same technique as above :

road transport	= 52% * 4.6	= 2.39
power stations	= 26 % * 1	= 0.26
others	= 22% * 2.3	= 0.506
revised total		= 3.158

Hence:

road transport = 2.39/3.158 = 75% responsible for urban concentrations of NO_2.

OZONE

Ozone (O_3) is a gas which occurs quite naturally, and through its presence in the upper atmosphere provides a vital shield against harmful radiation from the sun penetrating the Earth's atmosphere. O_3 in the lower atmosphere (troposphere), or 'ground-level' ozone, is formed indirectly by the action of sunlight on nitrogen oxide, oxygen and volatile organic compounds (VOCs). VOCs comprise some 87 compounds in all, but a mere 26 of them contribute 85 per cent of ground-level ozone. VOCs are usually divided into methane – dealt with in Chapter 3 – and non-methane VOCs (NMVOCs). Some NMVOCs seem to cause cancer, and are examined separately below. Ozone, the result of the reaction of NO_x with VOCs, can cause a range of health effects: eye, throat, and nose irritation, chest discomfort, coughs and headaches. It is the link between ozone and asthma that has created recent controversy. Ozone has also been linked to increased rates of premature mortality.

Attributing the responsibility of the transport sector in ozone formation is particularly difficult. If the ratio of the ambient level of VOCs to NO_x is high, ozone formation is said to be 'NO_x limited'. At the margin it is the emission of NO_x that is responsible for ozone formation. O_3 can also be 'VOC limited'. It is usually assumed that both primary pollutants are equally responsible. Recent evidence presented by Small and Kazimi (1995) suggests that natural levels of VOCs in the USA are in fact very high and therefore ozone is NO_x limited. This chapter assumes that both primary pollutants are equally responsible.

Box 4.9
SUMMARY OF HEALTH EFFECTS OF OZONE

| Endpoint | Events/person/ppm | | | Source |
	Upper bound	Central	Lower bound	
Mortality	$2.4*10^{-3}$	$1.2045*10^{-3}$	0	Kinney and Ozkaynak (1991,1992)
Respiratory hospital admissions	$19*10^{-6}$	$13.7*10^{-6}$	$8.4*10^{-6}$	Thurston et al 1992
Asthma attacks	0.520	0.188	0.106	Whittmore and Korn (1980), Stock et al (1988)
Minor restricted activity days	$7.4*10^{-2}$	$4.67*10^{-2}$	$1.93*10^{-2}$	Ostro and Rothschild (1989)
Acute respiratory symptoms	0.204	0.137	0.07	Krupnick et al (1990)

Source: Rowe et al, 1995

Mortality estimates are taken from two studies by Kinney and Ozkaynak (1991, 1992) which find a statistically significant relationship between previous and concurrent maximum hour ozone levels and mortality rates in the USA (Box 4.9). Other epidemiologists have found no evidence for a link between mortality and ozone (Dockery et al, 1993), but typically these studies have failed to address some statistical issues about the independent effect of the season very well. Anthropogenic responsibility is assigned from a reference in Small et al (1995) that states that only one-half of ozone levels are attributable to anthropogenic sources. Box 4.2 and the Eyre factors are applied, assuming NO_x and VOCs equally responsible.

BENZENE

Considerable controversy surrounds the effects of benzene on human health. Benzene is a volatile organic compound (VOC), and is classified as a 'probable' carcinogen. At a sufficiently high level of exposure, it may be linked with cases of leukaemia. Although at normal ambient temperatures benzene is a liquid, at ground level small quantities of evaporated benzene are detectable, almost exclusively derived from motor vehicle use. Recent debate has centred on the relative emissions of benzene from leaded and unleaded fuel, particularly super-unleaded fuel. This fuel was designed for cars without catalytic converters and, according to the House of Commons Select

Committee on Transport (1994), presents a greater health risk because of elevated benzene levels, to compensate for the lack of lead. According to Shell (1995) the amount of benzene does not alter significantly between the two types of unleaded fuel, although both may alter with respect to refinery practice. The Expert Panel on Air Quality Standards (Department of the Environment, 1993) claims that average concentrations to which the general public are exposed present an 'exceedingly small risk to health'. Petrol retailers have also claimed that the health risks of benzene have been overstated, and that previous work has been based on a 'tissue of wrong assumptions' (ENDS, 1995).

The epidemiology literature contains several studies that present dose–response relationships for benzene, and most notably a United States Environmental Protection Agency (USEPA) review (Glickman and Hersh, 1995). The dose–response function between benzene and all-age leukaemia has been derived from occupational exposure tests, and is analysed by the USEPA(1992), Wolff (1993) and Glickman and Hersh (1995). All-age risk is related to the cumulative dose of benzene per kilogram body weight:

$$\Delta Pr(LEUK)/person = 2.0*10^{-6}mg^{-1}kg^{-1}*dose*bodyweight \qquad (3)$$

where $Pr(LEUK)$ is the probability of contracting leukaemia at all ages. Adults are assumed to weigh approximately 50 kilograms on average, with children at 25. Wolff has stirred further controversy by arguing that children are five times more sensitive to benzene than adults, and that benzene emissions from road transport may go a long way to explaining clusters of child leukaemia. Wolff assumes that there is no threshold below which a dose of benzene does no harm. The dose–response function is based on occupational risk of benzene exposure some 1,000 times higher than in the ambient urban environment. However, the UK Highway Agency acknowledges that the carcinogenic potential of benzene at lower concentrations is not known and there is no known safe level below which there is no carcinogenic effect (Wolff, 1993). The Expert Panel on Air Quality Standards (Department of the Environment, 1994) also concludes that, 'it is impossible to determine a concentration to which people might be exposed at which there is no risk detectable by existing methods' (their emphasis, pg 1). Wolff also assumes that the function is linear. There seems little evidence to suggest what the shape of the relationship actually is. In light of this, we have adopted the no-threshold and linear assumption. Wolff states that outside air levels of benzene (which he claims are chiefly derived from the petrol engine) are in the 1–10 parts per billion range (3.2–32 μg/m^3) depending on local traffic levels. The Department of the Environment (Department of the Environment, 1995) measures benzene levels across several urban areas in 1994, at an average of 1.2 ppb. This is assumed to hold for 1993. Data on rural ambient concentrations is scant, and a level of half that of urban areas has been assumed.

The 1995 Digest of Environmental Protection and Water Statistics suggests that 80 per cent of emissions of benzene are from road transport sources. Benzene is both present in petrol and formed by the partial combustion of the broad group of aromatics: population exposure is the result of both fuel evaporation and car exhausts. The breakdown of responsibility for emissions is placed at one-half from petrol vehicles and one-half from unleaded vehicles.

LEAD

The links between human health and lead have long been recognised. As far back as 370 BC Hippocrates raises concerns over adverse health effects (Moore et al,1990), while evidence on the effect of lead exposure on the neurological development of children has been gathered over the last 50 years (Ratcliffe, 1981). More recent work has been done on the links between exposure to lead and urban adult male hypertension, heart attacks and general mortality. Although the ultimate source of lead intake is recognised to be predominantly petrol engines, there is a multitude of pathways through which emissions enter the human bloodstream. Chance ingestion of lead-rich dust through food, or on the hands, as well as direct inhalation seem important. Road transport emissions have, however, fallen considerably over the past two decades, although concentrations still remain well in excess of 'natural' levels.

The relationship between airborne lead levels and human mortality rests on the effect of air lead on human blood lead levels, which in turn influence blood pressure levels. Higher rates of blood pressure are associated with both increased mortality, hypertension and heart disease.

It is unlikely that any one air lead: blood lead conversion factor will be adequate across all people. A person's diet, sex, smoking habits and so on all determine individual conversion rates. However, in 1980, a UK Department of Health and Social Security Working Party (DHSS, 1980) made a working assumption of a ratio of 2.0 between air lead and blood lead, and according to Dubourg (1995) this is in reasonable agreement with other studies. Ostro (1994) employs the same figure. The same linear assumption between air lead and blood lead is adopted for this study.

$$\Delta Pb_{BLOOD} = 2\ [Pb_{AIR1} - Pb_{AIR2}] \tag{4}$$

where Pb_{BLOOD} is blood lead concentration, in micrograms per decilitre, and Pb_{AIR1} is air lead concentration before and after the change in question, measured in micrograms per cubic metre.

Ostro reports that several studies have found strong statistical relationships between blood lead and blood pressure in adult men, without any evidence of a threshold. Again we follow Ostro, who in turn relies on the studies of Pirkle et al (1985) and the US Environmental Protection Agency (USEPA, 1986), to specify the following relationship:

$$\Delta DBP = 2.74 \ (\ln Pb_{BLOOD1} - \ln Pb_{BLOOD2}) \qquad (5)$$

where DBP is diastolic blood pressure, and PB_{BLOOD1} is blood lead concentration before and after the change in question. This relationship applies to urban men only, and therefore this section may underestimate actual damage.

The final link that needs to be established in calculating change in mortality is that

$$MORT = (1 + e^{-5.3158 + 0.03516(DBP1)})^{-1} - (1 + e^{-(-5.3158 + 0.03516(DBP2))}) \qquad (6)$$

between blood pressure and mortality rate. The positive impact of blood pressure upon mortality and rates of cardiovascular disease has been well documented (Levin, 1986). Ostro uses a function from the Levin study, which we use, where:

$MORT$ is the 12-year probability of death from all causes. Again this is applied exclusively to adult urban males.

To use the relationships discussed above requires rather specific data. The 1995 Digest of Environmental Protection and Water Statistics is the main source of information on air lead concentrations in urban areas. Less current data exists for average urban blood lead and blood pressure levels. The 1990 UK Blood Lead Monitoring programme (Department of the Environment, 1990) reports that over a sample of 1,500 adults, blood lead levels of urban males was 9.7 micrograms per decalitre. The diastolic blood pressure of males across England and Wales in 1986-87 was 77.6 mm Hg (Office of Population Censuses and Surveys, 1990).

The paucity of 1993 data presents something of a difficulty. As air lead levels have dropped between 1987 and 1993, so equations 4 and 5 predict that blood pressure levels will have dropped. Using a technique described in Dubourg (1995), the 1987 results have been extrapolated to 1993. These are then used as the base against which to estimate the number of mortalities without any road transport. It is also difficult to estimate accurately the proportion of all emissions derived from road transport. This study assumes 70 per cent of all emissions are from petrol engines, as suggested by the Energy Digest (1993).

MODEL RESULTS

On the basis of the information presented above, we have estimated the total external cost imposed on the UK economy by air pollution from the road transport sector during 1993. Box 4.10 presents the estimated total external damage per pollutant. Most damage is done by emissions of NO_x, largely because they are implicated in both PM_{10} and ozone formation, as well as having a direct effect in its own right. SO_x and direct emissions of PM_{10} also inflict considerable costs. VOCs, lead and benzene seem to inflict significantly less damage. Total external costs are approximately £19.7 billion per year. When 'low' and 'high' damage scenarios are used, the estimates vary from approximately £10.6bn to £32bn respectively.

Box 4.10
ESTIMATED EXTERNAL HEALTH COSTS PER POLLUTANT
(All prices refer to 1993)

Pollutant	Effect	Number of premature mortalities per year	Total external health costs/ £ millions
Direct PM_{10}	Mt	1,725	3,450
	Mb		2,100
SO_x (inc. indirect PM_{10})	Mt	1,880	3,760
NOx (inc. indirect PM_{10} and ozone)	Mt	2,000	3,990
	Mb		2,160
VOCs	Mt	1,010	2,020
	Mb		850
Lead	Mt	20	40
	Mb		240
Benzene	Mt	30	70
Total		6,665	19,720

Source: Calthrop, 1995
Note: Mt = mortality, Mb = morbidity

These total estimates can be broken down by different fuel types. To do this requires data on the contribution of each fuel type to total road transport emissions. The Quality of Urban Air Review Group Second Report (1993) provides this data for both petrol and diesel fuel in relation to most pollutants. Other sources have been used to estimate the breakdown between unleaded and leaded fuel, and should be treated with more caution. Once the total costs per fuel type have been established, it is straightforward to divide by the number of litres of fuel sold, and thus calculate the average cost per litre of fuel. This is done using data on fuel sales from the Institute

Box 4.11
MARGINAL EXTERNAL HEALTH COSTS PER LITRE OF FUEL
(All prices refer to 1993)

Fuel type	Total external cost/£ millions	Fuel sales/million litres	Marginal external cost/litre/pence
Diesel	11,765	14,000	84
Petrol	6,375	15,000	43
Unleaded	1,569	17,000	9
City Diesel	–	–	33[1]

Source: Calthrop, 1995
1 The figure with respect to City Diesel is merely an estimate based on advertised reductions in certain pollutants when compared to ordinary diesel.

of Petroleum (1994). This approximates the marginal external cost. Box 4.11 presents the results of this exercise. Each litre of diesel currently sold in the UK on average inflicts 84 pence damage on society. This is a very important result and is generated by the fact that diesel engines are so much more responsible for both PM_{10} direct emissions and SO_2 emissions. In contrast, leaded fuel inflicts approximately 43 pence of damage and unleaded fuel a mere 9 pence.

Emissions per litre of fuel vary enormously even within the same engine. Whether the engine is hot or cold dramatically affects the amount of emissions, as does the speed of the vehicle, vehicle age and maintenance record. Even if all engines emitted the same amount of emissions, the actual damage done by each litre of fuel would still vary enormously depending on the number of people exposed to emissions. Each emission in a crowded city centre does more damage than in remote areas.

While petrol engines are used almost exclusively by cars, diesel engines are used by a variety of different vehicles, and predominantly by Heavy Goods Vehicles (HGVs). The damage figure of 84p per litre masks variation between these vehicle types. It is interesting to try and disaggregate between vehicle types. This can be done by relying on data provided by the Quality of Urban Air Review Group Second Report on the contribution of each vehicle type to total diesel emissions (QUARG, 1993). This can be used alongside Department of Transport estimates of the quantity of total diesel sales to each vehicle type to estimate average damage per vehicle type (Department of Transport, 1994). Data is also provided on the kilometres driven by each vehicle type, which is used to estimate damage per kilometre.

Box 4.12 present the results of this exercise. While diesel cars inflict around 33 pence damage per litre (broadly similar to petrol cars), HGVs and Light Goods Vehicles average at 91 pence per litre,

Box 4.12

MARGINAL EXTERNAL HEALTH COST BY VEHICLE TYPE PER LITRE

(All prices refer to 1993)

Vehicle type	Total external cost/ £ millions	Fuel sales/ million litres	Marginal external cost/litre/pence
Diesel car	840	2,520	33
Leaded petrol car	6,375	15,000	43
Buses and coaches	1,659	1,260	132
HGVs and LGVs	9,255	10,220	91

Source: Calthrop, 1995

while buses and coaches inflict a staggering 132 pence per litre. Although when converted into damage per passenger–kilometre these figure appear much less dramatic, the basic magnitude reflects two factors: the typical urban driving conditions facing buses, with congested peak period trips, and the very old stock of buses still in operation. Department of Transport data (1994) shows that 28 per cent of bus stock dates from pre-1980. This is far higher than any other vehicle type category. It would have been interesting to disaggregate damage done by buses by age group to see the difference between new buses possibly equipped with particulate traps and pre-1980 buses. One suspects that the difference may be marked.

Box 4.13 presents the same data in terms of marginal cost per kilometre driven.

Box 4.13

MARGINAL EXTERNAL HEALTH COST BY VEHICLE TYPE PER KM

(All prices refer to 1993)

Vehicle type	Total external costs/ £ millions	Total kilometres travelled 1993/million km	Marginal external cost/km/pence
Diesel car	840	33,600	2
LGVs	777	18,200	4
Buses and coaches	1,659	4,600	36
HGVs	8,478	28,300	30

Source: Calthrop, 1995

POLICY IMPLICATIONS

The total external costs of air pollution currently being imposed on the UK economy by road transport are clearly very significant. Theory suggests that a tax should be imposed on the source of these emissions equal to the marginal external damage caused to society.

However, unlike the problem of carbon dioxide emissions discussed in the last chapter, air pollution damages vary substantially according to type of vehicle, as well as where, when and how a vehicle is driven and maintained.

The best solution to the problem of air pollution, at least from an economist's point of view, appears to require the use of remote sensing of emissions using infra-red beams. This technology has already been demonstrated in the US (Glazer et al, 1995). Remote sensing of emissions would form the basis for a set of charges providing motorists with a variety of incentives including reducing the overall number of trips, purchasing a low-emission vehicle with anti-pollution devices fitted (and working) as well as to keep the vehicle in a good state of repair. Problems with the technology, however, include the fact that vehicles have to move in single file past the monitor and that the reading taken is only a snapshot of the emissions. Even with the same vehicle, emissions per litre will vary because emissions from a cold engine of either variety are significantly higher than when hot. It may take 5–10 kilometres before the engine is fully warmed and operating sufficiently. Only emissions from the exhausts are monitored and particulate emissions cannot yet be monitored at all. Until this technology is developed further (and costed) much less direct means of confronting motorists with the damage done by their vehicle's emissions have to be found.

Total emissions are not linked particularly closely to total consumption of fuel. Nevertheless, higher fuel taxes are often seen as a viable means of securing improvements in air quality and given the scale of the problem an increase in fuel prices may be a useful component in a mixed policy response. The evidence would indicate that for every 10 per cent increase in fuel prices, demand falls by between 7–8 per cent once adjustments have been made to the fuel efficiency of the vehicle fleet (Goodwin, 1992). The damage caused by emissions, however, depends strongly upon location in a way which fuel taxes cannot reflect. Rural car drivers will be needlessly penalised by a system which increases the price of fuel on which they are dependent through an absence of public transport alternatives.

Whereas changing the absolute level of taxes may not (for a variety of reasons) constitute the least-cost way of solving air pollution problems in cities, relatively large effects can be achieved by creating small tax differentials between fuels simply because they are such close substitutes (particularly so over periods of time long enough for the vehicle stock to turn over). The prime example is the tax differential which was created between leaded and unleaded petrol. More interesting is the existence of differential tax treatment given to diesel and unleaded petrol in most European countries including, to a much lesser extent, Britain. This has variously been justified in terms of lower carbon monoxide and carbon dioxide emissions from diesel engines; as well as the argument that diesel is an 'intermediate' good, or one used by industry, and that in an efficient tax system the burden of revenue-raising taxation should fall on consumer goods, or 'final consumption'. But as Crawford and Smith (1995) note, the distinction between diesel and petrol engine vehicles now no longer coincides with the distinction between final and intermediate consumption uses of motor fuels. The tax differential in favour of diesel appears to us hard to justify on either economic grounds or on environmental grounds. In fact, given our estimates of the damage per litre of fuel, it would appear advisable to create a healthy tax differential in favour of unleaded petrol. We would, however, want to make an exception to this: City Diesel currently being introduced by some retailers (Sainsbury's plc, 1995) claims to reduce particulate matter emissions by up to 40 per cent and with no impact on performance. Most other pollutants are also reduced, including carbon monoxide by 17 per cent, sulphur oxides by 99 per cent and nitrogen oxides by 7 per cent. If these estimates are accurate, and if there are no significant increases in emissions at the manufacturing stage, then City Diesel clearly deserves to receive a sizeable tax advantage over ordinary diesel. Low sulphur fuel has been available in Scandinavian countries for over five years. The EU is currently regulating to make provision of low-sulphur fuel mandatory from 1996. Particulate traps require vehicles to use low-sulphur fuel. They operate on larger vehicles such as buses and HGVs and significantly reduce emissions of most pollutants, especially PM_{10}. Depending on the cost of purchasing and fitting the trap (one type currently costs £3,500-£4,000), this seems an attractive means of reducing the very considerable air pollution from HGVs and buses. By our calculations the average external costs associated with the consumption of a litre of City Diesel is 33 pence compared to 80 pence for conventional diesel.

The establishment of tax differentials is crucial to the development of alternative fuels. The capital cost of alternative fuel vehicles tends to be higher and without tax differentials which reflect the environmental impact of the various alternative fuels relative to the conventional ones then alternative fuels will not begin to penetrate the market. Given emissions factors for alternative fuel-propelled vehicles it would be relatively straightforward to calculate appropriate taxes for each of the fuels and then compare them on a per kilometre basis to other fuels. Announcing that emissions will form the basis for the taxation of fuels along with shadow values for particular pollutants is important. Without the assurance that alternative fuels will be favoured it is hard to see private industry promoting these fuels. The Royal Commission on Environmental Pollution (1994) see particular environmental advantages associated with the use of compressed natural gas as a means of powering heavy vehicles in urban areas specifically because of the virtual absence of any particulate emissions. Buses might also be electrically propelled.

Creating tax differentials on the basis of external effects, however, presupposes an ability to quantify the relative external effects. In many instances the external effects remain elusive.

But fuel taxes alone are inadequate in that they do not encourage the take up of devices such as catalytic converters and other modifications which lower average emissions per unit of fuel burnt. Where these devices and modifications are costly, differentiated sales taxes on new motor vehicles or differentiated annual charges are required. A number of countries have begun differentiating vehicle taxes in accordance with such factors as engine size which may influence vehicle emissions. In the period before the fitting of catalytic converters became compulsory, the Netherlands and Germany both created fiscal incentives for the immediate fitting of these devices. There are no differentiated charges in the UK at the moment and as a consequence the retrospective fitting of emissions technology has been limited. Both sales taxes and recurrent taxes have the advantage of being cheap to administer. The major drawback with this type of tax is that once the owner has paid the fee there are no marginal incentives to reduce vehicle usage.

Vehicle emissions standards are employed throughout the EU as a means of exercising control over pollution from motor vehicles. These standards apply only to new cars sold in the EU and are in terms of grams of pollutants per kilometre as measured over a prescribed test cycle. In some ways, the setting of vehicle emissions standards and the tax differentiation of purchase or ownership of vehicles are alternative policy measures. Both attempt to favourably influence the composition of the vehicle fleet. There are, however, reasons to prefer tax differentiation since this gives motorists and vehicle manufacturers an incentive to exceed the minimum standards of compliance. At the moment there is no financial incentive for a motorist to purchase a vehicle which complies with the more stringent EU Stage II emissions limits which come into force in 1997, even though there are vehicles currently available which can meet these standards. Similar incentives could be used to encourage hauliers to purchase HGVs which exceed currently enforced standards. Certainly a reliance on vehicle standards is not on its own a sufficient policy.

A further complexity is that neither vehicle standards, fuel taxes nor differentiated taxes on purchase or ownership can adequately reflect the fact that on a mile-for-mile basis a small percentage of cars typically account for a high proportion of the pollution problem. To some extent these 'gross polluters' are older vehicles. The gradual rise in standards required for emission rates from new vehicles over the past twenty years means that vehicle age may proxy emissions technology quite well. Alberini et al (1994) comment that while pre-1980 cars make up a mere 18 per cent of the USA vehicle stock and account for only 8 per cent of miles driven, they contribute over 40 per cent of total emissions from vehicles of hydrocarbons and 25 per cent of nitrogen oxides.

Specifically to deal with the problem of older vehicles, a variety of Accelerated Vehicle Retirement (AVR) programmes have been advocated in the US (Alberini et al, 1994). The aim is to remove old vehicles from the fleet (although this also coincides with the aims of vehicle manufacturers in increasing the market for new vehicles). The cost-effectiveness of such a scheme, however, is difficult to ascertain. First of all there is no necessary linkage between the age of a car and the pollution which it creates. Older vehicles may be driven less and the state of a vehicle's maintenance is also very important in determining its emissions. It seems that any scheme would need to be based on generic type rather than purely on age. Typically there may be a self-selection problem with the scheme whereby only those owners who were about to scrap their car anyway enter the programme. If new vehicles are purchased, additional pollution through the manufacturing process as well as the disposal of the old vehicle are also potentially important. Greece operates a system of fiscal incentives to remove the most polluting vehicles from the fleet.

Alberini et al also discuss a General Motors and Environmental Defense Fund proposal that involves setting up private brokers who receive credits upon buying an old car which can be sold to stationary sources of pollution to offset their pollution abatement requirements. The price of the vehicle is negotiated between a private broker and the owner of the vehicle based on generic type and the regional market for emissions reductions. The broker who purchased the vehicle receives a credit which can then be sold to stationary sources. This amounts to a tradeable permit scheme and would ensure least-cost abatement across several sectors of the economy. This remains at the proposal stage in the USA and clearly needs careful attention to practical details. It is, however, an interesting policy option partly because it may receive some backing from motor manufacturers and partly because it introduces the idea of trading between different emissions sources in an attempt to minimise the cost associated with complying with air quality standards.

Irrespective of age and generic type, a poorly maintained vehicle (particularly a petrol-engined one) will emit higher amounts of carbon monoxide and hydrocarbons than a regularly serviced one. A recent study (Betts et al, 1992) found that 6 per cent of diesel cars needed adjustment while nearly 30 per cent of catalyst-equipped cars tested required some tuning. Eighty per cent of standard petrol cars needed attention. Recent checks in the UK by the RAC (1994) revealed that in London 10 per cent of cars produce 44 per cent of the pollution. Potentially, significant reductions in emissions are possible if the state of repair of the vehicle fleet can be improved. Catching poorly maintained cars requires monitoring and inspection programmes.

Use of roadside checks may seem superfluous if emissions checks are also incorporated in to the MOT test. The effects of the two schemes, however, would probably be different. There is evidence that the MOT requirements have little practical effect on emissions. The Royal Commission on Environmental Pollution cites research by the RAC which suggests that out of a survey of 25,000 cars, one-third would have failed the MOT emissions test. Evidently then, with an MOT test the only incentive to tackle an emissions problem in the vehicle is just before the test is due. Glazer et al (1994) in their analysis of California's smog check programme also take the view that anticipated inspections are relatively ineffective. With a programme of roadside spot checking, on the other hand, there is always an incentive for the vehicle owner to tackle emissions problems as they arise. With such checks, however, there are questions regarding whether anyone other than a uniformed police officer should be given the authority to stop vehicles. Instead, remote sensing of emissions might be used to automatically screen which cars should be checked by photographing their licence plates and asking them to present their vehicles for testing within a short time. Some motoring organisations such as the RAC strongly favour such an approach. Instrumented smoke tests for London taxis are to be introduced next year but these are only on an annual basis.

The tax treatment of substitutes and complementary goods such as additional parking charges and the subsidisation of public transport will also affect the level of air pollution, although in the case of the latter it appears that the sensitivity of car travel to public transport prices is very low. Much more important are the links between the level of air pollution and road tolling. These work through increasing vehicle speeds and the elimination of stop–start driving conditions which are detrimental to fuel efficiency. A discussion of the potential contribution of road pricing to improving air quality is deferred to a later chapter. To summarise some of the arguments contained in that chapter, it also appears that the same instruments used to tackle congestion in cities might also be used to reduce transport-related emissions at times when meteorological conditions serve to elevate the risks posed by air pollution. At the moment the Government merely requests motorists to avoid unnecessary journeys.

On the whole, given the complexities outlined, it seems clear that a fuel tax on its own will not be a particularly desirable or effective instrument. Fuel taxes must be coupled with instruments to target older vehicles, particular types of vehicles such as buses and improvements in vehicle emissions standards and maintenance. It is equally clear that there exists considerable potential to amend the current fiscal system in order to better reflect the economic costs in terms of air quality associated with road transport. The House of Commons Environmental Committee Report (1995) states that insufficient consideration has been given to encouraging the sale and purchase of less-polluting vehicles.

Improving air quality may involve a variety of technical solutions, and changes in consumer behaviour. It is worth stressing, however, that the mechanisms adopted are not of great concern to the economist. If drivers pay according to the amount of emissions they discharge per litre, then a perfect incentive pattern emerges. Consumers will find the best balance of reducing mileage, buying more fuel efficient cars, driving in a more emissions-friendly manner, and investing in whatever technology exists to reduce emissions. In the absence of a perfect charging system, we believe the policy suggestions put forward here closely proxy this system, and air quality will be improved at the lowest overall cost to society.

Lastly, there also needs to be more comprehensive monitoring of air pollution throughout the UK to provide information for subsequent studies of the impact of air pollution on human health. The existing studies can all be questioned on methodological grounds for a variety of reasons and there are reasons to doubt whether they can always be successfully applied to other countries. A proper knowledge of the relative impacts of various pollutants is a prerequisite for sensible policy choices since technologies often present trade-offs between different types of pollutants, for example, as in the debate over whether super unleaded petrol is a 'green' fuel or not. Modelling techniques need to be developed that will shed light on the exposure of the public to emissions arising from various sources. Rural sources and urban low-level sources cannot be counted as equivalent in terms of their contribution to poor urban air quality. Both these recommendations are also made in the Royal Commission on Environmental Pollution's (1994) report. Information on air quality in cities should be made as readily available as possible. Information helps vulnerable people make decisions about how to plan their day. Vienna, for example, has a large public display of real-time monitoring of emissions of the major air pollutants and an interpretation of them. London should have the same.

Chapter 5

Noise Pollution

INTRODUCTION

Due to the growth in road transport, silence is becoming an increasingly scarce commodity in our towns and cities. UK noise levels have been measured on a regular basis only since 1986 (Box 5.1). It appears that road transport is the main source of noise pollution by a considerable margin (Box 5.2). There are few locations which are not now afflicted by noise generated by road transport.

Year	Average noise level L_{Aeq}	Percentage of population exposed to dBL_{Aeq} greater than:		
		50	60	70
1986	52	58	21	4
1987	52	55	18	3
1988	52	57	18	2
1989	52	55	15	2
1990	53	58	23	4
1991	53	60	25	4

Box 5.1
EVOLVING NOISE LEVELS 1986–91

Source: Department of the Environment, 1992; 1994

Pollution of the acoustic environment is associated with numerous ill effects. Exposure to noise during the night changes the duration and quality of sleep, which can impair health in a variety of ways. The number of medical prescriptions, psychotherapy sessions and the number of tranquilisers and sleeping pills all tend to be higher in noisier areas. There is a heightened risk of cardiovascular and circulatory disorders. Traffic noise also affects childrens' learning. Noise is also responsible for productivity losses caused by an inability to concentrate at work or through tiredness resulting from disrupted sleep. References in support of all these propositions may be found in an Organization for Economic Cooperation and Development (OECD) booklet (1991). The National Noise Incidence Study carried out in 1990 confirmed that over half of the dwellings in England and

Box 5.2
NOISE SOURCES OUTSIDE DWELLINGS 1986–91

Noise source:	Percentage main source:	Percentage of sites recording source of some noise:
Road traffic	66	93
Aircraft	3	31
Railways	1	14
Construction	1	4
Industry	1	2
People	13	73
Animals	2	38
Birds	4	8
Mowers	2	11
Wind	5	7

Source: Department of the Environment, 1992

Wales suffered from daytime noise levels which exceeded World Health Organization recommended daytime maximum levels. Noise in excess of these limits is deemed to cause an annoyance (Department of the Environment, 1994). The survey also found that 7 per cent of the homes in the survey experienced such a level of noise pollution that sound insulation improvements would mandatorily have to be provided were there any further increase in noise due to a new road.

An obvious question to ask is whether society is devoting sufficient resources to noise abatement. The answer to this question requires knowledge of the willingness of society to pay for reductions in noise levels. This chapter considers the measurement of noise as a physical concept and the techniques that have been applied to the measuring of willingness to pay for noise reductions in different contexts. On the basis of a survey of empirical findings, the cost of noise generated by road transport is estimated for the UK. The possibilities for using market based instruments and other measures to reduce ambient noise levels are considered.

THE MEASUREMENT OF NOISE

Noise is measured in decibels (dB). This is the unit measure of sound pressure related to a standard reference of $0.00002Nm^{-2}$. The dB scale is logarithmic such that a wide range of audible sound can be expressed manageably. The 'A weighted' index (dB(A)) is a measure of sound in which greater weight is attached to those frequencies to which the human ear is more sensitive. Equivalent continuous sound level (L_{eq}) is that constant level of sound which conveys the same energy as that from a fluctuating source. The measure L_{50} gives that sound level which is exceeded 50 per cent of the time. L_{10} gives the sound level which is exceeded 10 per cent of the time and therefore some indication of the peaks in sound levels which would otherwise be obscured.

Noises with a large variation in level are generally held to be more annoying and there is evidence that people do judge the intruding noise by reference to the background level. A measure of the intrusiveness of noise is sometimes taken as $L_{10}–L_{90}$. Because the sound signal varies through the day, all indices are averaged usually over the period 0600–2200 or 0800–2000. Although daytime L_{eq} tends to be presented as the most appropriate indicator of noise it clearly needs to be supplemented by nighttime equivalents as well as by indicators of the peaks in noise levels, possibly in relation to background levels. As regards the single most appropriate index of noise only one study (Allen, 1980) has attempted to discriminate between alternative noise indices. Allen concludes that L_{10} is superior to either L_{eq} or $L_{10}–L_{90}$.

MEASURING THE DISAMENITY OF NOISE POLLUTION

Noise costs have been measured by a number of techniques each of which can be used to value the cost of noise in different contexts (Box 5.3). The measurement of noise costs in different contexts is crucial: exposure to traffic noise at work, at home, at leisure and while travelling all need to be considered if the effects of noise pollution are not to be understated. Estimates of noise costs will obviously differ unless they attempt to measure noise in the same context.

The only methodology for valuing noise nuisances to private individuals in all contexts is based upon the use of Contingent Valuation Method (CVM) surveys of willingness to pay. The typical CVM study generally comprises three parts: firstly, a description of the scenario in which the respondents are to imagine themselves placed; secondly, questions from which values are to be inferred; and, finally, questions relating to the respondents themselves. The latter are required to demonstrate that socio-economic characteristics determine the responses rather than random impulses. The strength of the CVM approach is that not only is it applicable in all contexts but also that it purports to provide exact measures of willingness to pay for noise abatement rather than dealing in terms of approximations as so many other techniques do. A recent example of application of the CVM technique to noise is provided by Soguel (1994) who estimates the willingness of the inhabitants of Neuchatel in Switzerland to pay for a halving of their exposure to road traffic noise. The average monthly payment is reported to be SFr70 (which is approximately £480 per year). Dogs et al, (1991) conduct a similar

Box 5.3
SELECTED ESTIMATES OF THE COSTS OF TRAFFIC NOISE

Author	Date	Country	Per cent GDP	Method
Ringheim	1983	Norway	0.22	Loss in property value
			0.17	Loss of sleep
			0.07	Existing protection
			0.12	Potential vehicle protection programme
Wicke	1987	West Germany	0.15	Productivity losses
			1.45	Loss in property values with 30 dB(A) norm
IRT	1983	France	0.30–2.27	Insulation costs for a 50–40 dB(A) norm
Lambert	1986	France	0.04	Loss in property values
UIC	1987	Netherlands	0.02	Government expenditure on abatement
Opschoor	1987	Netherlands	0.02	Loss in property value
Sharp et al	1976	UK	11.18	Reducing traffic noise by 10 dB(A)
Quinet	1989	General	0.10	Comparison of studies
Kanafani	1983	Europe	0.10–0.20	Comparison of studies
		USA	0.06–0.12	Comparison of studies
Bouladon	–	General	0.30–1.00	Abatement at source
Bleijenberg	1988	Netherlands	0.03–0.08	Extra prevention and remaining loss in property values
Van den Meijs	–	Netherlands	0.03–0.08	Potential insulation
			0.12–0.24	Abatement at source
Dogs et al	1991	West Germany	0.03	Roads: avoidance cost
			0.03	Rail: avoidance cost
			0.52	Roads: willingness to pay
			0.22	Rail: willingness to pay
Grupp	1986	West Germany	0.02–0.05	Loss in property value

Source: Verhoef, 1994

exercise for Germany and determine that aggregate willingness to pay to avoid noise generated by road traffic amounts to 0.52 per cent of GNP. Applied to the UK this amounts to £3.1bn. It must, however, be conceded that transferring benefits in this manner has little merit to it; it cuts across all manner of important differences between countries, not least that ambient noise levels may be completely different in Germany and the UK!

Although these 'stated preference' techniques may in general appear to present much less formidable data requirements than some of the methodologies which follow, there are many potential pitfalls associated with their use. The main concern is whether the means of extracting replies to hypothetical questions results in some kind of bias in the response. Some problems are general to all hypothetical methods for valuation, but there are particular problems connected with the use of CVM surveys that seem highly relevant in the case of the evaluation of noise pollution.

By necessity the CVM questionnaire must provide a description of the setting in which the respondents are asked to imagine themselves. Few members of the public will be familiar with the dB(A) scale. If one is to elicit values of noise reduction it must be in terms that the respondent can recognise, such as 40dB (a 'light breeze in the countryside'). It may not be easy for individuals to conceive of such a reduction actually occurring (resulting in a large number of non-responses) so the question is often framed along the lines of 'How much additional monthly rent would you be willing to pay in order to move to an otherwise identical area but where noise levels are reduced by half?' At this point care must be exercised since a halving in the reduction of perceived noise does not imply a halving in the dB(A) scale but rather to a 10dB(A) decrease. Furthermore if, in answering this question, respondents imagine a general reduction in road traffic then it is clear their reported willingness to pay will also include assumed benefits from reduced traffic pollution and the barrier effect, etc. This is known as the 'embedding effect' and drives a wedge between what the respondent understands about the choice situation and what the investigator intends the respondent to understand. The embedding effect is consistent with the observations of Verhoef who notes that hypothetical approaches tend to estimate noise costs eight times greater than those from other techniques. In order to demonstrate the absence of the embedding effect, follow-up questions are required to establish what the respondent has included in his or her reply. Equally, however, this could also be because CVM questionnaires attempt to evaluate noise in many different contexts. There is some evidence that individuals are willing to contribute towards general reductions in noise levels even when they themselves claim not to be bothered by noise in the context of their home. It would be interesting for future studies to look at the relative magnitudes of the payments offered by those who are and are not bothered by noise in the contexts of their homes. This would provide evidence on the extent to which those techniques outlined below, which measure noise solely in the context of the home, are likely to understate the overall scale of the problem.

The other problem with CVM studies is that they rely on confronting people with hypothetical choices rather than observing actual behaviour. This leaves open the possibility for respondents to deliberately misrepresent their views particularly if they suspect that they can increase their provision of a public good, such as noise abatement, without affecting their payment obligation. The only sure way of avoiding the problem of deliberate misrepresentation or respondents not taking the survey seriously is to rely on methodologies based upon observable behaviour. This means looking either at the expenditure decisions or the locational choices of different individuals and how these decisions are affected by noise pollution. Such studies, however, tend to limit themselves to measuring noise disamenities in the context of the home and are thus apt to understate the scale of the problem.

The simplest technique, known as the avoidance–cost method, considers the voluntarily incurred costs of soundproofing a house to reduce noise levels as a measure of the welfare impact of the noise nuisance. But it should be apparent that there need be no link at all between the two amounts of money. Apart from the problem of deciding whether particular investments can be attributed solely to the desire to reduce noise levels, expenditures on defensive measures by individuals understate the overall scale of the problem since they are made only up to the point at which the marginal benefit of insulation equals the marginal cost of obtaining it. Noise damages beyond that point are not valued by the technique, which helps to explain why the voluntarily incurred avoidance–cost technique yields such low estimates of noise nuisance (see Box 5.3). Alternatively, one could estimate the cost of investments required to reduce indoor noise to a given level. Again, these need not bear any association with the willingness to pay for noise abatement. Despite the shortcomings of the avoidance–cost technique, we can in principle infer something from the observed expenditures of households afflicted by noise pollution. In some circumstances differences in expenditures between individual households exposed to different levels of environmental disamenities can be exploited to reveal the implicit values placed on these amenities. This forms the basis of the so-called Household Production Function (HPF) technique. For a number of reasons, however, use of the HPF technique in practice is problematic when applied to the evaluation of noise pollution.

Most of the work on placing money values on noise has been conducted through the hedonic technique. The Hedonic House Price approach to valuing noise sees individuals as selecting between locations characterised by different quantities of environmental disamenities. Hedonic studies value noise by considering the reduction in house prices which can only be explained by ambient noise levels. The basic assumption underlying Hedonic studies is that, given the supply of noisy and quiet areas is fixed, the action of markets ensures that relative house prices adjust to reflect the supply and demand for various characteristics in any given area. The market price of a home is then a function of the attributes of the home itself, the neighbourhood's characteristics, local taxes, local services provided and variables describing environmental quality. After the 'house price locus' has been estimated by regressing property prices on a set of characteristics, the marginal willingness to pay can be determined by considering the additional cost of moving to a location with marginally less noise with everything else held constant. There obviously exists a tension between choosing a sufficiently large area across which noise levels vary considerably while at the same time controlling for numerous other factors which affect house prices. Fortunately noise levels from road traffic can vary considerably even in a relatively small area, so the Hedonic technique lends itself well to the evaluation of noise, as many environmental variables can be considered fixed over tracts of land across which noise levels vary quite considerably.

For any household the marginal willingness to pay for noise reductions can be calculated by considering that household's chosen position on the 'noise–price locus'. Since houses are durable assets these estimates of marginal willingness to pay are discounted present values and need to be annuitised. If, on the other hand, annual rental prices are to be used, the implicit price of noise reflects the value of noise as perceived over the duration of the rent. Sometimes, however, this process of price stratification is prevented by regulations governing the market for rented property. In such cases application of the Hedonic technique might reveal not the preferences of those dwelling in particular properties but the preferences of those who regulate the rents.

House price studies value noise solely in the context of the home but the Hedonic method could equally be applied to the prices of office floor-space to determine the value of traffic noise in the workplace. To the best of our knowledge, however, there are no examples of the latter. But since there is considerable evidence that performance at work is related to noise levels, it seems highly likely that commercial property prices would also reveal a noise–price relationship.

Further complexities associated with the Hedonic technique are that for large, or non-marginal, changes in noise levels there exists a problem of identifying the bid curve for noise–price combinations. The noise–price locus is not synonymous with the bid curve for any individual unless individuals happen to be alike in all respects (Box 5.4). Despite this the noise-price locus is almost invariably interpreted as the bid curve in the literature. The noise–price locus plots out the marginal willingness to pay for noise reductions of different individuals. But the individual bid curves are not identified. All that can be construed from the point where each individual has chosen to locate on the noise–price locus is his or her marginal willingness to pay. The only means of identifying the bid curve for individuals is to confront individuals who are alike in all respects with a different set of prices for obtaining the same set of environmental characteristics and observe their behaviour.

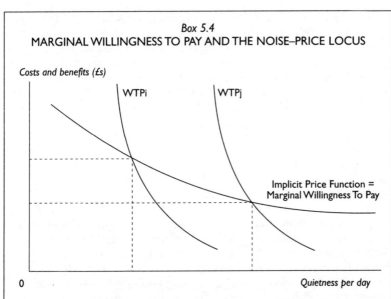

Box 5.4
MARGINAL WILLINGNESS TO PAY AND THE NOISE–PRICE LOCUS

Costs and benefits (£s)

WTPi

WTPj

Implicit Price Function =
Marginal Willingness To Pay

0

Quietness per day

The Hedonic technique identifies the implicit-price locus, which for a small change in noise level corresponds with an individual's willingness to pay function (WTPi). This poses a problem for valuing large, or non-marginal, changes in noise levels, which requires information on the WTP function, or bid function. Many studies simply use the implicit price function to calculate the value of large changes in noise levels.

Although some methods for ensuring the proper identification of the demand curve have been suggested in the literature, the use of cross sectional data from different cities is the only surefire means of dealing with the problem. The technique would be to estimate the house noise–price relationship for each city and then calculate the marginal implicit price paid by each individual. These implicit prices are then regressed on other factors affecting the bid function such as household composition and income levels. Assuming sufficient variation across the markets and the identical preferences of individuals with the same characteristics this will identify the bid functions. To the best of our knowledge there are no Hedonic house price studies of noise which satisfactorily address the identification problem. Accordingly there is no information on how households at different levels of income vary with respect to their willingness to pay for the same noise reduction and no information about the willingness to pay for non-marginal changes.

The other statistical problem which impinges on Hedonic house price studies is multicollinearity, which is an inability to distinguish between the manifold effects of road traffic which tend to be supplied in fixed proportions to traffic volumes, eg noise, pollution and the barrier effect. This has led some researchers to drop those variables which are not the focus of interest, which unfortunately leads to the estimated coefficient on the noise variable to become an amalgamation of both the noise and the omitted variables. A misleading sense of the marginal willingness to pay for noise avoidance may result, just as in the case of CVM studies in which respondents are unable to unbundle the different effects of road transport. A particular problem is in distinguishing between night-time noise and day-time noise which tend to be highly correlated. Yet the distinction between day-time and night-time noise levels is an important one in determining the most cost-effective means of reducing the cost of acoustic pollution. The existence of a premium on night-time noise deserves more attention.

The main findings from house price studies can be summarised by means of a Noise Depreciation Sensitivity Index (NDSI). This index gives the average percentage change in property prices per decibel. A number of literature surveys are available. Nelson (1982) concludes that the average change in property prices is 0.4 per cent per dB. A recent survey by CSERGE/EFTEC (1994) considers a wide range of studies and concludes that the mean property price change is 0.67 per cent per dB (Box 5.5). Although useful as a means of comparing diverse studies, the Noise Depreciation Sensitivity Index does tend to leave the impression of a linear relationship between noise levels and the percentage change in property prices which might not be the best description of the relationship. There is evidence that the NDSI tends to increase somewhat with noise levels (Soguel, 1991). It is apparent that these studies sometimes make quite different estimates of the costs associated with noise on property prices. Sampling differences apart, some studies may present different values because they employ a different concept of noise over a different part of any given 24-hour period. Studies also differ in that they are drawn from countries with different levels of per capita income and different societies may react to noise levels in different ways.

AGGREGATE NOISE COSTS FOR THE UNITED KINGDOM

What proportions of the British people are exposed to given levels of noise from road transport? Obviously not all recorded noise is from this source. While there are a few figures for overall noise levels in the UK, these make no attempt to attribute noise to particular sources. Without such attribution to a particular source it is impossible to derive the cost share for road transport. This raises the question of how such an attribution may be done properly. The second issue is that of whether there is any difference between the marginal and average external cost of noise. We have argued that,

---

Box 5.5
IMPACT OF NOISE LEVELS ON RESIDENTIAL PROPERTY PRICES

Reference	Date	Location	Net Depreciation Sensitivity Index
Nelson	1978	Washington DC	0.88
Vaughan et al	1978	Chicago	0.65
Anderson et al	1977	Towson, USA	0.54
Palmquist	1980	Kinsgate, USA	0.48
Bailey	1977	N Springfield, USA	0.38
Allen	1980	N Virginia, USA	0.15
		Tidewater, USA	0.14
Hall et al	1977	Toronto	1.05
Pommerehne	1986	Basel	1.30
Soguel	1991	Neuchatel	0.90
Iten and Maggi	1990	Zurich	0.90
Average			*0.67*

Source: CSERGE/EFTEC, 1994

---

for the purposes of investigating the economic efficiency of the road transport sector, the relevant concept is the marginal external cost. The average external cost is interesting only if we wish to calculate the unpaid bill road users inflict on the rest of society. In order to determine the marginal and average external costs of road transport one requires a mathematical relationship between traffic flow and noise levels to deduce the impact of the marginal car user in terms of decibels. This expression should be substituted into a damage function which converts ambient noise levels into total damage costs. This expression can either be divided by traffic flow to give average external costs or differentiated with respect to vehicle flow in order to determine marginal external costs. Lamure (1990) suggests the following relationship between vehicle flow and noise levels:

$$L_{eq} \ (dB(A)) = a + 20 \log s - 10 \log d + 10 \log q \qquad (1)$$

where:
a is a constant
s is speed
d is distance from the road, and
q is traffic flow per hour.

The marginal increase in noise levels is a decreasing function of traffic flow. If the perceived damage was a linear function of the number of decibels then the marginal external cost would be below the average external cost. But although the functional form of the damage function varies between studies, it is typically highly non-linear. It is usually (implicitly) assumed in the literature that this serves as a counterbalance, leaving the marginal and average external cost equal.

Box 5.6
COST OF NOISE POLLUTION IN THE UK
(All prices refer to 1993)

Noise levels dB	Population exposed millions	Households millions	Loss in property value £bn
55–60	17.2	7.1	7.3
60–65	9.2	3.8	11.6
65–70	4.6	1.9	9.7
70–75	0.5	0.2	1.4
75+	0.6	0.3	2.8
Total	32.1	13.4	32.8
Annual cost:			2.6

Source: Authors' calculation and OECD, 1993
Notes: These studies assume a base level of noise of 55dB and a NDSI of 0.67 per cent. The average house price is taken as £61,000 (CSO,1995) and the discount factor used to annuitise the values is 8 per cent. 55 dB(A) is taken as the zero annoyance level and there are 2.4 people per household (CSO, 1995).

These problems notwithstanding, data for noise pollution is drawn from the OECD's Environmental Data Compendium (1993). For the United Kingdom the number exposed to particular noise levels solely from road transport are as shown in Box 5.6. The study is not based on the year 1993 but it is all that is available for the purposes of this exercise. The technique to value noise damage follows that of Lambert et al (1986) and represents an approximation to willingness to pay in that it integrates under the noise–price locus and the emergent results depend very much on the zero annoyance level of noise. The damage function is assumed to be piecewise linear. The result is an estimate of £2.6bn annually and would constitute an exact measure of willingness to pay only if all individuals were alike. Furthermore, as argued above these figures value noise only in the context of the home and as such are likely to understate the true costs of noise to an unknown extent.

Based on a survey of the available literature Quinet (1989) suggested that traffic noise may give rise to damages in the form of productivity loss and annoyance amounting to 0.1 per cent of GNP in the OECD countries. For the UK this was equivalent to £0.6bn in 1991 and this was the figure taken as the cost of noise pollution from road transport in earlier work (Pearce et al, 1993). This figure now appears too low by a factor of at least four (Box 5.6). Some authors have further attempted to allocate these noise costs from road transport to particular modes. Various weighting schemes are used to account for the comparative noisiness of a vehicle kilometre. Peirson et al (1994), for example, use the weighting scheme 3:2:1 for heavy goods vehicles, buses and motorbikes, and cars and vans respectively. Applying this weighting scheme allocation on a per kilometre basis is shown in Box 5.7. On a passenger kilometre basis, motorbikes are the noisiest form of transport.

Box 5.7
NOISE COSTS PER KM PER VEHICLE TYPE
(All prices refer to 1993)

Mode	Billion km	Noise weighted	Total cost/ mode/ £ billion	Occupancy	Noise cost per passenger/ km/pence
Car	373.2	373.2	2.43	1.6	0.41
Bus	4.6	9.2	0.06	13.5	0.097
Motorbike	4.2	8.4	0.05	1.1	1.18
HGV	28.3	84.9	0.55	1	1.96

Source: See text

CHARGING FOR NOISE POLLUTION

It is rather difficult to devise an entirely satisfactory way of charging for noise pollution. In theory one would wish for a charge related to the marginal damage caused by the sound emissions from a vehicle. But even apart from the impossibility of continuously monitoring a vehicle's noise emissions, the marginal damage done depends upon the time and place in which the vehicle is being driven. Accordingly simpler though less direct means of limiting noise pollution need to be considered and different countries have evolved different methods of controlling noise pollution. These typically tend to involve the use of regulations governing the construction of vehicles, restrictions on their use and the use of financial incentives. It is also interesting to note the extent to which vehicle speed determines the level of noise created since this suggests a further means of reducing noise nuisance through speed restrictions. Alternatively propelled vehicles may also be a means of reducing noise levels in cities. Since at high speeds a significant proportion of traffic noise is produced by the tyres of a vehicle, noise levels can be influenced by the nature of the road surface. The Royal Commission on Environmental Pollution (1994) suggests that some types of road surface may be between 4dB(A) and 8dB(A) quieter than conventional road surfaces, although more expensive. Physical barriers can also reduce noise levels to an even greater extent although they are often unsightly. Finally, it is apparent that reducing the overall amount of road transport and mode switching also constitute effective means of dealing with noise from road transport. There are thus a range of alternative measures which may be employed to reduce noise nuisance from traffic.

The extent to which any measures at all are justified must be determined by reference to the value of given noise reductions to households. Such a cost–benefit based approach seems preferable to setting targets in the manner suggested by the Royal Commission on Environmental Pollution. They advocated reducing daytime exposure to noise from road and rail to not more than $65\text{dB(A)}_{\text{eq,16h}}$ at the external walls of housing, and to no more than $59\text{dB(A)}_{\text{eq,8h}}$ during the night-time with no obvious thought given to the costs and benefits involved in different locations.

In Britain road vehicles noise emission limits are currently governed by the EC. The maximum limits for noise are currently 84 dB(A) for heavy goods vehicles and 77 dB(A) for cars. The traditional criticism of standards is that they encourage neither the development of, nor the purchase of, quieter vehicles even where they are available. Accordingly there should be financial incentives for motorists to purchase quieter vehicles. Such a scheme was at one time operating in the Netherlands. Originally it was intended that there would be subsidies for the purchase of vehicles whose noise emissions were below legally required standards and charges for the owners of noisy vehicles in accordance with the potential noise nuisance of their emissions. In the case of lorries the charges were steeply progressive and would double for every additional 3dB(A). But the charges were never implemented and instead the subsidies became the main focus of policy. Although successful in terms of encouraging the purchase of low-noise heavy goods vehicles, the system was subsequently abandoned for budgetary reasons.

Of course the noise limits of the car deteriorate with its age and state of maintenance so in-use testing of vehicles will be necessary too. There is unfortunately no metered testing of the noise levels of vehicles in the UK either in the annual MOT test or at the roadside. We hope that this might change in the future. In Japan and Australia by contrast vehicles may be subjected to close proximity exhaust noise tests at the roadside. Vehicles which fail to meet prescribed standards are liable to a fixed penalty or to present their vehicles for inspection. In New South Wales thousands of vehicles are tested each year and average reductions of 9dB(A) are achieved. A pilot study has shown that the additional costs for noise enforcement would be quite small.

In much of Greater London a scheme exists in which the movements of heavy goods vehicles are subject to control between 21.00 and 07.00 on weekdays and at periods over the weekend. Some freight hauliers are exempt on the basis that they 'need' to operate. These restrictions may be warranted, but we believe that in order to operate in residential areas at night more has to be known regarding the premium on night-time noise and proper incentives need to be given to the operators by charging. In urban areas where road pricing is undertaken the noise costs associated with different modes of transport might usefully be reflected in the per kilometre road charges which the users are required to pay, or at least some average charge representing typical noise costs. A system somewhat similar to that in London operates in Bad Reichenhall in Germany where only low-noise lorries are exempt from certain lorry restrictions. The local authority also offers subsidies for the purchase of such vehicles by firms operating predominantly in the Bad Reichenhall area.

More than anything however, research is desperately required into the willingness of British people to pay for the preservation of the acoustic environment as well as the resource costs of securing improvements in the vehicle stock or regulations governing its usage. This would overcome the need to rely upon valuation studies from overseas which may turn out to be inaccurate representations of the British situation. Not knowing enough about night-time noise premiums, willingness to pay for noise reductions outside the context of the home or the willingness to pay for non-marginal changes in noise levels are three outstanding problems which need to be solved. Even then it is necessary to improve dramatically the monitoring of the acoustic environment in the UK. The contribution to overall noise levels of different modes of transport needs to be better understood in order to allocate the costs appropriately. Just considering noise nuisance in the context of the home, using a set of rather old figures, reveals a willingness to pay of £2.6bn annually for the UK. This is approximately 0.4 per cent of the UK's GDP. If on the other hand one were to take the willingness to pay estimates of Dogs et al (1991) which attempt to measure road noise in all contexts, these costs might rise to £3.1bn. Productivity losses would be additional to this.

Chapter 6

Congestion Costs And Road Damage Costs

INTRODUCTION

Due to the growing volume of traffic, average traffic speeds in London have fallen over the last 20 years (Box 6.1) after having been stable for most of the century. It is clear to just about everyone that the current practice of permitting open access to the roads network is extremely wasteful. Goods whose delivery is urgent, or people whose time is valuable, are delayed by drivers on relatively unimportant trips. One possible response to congestion is to advocate road pricing. This chapter explains the theory underlying road pricing. The basic idea is that by charging all users of the road a fee equal to the marginal congestion costs which they impose on other road users, congestion costs are reduced. This occurs partly by dissuading those whose journeys are relatively unimportant from travelling by private car and partly by encouraging them to reschedule their journeys away from peak times.

Box 6.1			
AVERAGE TRAFFIC SPEEDS IN GREATER LONDON			
Year	Morning peak speed/kph	Daytime off peak speed/kph	Evening peak speed/kph
1968–70	18.1	21.3	18.6
1971–73	17.7	21.6	18.3
1974–76	17.9	21.7	18.3
1977–79	16.9	20.9	17.2
1980–82	17.5	20.6	18.0
1983–86	16.9	20.9	17.2
1986–90	16.0	18.9	16.5

Source: Department of Transport, 1992

Perhaps part of the solution to the UK's problems of road traffic congestion lies also in expanding the roads network itself. For the UK as a whole the British Road Federation (1994) has calculated what would happen to congestion with the current trunk road programme, and what would happen if the trunk road programme were increased or decreased by 50 per cent from now until the year 2010. The results are that with the current trunk road programme congestion on the network as a whole would get worse each year, cutting average speeds by 5 per cent, and that even if the amount of money spent were increased by half, congestion would still imply a reduction in average speed of 3 per cent. A cutback in the road building programme of 50 per cent, on the other hand, would be likely to see an increase in average road speeds of about 9 per cent. Apart from the time losses that this would inflict, nothing pollutes quite as much as a row of stationary vehicles, leading some to argue that anything which relieves congestion is environmentally friendly (McWilliams, 1994). But others suspect that the construction of new roads is in some sense self-defeating: they seem to fill up with traffic almost as soon as they are opened. Does it make sense to construct new roads simply because there is traffic congestion? Does the opening of new roads really generate extra traffic and if so what does this imply for new road appraisals? Many road projects are anyway intended not so much to relieve congestion as to take road transport out of city centres and with it the noise, grime and danger to pedestrians. But here exists an all too obvious tension between reserving landscapes on the outskirts of cities for recreational purposes and building new roads over them. How can a balance be struck between these two goals?

This chapter attempts to show how the current system for road traffic appraisals is misguided and has facilitated the expansion of the road network or at least put roads in the wrong places. It is argued that the appraisal system must be rectified by accounting for generated traffic and by according environmental impacts the same status as construction costs and time savings in road traffic appraisals. This chapter also discusses the much vaunted idea of road privatisation as a means of solving traffic congestion and shows why this proposal won't work in practice. The distributional aspects of road pricing are considered and the political supportability of road pricing assessed. Empirical estimates of the scale of congestion in the UK are presented, including an analysis of the extent to which road pricing in London would also succeed in dealing with the capital's air pollution problems. Road damage costs are analysed and policy recommendations made for cutting traffic congestion in urban areas.

THE THEORY OF CONGESTION COSTS:
A DIAGRAMMATIC ANALYSIS

Abstracting from the other external costs of road transport, the costs of using a road have three elements: firstly, the own costs of using the uncongested road (time, fuel, own risk assumptions, etc), depicted in the diagram contained within Box 6.2; secondly, the congestion cost faced by the marginal road user (which increases with the flow of traffic due to slower journey times); and, finally, the congestion costs imposed by the marginal road user on everyone else. The first two costs are internal and represented by the average social cost curve. It is assumed that the average social cost curve is rising as the number of vehicle kilometres increases. This occurs because as the flow of traffic increases the vehicles start to impede one another and this reduces their speed. This effect is not sufficient to reduce the flow of traffic but does increase the time necessary to make any given journey. Given that the average social cost of travel is rising as the flow of traffic increases, the marginal cost curve must lie above the average social cost curve. This reflects the fact that the last kilo-

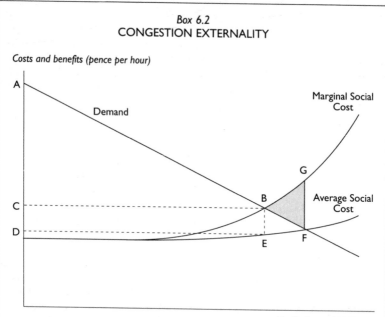

Box 6.2
CONGESTION EXTERNALITY

Costs and benefits (pence per hour)

Traffic flow: vehicles/hour

In an unregulated market, people drive up until the point that average social cost equals demand; ie point F. The socially optimal flow of traffic is that associated with point B where marginal social cost equals demand. For all trips over and above point B, the benefit to the driver (shown by the demand curve) is less than the cost they are imposing on other drivers (the marginal external cost). It is better for all society if these trips are not made.

   A tax can be introduced to induce people to drive up to the socially optimal point, B. This would be set at the rate BE. This would generate revenue equal to the area CBED. The benefit to society from the tax is equal to the shaded area BGF.

metre driven increased average social costs and so must be more expensive than all those that preceded it.

The tendency is for traffic flows to expand to the point where the average social cost curve cuts the demand curve. At that point the private cost incurred by the last motorist is just equal to the benefit which he obtains from his journey, despite the fact that he is imposing positive congestion costs on all other road users. In contrast the efficient flow of traffic is where the marginal social cost curve crosses the demand curve at which the net private benefit enjoyed by the last motorist is equated with the additional time costs imposed on all other motorists.

Without pricing incentives there is no easy way of regulating the traffic in an economically efficient manner. It is almost impossible to discriminate among different road users with respect to the value of their trips. The socially optimum traffic level may, however, be achieved by the imposition of a tax as illustrated in the diagram and results in a welfare gain equal to the area shown in the diagram. The total amount of revenue which this would yield is given by the rectangle indicated. Note that as the demand for the use of the road increases (eg during the rush hour) the demand curve shifts out and the optimal tax increases as well as the traffic flow and the level of congestion.

The analysis offered thus far refers to a short run situation in the sense that the capacity of the road network is assumed to be fixed. Clearly in the long run the capacity of the road network can be expanded. The circumstances under which the publicly funded expansion of capacity might be merited are now considered and compared with what is common practice (Box 6.3). Suppose we consider the case for the expansion of a road link which is currently being optimally taxed to deal with the congestion. As the road network is extended, the average and marginal cost shift right representing the partial relief of congestion. This reduction in the private cost of motoring will to some extent manifest itself in an increase in traffic and this is what people mean when they speak of some transport investments being self-defeating. In an extreme case average speeds can fail to improve at all. The argument is that part of the time savings generated by the expansion of capacity is ploughed back into undertaking more journeys both on new and existing capacity explaining why the extent of the relief provided is often less than envisaged by the road planners. However, the fact that new roads generate more traffic is not necessarily a reason for not building more roads. Expansion results in a change in consumer surplus (defined by the area between the demand curve and the marginal social cost curve) which should be compared with the costs of expanding the network. It does not make sense to expand the road network simply because the existing network is encountering congestion costs but rather it depends upon the costs of expanding capacity.

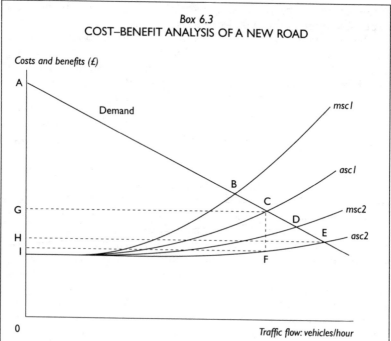

Box 6.3
COST–BENEFIT ANALYSIS OF A NEW ROAD

Building a new road reduces the cost curves faced by drivers, and hence the average social cost curve is reduced from *asc1* to *asc2*. However, simple cost–benefit analysis may produce misleading policy conclusions: time savings may be calculated as the area GCFI. This will then be balanced against the costs of the new road. In fact in lowering costs new demand in generated to equilibrium at point E. Hence real benefits of the road are only GCEH. In practice this may be considerably lower than GCFI.

Whether the costs of expanding capacity extend to more than the construction costs plus the market value of the land required will be considered in a moment. For now consider what happens if the public agency chooses not to optimally charge for the roads and instead tries to evaluate the case for increasing capacity on the assumption that such expansion will not generate more traffic. The system of appraising new roads has indeed typically been based on the assumption that the volume of traffic will be the same with or without road improvements – 'road building does not generate new traffic'. This position has recently been partially abandoned by the Government (Standing Advisory Committee on Trunk Road Assessment: SACTRA, 1994). The apparent change in consumer surplus is the reduction in average social costs multiplied by the original volume of traffic. The generated traffic, however, will take traffic flow to a new equilibrium and average social costs will be higher than anticipated through the congestion which this causes.

The real change in consumer surplus is given by the area under the demand curve minus the new average social costs multiplied by the new and greater volume of traffic. These benefits could be very much smaller than those anticipated particularly if the demand curve is quite flat. It is therefore apparent that omitting generated traffic from the cost–benefit analysis of a new road can result in lower than anticipated and perhaps even negative rates of return (Newbery, 1992).

Furthermore, not only are the environmental costs generated by the use of the infrastructure ignored, the environmental costs associated with the construction of the links are also ignored in the appraisal or at least their value never tested against what people profess to be their willingness to pay to avoid such impacts (Bateman et al, 1994). By failing to monetise these things neither the environmental costs associated with construction nor with usage of the link are accorded equal status with the purely financial costs involved (see Box 6.4). The reason offered is that these costs are 'uncertain' and 'difficult to pin down'. But whether these values are difficult to calculate or not they are nevertheless implicit in the decision that is eventually reached over whether to proceed with a particular project or not. We do not argue that environmental degradation currently receives no weight in the decision making process, but rather that these weights should be made explicit. They can then be compared with the evidence on what people are willing to pay to avoid environmental degradation. Our view is that failing to monetise these costs probably imparts a bias in favour of road construction or at the

---

Box 6.4
ELEMENTS IN THE CONSTRUCTION OF NEW ROADS

Items monetarised in COBA[1]	*Items not monetarised in COBA*
Construction costs	Recreation/Amenity loss
Land costs	Traffic noise
Demolition costs	Visual obstruction
Compensation costs	Visual intrusion
Maintenance costs	Air pollution
Vehicle operating costs	Built environment/heritage
Time savings	Community severance
Accident reductions	Ecological sites
	Pedestrian and cyclist impact
	Disruption during construction
	Climate change

Source: Bateman et al, 1994
1 COBA is the cost–benefit analysis manual used by the Department of Transport in appraising new road schemes.

very least results in inconsistencies throughout the planning process. Without considering the environmental costs of each proposed link or bypass carefully it is obvious that we are apt to build the wrong roads in the wrong locations.

Because of the failure to appreciate the consequences of generated traffic and the failure of planners to explicitly account for the environmental consequences of new road infrastructure and the vehicles which will use it, it is impossible to escape the conclusion that resources devoted to some road construction projects might well have been more profitably spent elsewhere.

OTHER PERSPECTIVES ON CONGESTION COSTS

Despite the apparent benefits to be gained from it, road pricing has its detractors. Moreover, it is often claimed that congestion costs are not external costs at all since they are borne only by other road users (Adams, 1995). While this argument does have a superficial appeal it is quite incorrect. As the preceding analysis made clear the average private cost paid by the driver of the last kilometre is less than the marginal social cost inflicted on all other road users. The Royal Commission on Environmental Pollution (1994) alas took the same view as Adams arguing that, 'although they are sometimes included in estimates of the social or external costs of road transport, and given a very high money value, congestion costs....are not external to road users as a group.'

The Royal Commission on Environmental Pollution thus took external as being defined in a sectoral sense and quite differently from the sense in which it is used in economics. If the concern is economic efficiency then the appropriate analysis is at the level of the individual. This error invalidates their subsequent attempt to assess the economic efficiency of the transport sector by comparing the tax revenues from road transport with the remaining environmental costs. Newbery (1995) makes the same observation on their work. But there is nonetheless a related point of some current interest: the opportunity for resolving the problem of the inefficient allocation of road space through privatising roads. The reader will recall from Chapter 2 that there are two different perspectives on dealing with external effects. These are the use of taxes to internalise the externalities or alternatively the creation of private property rights over what was previously an open access resource (the 'Coasian' solution). Although the tax approach has been the focus of most of the academic discussion so far it is certainly possible to conceive of defining private property rights over roads. Indeed, the private ownership of roads was the norm in medieval times and even as recently as the start of the 20th century there were more than 1,000 turnpike trusts. Theoretically, as long as there were a large number of buyers and sellers of road space, then the private charges made by the operators of the roads would be exactly sufficient to cover the costs of their construction and maintenance. Road space would be bought and sold like any other commodity and the route which·one takes would be determined by whether one is in a hurry and prepared to pay for a fast journey time. This parallels what happens in almost every other market in which people have the choice of paying more for a higher quality service.

Such an institutional arrangement would undoubtedly have certain advantages compared to the present one in which organisations with special interests press for the construction of roads that they themselves will benefit from, but do not have to pay for. The charges and revenues also serve a role as an indicator of the desirability of further extensions to the road network. With privately owned roads, any repairs are likely to be done promptly since neglect would result in a loss of revenue as drivers chose other routes. Repairs to roads would depend less upon the budgetary requirements of the Government. Furthermore, since markets would efficiently allocate road space between different road users the responsibility of the Government would be reduced to regulating the external costs imposed by the 'club' of road users on everyone else. With the current institutional arrangements, however, taxes have to play a dual role of charging road users for the congestion costs they impose on others as well for air pollution and noise.

Since a return to the private ownership of roads is often mooted as part of a solution to Britain's transport problems (eg *The Economist*, 1 April 1995) it seems important to ask what history and economics teaches us concerning the private provision of roads. Rothengatter (1994) argues that:

> Physical networks are natural monopolies, both because their cost functions are sub-additive and because capacity investment decisions are not reversible in the sense that fixed costs are sunk. An incumbent of a given network component is able to protect his domain against entry by competitors, such that any attempt to privatise would result in general in a technological monopoly.

Rothengatter argues that the road network is a natural monopoly, and that any attempt to privatise roads will not result in a market with lots of rivalrous sellers of road space. Moreover, a certain power arises from the fact that the costs of constructing a road are irretrievable. An incumbent road owning consortium will be able to threaten to underprice any potential competitor, thus deterring them from constructing parallel links. This will lead to higher prices for the road user and less supply of road space than is socially desirable. Therefore privatisation of all or even small but key parts of the road network might generate a problem in the exercise of monopoly power. Much of the history of turnpike roads suggests that without some regulation, private roads become an institutionalised form of highway robbery and such bad experiences might explain hostility to the concept of road pricing. Some have seen these issues as not only applying to privately owned roads and have argued that the Government also has a perverse incentive. As it is a monopoly supplier of roads it has an incentive to over-price road space in order to maximise revenue. In any case, our conclusion is that privatisation of road space will not provide a solution to the UK's problems of traffic congestion.

THE DISTRIBUTIONAL IMPLICATIONS OF ROAD PRICING AND SOME IMPLEMENTATIONAL ISSUES

It is possible for one to support the idea of road pricing as a theoretical solution, but to balk at the practical problems likely to be encountered in ever enacting such a measure. Likely implementational problems include questions concerning its political feasibility and issues relating to technological feasibility and issues of privacy. We deal first with the question of the distributional incidence of road pricing and its implications for the political feasibility of its introduction.

In Box 6.2 the shaded area was presented as the gain to society from adopting a system of optimal road pricing. Critically, however, it is possible that road users could en masse experience a decline in welfare from the move to optimal road pricing. The congestion tax could make all commuters worse off since it prices some off the road altogether and remaining commuters may not realise a sufficient decrease in journey time to compensate for the road user charges (Evans, 1992). The reason is that there is a transfer of welfare from the road users to the rest of society. The rest of society could at least in theory compensate the road users in some manner that benefits road users without affecting their incentives to drive, and still be better off. But if the congestion tax revenues are not used to compensate road users then the net gain to society as a whole is at the expense of road users. But before rejecting road pricing on these grounds alone it is as well to remember that we are all road users to some degree or other and all taxpayers, too. The full distributional effect of road pricing depends upon who the beneficiaries of the faster travel times are and, crucially, how the congestion tax revenues are disbursed to keep the tax change revenue-neutral.

A more interesting analysis concerns the case of a heterogenous traffic stream in which the different road users have different valuations of time (eg the busy executive and the day-tripper). When groups with high and low values of time are present in the traffic scheme, the low-value traffic gives way, and the high-value traffic may enjoy time savings which more than compensate for the tolls that they pay. Thus not only are there important transfers between road users and non road users, but also within different classes of road users. Layard (1977) suggests that the congestion tax may even be regressive depending upon the type of journey being undertaken, although alternative means of transportation may offset some of the adverse effects. Small (1983) has calculated how the different elements associated with a switch to road pricing contribute to its overall effects in the case of the US (Box 6.5).

Box 6.5 INCIDENCE OF CONGESTION TOLLS *(US cents per workday per commuter)*			
Welfare effect	*Low income*	*Middle income*	*High income*
Price increase	−17.1	−20.2	−22.4
Uniform redistribution	19.7	19.7	19.7
Net financial effect	2.6	−0.5	−2.7
Value of time saved	7.2	13.8	21.9
Financial effect plus time saved	9.8	13.3	19.2

Source: Small, 1983

Is road pricing politically supportable? From the comments of past and present Secretaries of State for Transport one would certainly not think so (see *The Economist*, 11 April 1995). The evidence generated by surveys of public opinion, however, is less clear cut. Newbery (1992), for example, cites a survey by the Metropolitan Transport Research Unit (*The Independent*, 26 January 1990) which showed 87 per cent in favour of some form of traffic restraint and 53 per cent in favour of a fixed charge to drive into London. Charging per mile was widely supported. A report by the Harris Research Centre (National Economic Development Office, 1991) on the other hand found that less than half of those questioned thought that road pricing was acceptable to any degree. What this illustrates is that the opinions given in these surveys are highly dependent on the way that the question is framed and in particular on the assumptions made regarding how the revenue from road pricing (which could be substantial) is to be distributed. Some surveys of public opinion do not even mention the redistribution of the revenue or the time savings that are created by road pricing. There is little evidence that people consider such things for themselves before answering. In our view there is no reliable evidence to support the view that road pricing is an inherently unpopular policy. The questions that have been asked of the public are just too vague to make sense (Jones, 1991).

Some practical issues relating to the technical feasibility of road charging are now considered. Historically, road pricing involved tolling. But using conventional tolling involving lanes and booths to collect payment is not a very attractive option particularly for the UK. These tolling systems create backlogs of traffic and delays during peak times. To deal with the high volume of traffic found on the M25 motorway, toll plazas will require perhaps up to 30 lanes or even more. Such plazas would require a considerable area of land and be costly to construct. Given the unattractive features of the use of manned toll booths, the majority of attention in UK policy circles has now turned to the possibility of electronic direct charging (Department of Transport, 1993). Electronic charging could work by an electronic tag inside the car which communicates with a beacon on the side of the road. By observing the passage of individual vehicles a charge can be related to the stretch of the road along which the vehicle is travelling as well as to the time and day on which the journey is made. There are those who legitimately object to the recording of individual journeys, regarding it as an invasion of privacy. Fortunately, however, it is not necessary to record the identity of individual road users unless they fail to comply with the regulations. An electronic tag can be loaded with credit which is gradually spent as the vehicle passes more beacons. If the beacon fails to detect a signal from the car it assumes that the driver has contravened the rules and the vehicle's number plate is photographed. Eventually this system might be extended to provide a two-way flow of information between the car and a central computer. Unfortunately, direct electronic charging on all routes is not a practical proposition as not all routes can be monitored, and therefore there is likely to be a problem in preventing traffic diversion from tolled roads to non-tolled ones. It can be shown that there are circumstances in which tolling on some routes produces a less efficient outcome than tolling none. This observation has for some tended to reduce the perceived attractiveness of road pricing. It formed the core of the Transport Select Committee's objections to the Department of Transport's Green Paper 'Paying For Better Motorways' (1993). While this makes the planning more complex, it is not in itself an argument against the introduction of tolling along absolutely any route.

The conventional road pricing models are all based on a charge per mile driven and varied depending on the level of congestion. Such a model implies certain abilities on the part of those administering the system and in practice other bases for charging may have much the same effect and yet in practice be far easier to administer. There is likely to be a trade-off between the complexity of the technologies required to operate certain charging systems and the desirability of the systems viewed from a purely economic perspective. The simplest system involves nothing more than increasing parking fees which may reduce the demand for trips within the city. Higher parking fees will not, however, discourage through-traffic or short-stop deliveries. Slightly more sophisticated are proposals for cordon charging or area licence schemes. These schemes are different from each other; with the cordon scheme only vehicles passing through the cordon pay, whereas with an area licence scheme vehicles within the cordon also pay. Neither system relates taxes paid to distance or road conditions. Cellular methods aim to approximate distance charges by issuing a charge every time a cell boundary is crossed. Other options include charging schemes based on time spent in a particular area or congestion metering whereby charges are made if average speed falls beneath a certain level. As well as encouraging high speed driving, the effect of these charges is difficult to predict in advance, and they may not work very well.

Box 6.6
EFFECTS OF CENTRAL LONDON CORDON AND DISTANCE CHARGING
(All figures are in 1993 prices)

Percentage change in car kilometres	Inbound cordon		Distance per mile	
	£2	£4	40p	80p
Centre all day	−16	−29	−13	−23
Centre am peak	−16	−29	−14	−26
Centre pm peak	−17	−30	−15	−27
Inner London all day	−2	−3	−1	−2
Inner London am peak	−2	−3	−1	−2
Percentage change in:				
Fuel consumption	−2	−3	−2	−3
Pollution	−23	−40	−20	−32
Accidents	−1	−2	−1	−1
Tax revenue (£m pa)	150	260	210	400
Economic benefit (£m pa)	110	160	100	150

Source: MVA Consultancy, 1995

A considerable amount of work has been done in the UK examining the advantages of alternative charging mechanisms and the means of collecting these charges. Cities examined include London (Box 6.6), Bristol, Cambridge and Edinburgh. These studies have focused upon the alternative charging systems, the technological options to implement each system, the impact on travel patterns, administrative procedures and distributional issues. Clearly there are great advantages in harmonising any systems adopted in different cities of the UK. But it seems improbable that technologies currently suitable for charging on motorways would be suitable for charging within urban areas. And there are, as the next section will demonstrate, serious doubts as to whether motorway tolling is in general required at all.

EMPIRICAL ESTIMATES OF CONGESTION COSTS

Although relatively simple to develop a diagrammatic model of congestion costs, it is very difficult to measure the costs involved because the relationship linking costs to speed and speed to flow are not well understood. In part this is because of the extensive data required to estimate these relationships. Nonetheless, a description of the derivation of congestion cost estimates now follows and the classic reference here is Walters (1961).

The first task is to establish for a representative road user a relationship describing Marginal Private Cost (MPC) per kilometre travelled as a function of speed s measured in kilometres

$$MPC = ASC = a + \frac{b}{s} \qquad (1)$$

per unit of time, the value of a unit of time to the occupants of a vehicle b and a fixed cost a per kilometre.

MPC represents the additional costs as perceived by the individual road user choosing to drive another kilometre. It also of course represents the Average Social Cost (ASC) of a vehicle kilometre, there being no reason why the private costs of the last road user should differ from those experienced by everyone else. In practice a more sophisticated function might be used to account for the impact of lower driving speeds on car maintenance costs and fuel consumption (Fwa and Ang, 1992).

The next stage is to establish a speed flow relationship where F is traffic flow per unit of time. Although this is typically assumed to be a linear relationship, a more complex relationship can be postulated. Nevertheless a linear function has been found to give a reasonable fit when the relationship is estimated from observations on traffic flow:

$$s = \alpha - \beta F \qquad (2)$$

We can substitute this relationship into the expression for MPC and ASC to make them purely a function of F and a few parameters:

$$MPC = ASC = a \frac{b}{(\alpha - \beta F)} \qquad (3)$$

Multiplying equation 3 through by traffic flow gives Total Social Cost (TSC):

$$TSC = aF + \frac{bF}{(\alpha - \beta F)} \qquad (4)$$

Differentiating equation 4 with respect to traffic flow gives Marginal Social Cost (MSC):

Box 6.7

MARGINAL EXTERNAL COSTS OF CONGESTION IN THE UK

(*All figures in 1990 prices*)

Road type and time	Marginal external cost of congestion, pence per vehicle km
Motorway	0.26
Urban central peak	36.37
Urban central off peak	29.23
Non-central peak	15.86
Non-central off peak	8.74
Small town peak	6.89
Small town off peak	4.20
Other urban	0.08
Rural dual carriageway	0.07
Other trunk and principal	0.19
Other rural	0.05
Weighted average	*3.40*

Source: Newbery, 1992

$$MSC = a + \frac{ab}{(\alpha - \beta F)^2} \qquad (5)$$

Subtracting MPC from MSC (equation 3 from equation 5) and multiplying by F yields the Marginal Externality Charge (MEC) which is the concept we require:

$$MEC = (MSC - MPC)F \qquad (6)$$

In his empirical study using prototype relationships similar to these plus numerical estimates of all the parameters, Newbery (1992) suggests that the average of the marginal external costs on different roads in the UK weighted by the number of vehicle kilometres driven under the different conditions was, in 1990, 3.4 pence per vehicle kilometre (Box 6.7). Urban roads at peak periods have on average marginal external cost of 36.37p/vehicle km whereas average marginal external costs for motorways are much smaller. Estimates from Belgium by Mayeres (1993) suggest that the marginal external cost of congestion there is similar to that in Britain (Box 6.8). Adjusting Newbery's estimate for a unit value of 3.4p per vehicle kilometre to 1993 values, making an allowance for the increase in congestion since then and multiplying by the number of vehicle kilometres, gives an approximate marginal externality charge of £19.1bn (Newbery, 1995). Using Newbery's method and more recently estimated equations, road marginal external congestion charges have recently been estimated at £17.5bn (Peirson et al, 1994). Note that compared to congestion in urban areas, the marginal external cost of congestion on motorways is much smaller. This suggests that very little economic benefit is to be derived from congestion tolling on motorways.

Box 6.8
THE MARGINAL EXTERNAL CONGESTION COSTS IN BELGIUM
(All figures in 1993 prices)

Operating conditions	Cost per car km (pence)
Urban off peak	5.6
Urban peak	28.4
Highway – no congestion	0.0
Highway – light congestion	0.7
Highway – medium congestion	29.6
Highway – heavy congestion	168.1
Other – no congestion	0.0
Other – light congestion	1.0
Other – heavy congestion	9.8

Source: Mayeres, 1993
Note: Rate of exchange used is £1 = BF45

Given the need for other costs such as additional fuel costs and costs of wear and tear on the vehicle to be taken into account, as well as the uncertain value of time, an alternative procedure to that taken by Newbery is a survey type approach in which individuals are asked directly about their willingness to pay to drive on less congested roads. An oft quoted survey conducted by the Confederation of British Industry (CBI) in 1988 suggested that the costs of congestion to the UK might be £15bn. Details of the manner in which this study was conducted are not available and to some these figures are too casual to be worthy of quotation. It may be that the respondents to the survey were an unrepresentative group or a group that responded strategically believing that their response would be used to influence plans to build more roads for which they would not be required to pay. The CBI estimate and the Newbery/Peirson estimates are of course not comparable. The former (presumably) measures the additional costs incurred relative to driving on entirely uncongested roads whereas the latter refer to the marginal externality charge. Box 6.9 distinguishes these two concepts. For our purposes the latter estimates provide the relevant concept.

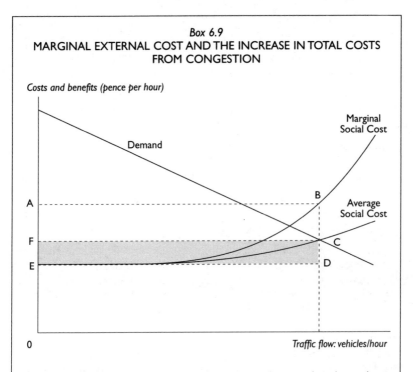

Box 6.9
MARGINAL EXTERNAL COST AND THE INCREASE IN TOTAL COSTS
FROM CONGESTION

The Newbery/Peirson estimates are of the marginal externality charge (area ABCF). The CBI estimates may be of the extra cost of travelling on congested rather than uncongested roads: (area FCDE).

THE IMPACT OF ROAD PRICING ON URBAN AIR QUALITY

Although not its primary purpose, there is evidence that road pricing (or any close variant thereof) is likely to have a very beneficial effect on urban air quality. This occurs partly because under a system of road pricing there are fewer vehicles on the road and partly because of the increase in vehicle speeds and the elimination of stop–start driving conditions. The deleterious effect of speed on emissions per kilometre has been widely documented by Dunne (1990) among others and it is possible to derive a relationship between speed and emissions per kilometre for a variety of vehicle types. This enables one to passively calculate the change in emissions following an optimally designed set of road prices. Furthermore, if one is willing to place money values on the various emissions it is possible to design a congestion tax which reflects not only the time delays imposed by the marginal driver on other road users but also the economic cost imposed due to the extra emissions now that the other vehicles are moving more slowly. Such calculations have indeed been performed

Box 6.10
REDUCTION IN VEHICLE EMISSIONS IN CENTRAL LONDON
FOLLOWING OPTIMAL ROAD PRICING

Pollutant	Charging for congestion, percentage reduction in emissions	Charging for congestion and emissions, percentage reduction in emissions
CO	42	43
VOCs	38	40
NO_x	21	23
Particulates	27	29
CO_2	37	39

Source: Austin, 1995

by Austin (1995) for London (Box 6.10). Austin finds that the time benefits accruing from road pricing are much more significant than the emissions benefits but that the quantitative reductions in emissions from road transport are very great indeed. Further results from the work of Austin suggest that the economic benefits arising from optimal road pricing in the central area of London amount to £40 per kilometre lane per hour on average whereas the tax revenue amounts to £111, thus highlighting the propensity of road pricing to transfer welfare away from road users. Average speeds are predicted to rise from just over 16mph to just over 22mph following the imposition of optimal road pricing.

Austin's study, however, has a number of important qualifications attached to it which may materially affect the results. Firstly, there is insufficient information to properly account for emissions from buses and heavy goods vehicles and he is forced to make assumptions in lieu of this information. Secondly, absolute emissions levels and the aggregate relationship between speed and emissions depends intimately on the composition of the vehicles being driven in London and in particular on the number of vehicles equipped with catalytic converters. Thirdly, the cold-start effect is ignored and, finally, the results depend crucially on the money values attached to the various emissions. These money values are taken directly from Pearce et al (1993) and are now regarded as far too low (see Chapter 4), not only because they do not include recent information on the health effects of small particulate matter, but also they might not apply to low-level urban emissions. The results provided by Austin are therefore to be interpreted as being suggestive only.

IMPLEMENTING DEMAND SIDE POLICIES:
THE EXPERIENCE ELSEWHERE

Singapore's Area Licensing Scheme (ALS) was implemented in 1975. This scheme required vehicles entering or leaving a central district to display a licence during peak periods. Vehicles with more than four occupants and commercial vehicles were exempt. These measures were supplemented by policies to discourage car ownership in addition to other restrictions. In 1990, the Singapore Quota System was introduced to further limit the purchase of new cars. Vehicles may be purchased only with a Certificate Of Entitlement (COE). Individuals wishing to purchase a vehicle enter a bid for the fixed number of COEs issued each month. The price is determined by the lowest accepted bid. These COEs may be resold. Snyder (1994) remarks that:

> The ALS scheme is successful in that it has effectively reduced peak demand for road use, however, too much restraint is economically wasteful. This non optimal tax results in pricing an inefficient number of drivers off the road and causes an inefficient allocation of trips to other modes and time periods.

It is therefore arguable that the road system of Singapore has been under-utilised for 15 years (McCarthy and Tay, 1993).

Most commentators would probably agree that any kind of restriction placed upon the purchase of a car is an inappropriate measure to deal with traffic congestion. Traffic congestion is not linked with ownership, but rather with when and where a car is driven. To deal with traffic congestion it must become possible to exclude certain sorts of road users from the road network – specifically those for whom the value of a journey is less than the value of the delays they would inflict on other road users. Which road users have valuable journeys and which do not is revealed by their willingness to pay an amount equal to the marginal congestion costs they impose on other road users.

France, Italy, Japan and the United States all have tolling booths along some of their major routes. Oslo, Bergen and Trondheim are surrounded by a toll ring which one must pay to drive through. Switzerland currently operates a system of motorway permits. This system requires all drivers wishing to use Switzerland's motorways to purchase a permit allowing access for a given duration (normally a year). Although relatively easy to implement and enforce, the scheme is unattractive because it cannot restrict demand during congested periods and it is not related to use. After the first journey has been made, all subsequent journeys are 'free'. Mexico City, Santiago and Athens have all instituted traffic bans based on license plate numbers (World Resources Institute, 1992) partly to deal with the congestion problems but also the very severe pollution problems experienced by these cities. But these schemes possess the flaw that as an attempt to bypass the regulations individuals now purchase a second vehicle (Goddard, 1994). The deficiencies of such a system hardly need to be pointed out: since so many individuals in Mexico City now possess a decrepit second vehicle (so that they can continue to travel on any day of the week) the air pollution is worse than before.

Due to its high population density coupled with rapid economic growth and sharply increasing levels of car ownership Hong Kong was first to experiment with electronic road pricing (Hau, 1990). The scheme began in 1983 and lasted until 1985. An electronic number plate was mounted on the vehicle and as it passed over a sensor in the road the vehicle's presence was recorded by a central computer and a monthly bill despatched to the driver detailing his movements. Vehicles with faulty or missing identity plates were photographed and the drivers traced. Cost–benefit analysis of the experiment indicated that the benefits outweighed the costs by a factor of 14 to 1; the net benefits of electronic road pricing were greater by a factor of two than the benefits from a system of restraining car ownership. Unfortunately the scheme was not permanently adopted. It failed because of public concerns over the lack of privacy, but also because of protests from drivers who felt aggrieved because taxis were exempt from the toll charges. At one time the Government of the Netherlands also had plans to commence electronic road pricing but political pressure once again led to these proposals being dropped (Button, 1993).

ROAD DAMAGE COSTS

The manner in which the maintenance costs are shared between different road users is important. Each road user must be made to pay a charge equal to the damage that they cause to the surface of the road. The damage done depends mainly upon the climate, the nature of the road surface and the axle weight. Damage rises extremely rapidly by a power of four as axle weight increases. Thus heavy vehicles with few axles cause a considerably greater amount of damage than cars per kilometre travelled. Any charge made for road damage must be related to the distance which a vehicle travels since those travelling greater distances cause more damage (although it also depends on the nature of the roads on which particular types of vehicles will travel). A tax on fuel cannot be used for this purpose because the damage caused is not by any means proportional to the quantity of fuel burned. Only one kind of tax appears to give a fair reflection of the variable costs of heavy goods vehicle (HGV) road traffic: the kilometre tax. Odometers have been successfully used in a number of countries (eg New Zealand, Finland, Sweden and Norway). Given the dominance of HGVs in causing road damage the kilometre tax ought to be confined to this class of vehicle. The tax should be related to the weight of the vehicle and to the number of axles it possess and, if possible, to the roads on which it is travelling.

Recently the maximum permitted weight of HGVs allowed on UK roads has been increased to 44 tonnes. These lorries, however, have to have more axles than normal in order that the damage does not become excessive. Under a system of a kilometre tax related to axle weight, private road hauliers would automatically be encouraged to use whichever vehicles constitute an efficient choice from a social perspective. The feasibility of using odometers in the UK clearly depends upon our continental competitors following likewise, given the number of foreign goods vehicles on British roads and British vehicles on the continent.

Privatisation of road space also has interesting potential implications for the appropriate attribution of damage costs (although these are not sufficient to overcome its earlier mentioned deficiencies). If there are a large number of buyers and sellers in the market for the provision of road space, no one road owner would permit road users to degrade the surface of their road without paying for it, and neither would any owner contemplate subsidising the damage done by one class of road users by increasing charges to another class. The second class would simply choose to drive on a competitor's road instead. Similarly, decisions taken by the owner concerning the thickness of the road would be made in the light of the nature of the anticipated traffic. Because the damage done by HGVs travelling on a thicker road is less, HGV owners would be expected to be charged less and could reduce their costs by driving on thicker roads. Heavy goods traffic is therefore likely to choose thicker roads to drive on (which is what they should do but currently have no incentive to choose). Moreover poor decisions concerning road thickness have financial repercussions for those in charge – quite unlike the present situation. Decision making is therefore likely to improve. Much traffic congestion appears to be the result of repairs to roads and the pipes and sewers underneath them. Anything which reduces the amount of damage done to roads is liable to ease traffic congestion. Newbery (1988) has calculated that annual damage costs in the UK are in the vicinity of £1.5bn annually.

CONCLUSIONS

Next to air pollution, congestion is one of the most important external effects of road transport. Although the construction of new roads to relieve congestion might in some cases be justified, the present appraisal process is flawed in that it fails to account for generated traffic, and fails to evaluate the environmental costs on the same basis as time savings, ie it does not monetarise them. Without accounting for these things, it is not surprising that roads are apt to be built in the wrong places. Some form of demand side restraint or institutional reform is an absolutely inescapable part of the solution to the United Kingdom's transport policies rather than continuing to allow open access to the road network.

Privatisation of roads, as advocated by some, is undesirable, and instead attention has fallen upon road pricing. Yet at the same time the technology required to implement road pricing, at least as it is envisioned in theory, is very complex and expensive. It is also apparent that charging for road space is likely to involve a significant transfer of resources from road users to non-road-users and in the eyes of policy makers this is at least as problematical as the onerous technological requirements.

The most attractive short-term policy seems to involve the use of tradeable area licences for London and other major cities, along the lines of those advocated for use in Mexico City (Goddard, 1994). Clearly these permits will not possess all the desirable properties of distance charging but they are a desirable and feasible interim step. The tradeable nature of these licences gives them advantages in that they will necessarily end up in the hands of those who value them most highly, irrespective of the way in which they are distributed. They might even be freely distributed and the excess bought back by the Government. This solves the problem of the large transfers by conferring the rents upon the road users rather than on society as a whole. Furthermore, although specifically directed at relieving congestion, road pricing schemes also contribute to reducing pollution by decreasing private road traffic generally as well as by encouraging a switch to mass rapid transit systems which have lower pollution emissions per passenger kilometre. These auxiliary benefits from the reduction of traffic volumes obviously have to be filtered into any analysis of the quantity of permits to be issued.

Another possibility is to differentiate these permits in terms of the likelihood of their being temporarily revoked on high air pollution days. Evidence suggests that most health damage from air pollution occurs on a few high pollution days, and a certain type of permit would not permit the driver to access the city on these occasions. Naturally these permits will exchange hands for different prices with those motorists who are flexible about their travel plans or mode of transport buying those permits likely to be revoked first. This system for dealing with the stochastic air pollution crises thus has considerable advantages over the kind of outright automobile bans implemented in some European cities or the UK's current reliance on moral persuasion, which very clearly doesn't work.

Chapter 7

The External Cost of Accidents

INTRODUCTION

The number of road accidents appears to be one of the few traffic statistics which has been steadily improving over time (Box 7.1). Moreover, it is a measure in which the United Kingdom compares favourably with other countries (Box 7.2). But such measures provide an incomplete picture in that they do not record the changes in the behaviour of unprotected road users as they try to adapt themselves to the growing volume of traffic. These adaptations can be readily observed and they are not without cost. Furthermore, with the notable exception of air transport (which accounts for only a very small fraction of travel within the United Kingdom) those modes of travel with the worst safety record are growing fastest.

Most attempts to calculate the external impacts of road transport

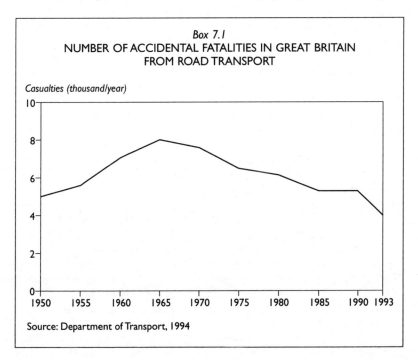

Box 7.1
NUMBER OF ACCIDENTAL FATALITIES IN GREAT BRITAIN
FROM ROAD TRANSPORT

Source: Department of Transport, 1994

Box 7.2
INTERNATIONAL ROAD DEATHS 1990

Country	Road deaths per 100,000 people	Car user deaths per billion car km
Great Britain	9.4	7.1
West Germany	12.6	10.1
East Germany	18.9	11.4
France	19.9	21.9
Italy	12.3	14.5
Luxembourg	18.7	16.7
Netherlands	9.2	9.1
Spain	23.2	62.9
Austria	20.0	28.7
Finland	13.0	10.3
Norway	7.8	7.4
Switzerland	9.0	8.5
Sweden	13.4	12.7
Yugoslavia	21.0	91.6

Source: Department of Transport, 1992

assign large values to accidents. There are actually three stages in computing the external costs of accidents involving road vehicles: the first involves identifying the cost elements involved in traffic accidents, the second involves considering whether and to what extent these costs are externalised and the third involves placing money values on those cost elements which are externalised. The penultimate section of this chapter goes on to discuss the adequacy of using accident statistics as a measure of the effect of road transport on unprotected road users. The final section considers measures to reduce road traffic accidents.

ACCIDENT COST COMPONENTS

Listing the social costs (ie including both external and private costs) of road accidents is a straightforward exercise (Box 7.3). But what exactly are the costs involved in an 'average' accident? How are these costs to be calculated in the case of intangibles such as physical pain and grief resulting from accidents? What fraction of these can be considered as being externalised by the road users themselves? Should the adaptive behaviour of pedestrians and cyclists be costed and if so how? Here there are a large number of unresolved issues.

The private costs of road transport include among other things the driver's (and passengers') assessment of the physical risks to their own safety. It may therefore seem that the human costs of accidents are internal costs in the sense that the drivers can choose the level of

---

Box 7.3
SOCIAL COSTS OF ACCIDENTS

Own human values
Other human values
Medical and ambulance costs
Police and administrative costs
Material damage costs
Loss of output

---

risk that they submit themselves to. But this involves a number of assumptions which are not self-evidently correct: firstly that the human values used by the individual include the pain and grief felt by the bereaved in the event of a fatal accident. Should these values be increased to reflect altruistic concerns for the safety of others? The surprising answer is that probably they should not. Bergstrom (1982) has shown that if altruism exists in its purest sense as a concern for the overall welfare of others then it is not appropriate to include any additional payments reflecting altruistic concerns. The reason is that this would result in the overprovision of safety to other individuals and a corresponding underprovision of all other determinants of their overall level of welfare. Only if altruism is purely safety focused (ie one derives satisfaction only from the survival prospects of other individuals) should these elements be included. Which is the case in reality appears to be an empirical matter.

Secondly, it is assumed that the individual motorists estimate correctly the likelihood of their being involved in an accident. In fact, the majority of people believe that they are safer than the average driver (the 'it'll never happen to me' syndrome). Misperceptions have a policy relevance in that there may be a case for intervening in order to make road users 'more aware' of the risk to which they are exposing themselves. Additional taxes could be required to correct endemic misperception of the risks.

Thirdly, there is the assumption that the physical risks faced by any motorist are not affected by the actions of others. This area is rather contentious. Some researchers are clearly impressed by the fact that when two or more cars collide they impose 'external costs' on each other. Therefore they reason that all collisions are external costs. This, however, is an abuse of the word 'external' as it is intended in economics. What is required is a less myopic view! Accident costs are external to the extent that an additional vehicle kilometre driven increases the probability of any other motorist having an accident. If the presence of an additional motorist makes no difference to the likelihood of any other motorist encountering a mishap then there is no externality. Mathematically, as demonstrated below, the number of pairwise encounters between vehicles (and presumably the number of accidents) should increase at the square of the flow of vehicles assuming that drivers do not take any additional care or modify their driving behaviour. But as mentioned in the introduction to this book over recent years traffic flow has increased considerably while at the same time the number of fatalities has fallen. This might be taken as implying that there is a negative relationship between flow and the number of accidents. However, not only have there been improvements in road design, car design and medical treatment but also greater driver education and tougher enforcement of driving laws. An empirical analysis would require cross sectional information on a large number of roads for which all these variables would be held fixed. Empirical evidence of a cross sectional nature gathered by Vickrey (1968) for the US more than 25 years ago suggests a more than linear relationship between traffic flow and the number of accidents. More recent evidence from the US suggests that this relationship might be closer to linear (Vitaliano and Held, 1991). The Department of Transport also assumes a linear relationship (Newbery, 1992). Given the policy relevance of this to determining the degree of market failure in road transport it is unfortunate that not more is known regarding traffic flows and accident rates.

The final objection to the view that all accident costs are internal is that there are three very definite external costs of accidents. In the first place it is clear that the administrative costs of clearing up the aftermath of an accident is a cost not borne directly by the motorist and neither is the cost of medical treatment given the universal entitlement to free medical provision. The output lost to the state in the form of the taxes paid by the individual is also an external cost. Nobody behaves in such a way as to take into account the increased tax burden on others in the event of their death while deciding whether to drive or not. The material costs of accidents on the other hand are already internalised through mandatory third party insurance payments for damage to private property. It is conceivable that not all physical damage done is paid for (eg damage to public rather than private property) and we ignore these costs.

It is possible to incorporate all of these elements into a simple model from which one is able to derive the marginal external cost of road transport in respect of accidents. It is also easy to demonstrate how these marginal external costs depend axiomatically on key parameters and assumptions for which there is very little information and as a consequence the true marginal external costs of accidents are subject to a wide margin of error (the model is adapted from Jansson, 1994).

$$TSC = (a+c+d)rF \tag{1}$$

where a stands for the expected cost to the road user and fellow passengers in the event of an accident while c stands for the cold-blooded financial costs of each accident such as the administrative and medical costs; d stands for damage costs paid for by the road user involved in an accident; r stands for risk: the risk of a representative road user having an accident per vehicle kilometre and F is vehicle flow per unit of time.

The expected number of car accidents per kilometre is itself likely to be an increasing function of the flow of traffic. The greater traffic density, the greater the opportunities for a collision. Accordingly it is possible to write:

$$r = \beta F^\gamma \tag{2}$$

More specifically, if doubling the density of traffic results in a doubling of the risk then the relationship between r and F is a linear one and γ is equal to unity. This seems intuitively sensible since doubling the density of traffic means twice as many cars coming in the opposite direction. This is a most uncertain relationship however: the empirical evidence offered by Vickrey is that γ takes the value of 0.5 while the position of the Department of Transport is that r is not a function of traffic flow at all (γ is equal to zero) which seems hard to believe. Substituting this relationship into the TSC function yields:

$$TSC = (a+c+d)\beta F^{1+\gamma} \tag{3}$$

The Marginal Social Cost (MSC) is simply:

$$MSC = (\gamma +1)(a+c+d)\beta F^\gamma \tag{4}$$
$$MPC = APC = (a+d)r = (a+d)\beta F^\gamma \tag{5}$$

The marginal private costs (MPC) are the expected private costs of an accident from the last vehicle kilometre driven. Again, there being no reason why the driver of the last kilometre is safer than any other road user, the marginal private cost is equal to the average private cost.

Note that this equation assumes that road users correctly perceive the risks involved in driving and that it omits net output costs and treatment and accident administration costs since these are not directly paid for by road users themselves. The Marginal Externality Charge (MEC) is the marginal social cost minus the marginal private cost multiplied by the traffic flow:

$$MEC = (MSC-MPC)F \tag{6}$$

This charge is necessary to reconcile the behaviour of motorists with the costs that they inflict on others as well as on wider society. Suppose now that the risk to the road user of making a journey is independent of the number of other road users (in other words that γ is equal to zero). In this case the charge to internalise the accident externalities can be shown to reduce to the sum of the cold-blooded costs inflicted on the rest of society. If on the other hand there exists a serious problem of misperceptions almost to the extent that people did not believe that they personally were at risk from an accident then the total revenue necessary to internalise accident externalities would be the marginal social cost multiplied by the vehicle flow. This would be a very considerable sum indeed, exceeding even the total social cost of accidents! It is also possible to relax the assumption that all traffic is composed of homogenous road users and to introduce different types of vehicles into the traffic flow, for example, cars and buses. These vehicles have different characteristics in terms of their effect on the accident rate. Taxes can be derived for road use in order to reflect any external accident costs and these may differ between different classes of road users resulting in changes in the composition of traffic (see Jansson, 1994).

Unlike collisions between cars, lorries and motorbikes, the physical outcome of a collision between a protected and an unprotected road user (by which we mean a pedestrian or cyclist) is clearer cut. If there were a linear relationship between traffic flow and the number of unprotected road user casualties (ie a constant risk of an accident per vehicle kilometre) and road users bore no cost in the event of their causing an injury to an unprotected road user then the costs of all such accidents are external to protected road users. They fall either on the unprotected road users or on society as a whole in terms of the medical treatment that the victim receives. We do not suppose that such a situation is very far from the truth, but there is the obvious question of the extent to which insurance payments or other sanctions internalise the cost of accidents involving injuries to pedestrians and cyclists. The important question is what courts of law award in cases of accidental death or injury. It appears that payments seldom reflect the estimated external costs of the accident and are more concerned with compensation or apportioning blame between the parties involved.

These simple models are applied to the calculation of accident externalities in Great Britain in a later section. Before doing so, however, the next section deals with the problem of calculating the major cost element in road traffic accidents: the value of a statistical life, and the economic value of pain, grief and suffering. These values inject further uncertainty into the ongoing calculations.

THE VALUE OF LIFE AND LIMB

The Value Of a Statistical Life (VOSL) refers to the marginal willingness to pay to avoid the risk of a fatal accident aggregated over a large number of people. Many activities increase or decrease the probability of a fatal accident and if life were infinitely valuable all resources would be devoted towards its preservation. But the fact that no individual behaves in such a way suggests that there are acceptable degrees of risk. Indeed, in many contexts individuals can be observed trading off risks against wealth. By using a single figure for the value of avoided fatalities one is better able to avoid inconsistencies whereby the implicit value of safety differs across different sectors. The exact values placed upon human lives and the avoidance of accidents can matter a great deal when it comes down to determining the nature of road investment projects. Increasing the cost of an accident relative to time savings seems to encourage projects whose main attraction lies in their ability to reduce the number of accidents rather than in, for example, relieving congestion. There is a widespread view that safety is seriously underprovided for in the UK (Jones-Lee, 1989) in the sense that the figures used by the various departments do not match stated preferences of individuals.

Originally, the present value of future income was used as an indicator of the value of road safety. Maximum willingness to pay was erroneously thought to equal lifetime earnings (see Freeman, 1992). Allowances were made for the value of non-marketed services such as those of the housewife as well as for direct economic costs associated with accidents such as medical bills. The problem with this approach is that people value safety for its own sake and not because of a desire to maintain the output of the economy. The approach was accordingly amended to include some more or less arbitrary element for pain, grief and suffering. A variant of the approach is to say that the discounted present value of the victim's consumption should be subtracted from gross output. This yields a measure known as the net output loss and reflects the economic impact of the death of an individual on the rest of society. The fairly obvious objection to this approach is that the death of a disabled person or anyone past retirement age is apt to be counted as a benefit.

Box 7.4
**VOSL IN THE UK BASED ON COMPENSATING
WAGE DIFFERENTIAL STUDIES**
(All figures in 1993 prices)

Study	Date	VOSL
Melinek	1974	0.5
Veljanovski	1978	5.5–7.6
Needleman	1980	0.2
Marin et al	1982	2.4–2.7
Georgiou	1992	8.6
Average		3.7

Source: Organization for Economic Cooperation and Development (OECD), 1994

Box 7.5
VOSL IN THE USA BASED ON COMPENSATING
WAGE DIFFERENTIAL STUDIES
(All figures in 1993 prices)

Study	Date	VOSL (£m)
Smith	1974	8.7–16.6
Thaler and Rosen	1976	0.7
Smith	1976	4.1
Viscusi	1978	1.4–4.3
Dillingham	1979	0.5–1.5
Brown	1980	2.0
Viscusi	1980	3.0–8.2
Viscusi	1981	4.0–7.1
Olson	1981	8.5
Arnould et al	1983	0.7
Butler	1983	0.9
Low and McPheters	1983	0.7
Dorsey and Walzer	1983	6.5
Smith	1983	1.9–5.8
Dickens	1984	1.9–2.3
Leigh and Folsom	1984	5.4–7.1
Smith and Gilbert	1984	0.5
Dillingham	1985	1.66–4.7
Gegax	1985	1.3–1.7
Leigh	1987	4.4–8.3
Herzhog and Schlottman	1987	5.3
Viscusi and Moore	1987	1.1–1.3
Garen	1988	4.1
Cousineau	1988	0.8–2.6
Moore and Viscusi	1988	1.2–5.7
Moore and Viscusi	1988	5.7
Viscusi and Moore	1989	5.4
Moore and Viscusi	1990	10.6
Moore and Viscusi	1990	10.6
Kneisner and Leeth	1991	0.4
Average		4.1

Source: Organization for Economic Cooperation and Development (OECD), 1994

Other suggestions were to use the implicit value of life reflected in past public sector policy decisions which risks circularity and completely avoids the question of how the public sector ought to value life. The life insurance method attempts to link the value of a statistical life with the sums for which people typically value their lives or limbs. Unfortunately many individuals who are nonetheless very concerned with their own personal safety may rationally decide not to hold any life insurance whatsoever, particularly if they are without dependents. In any case since they will not be around to pick up the insurance payout it is very hard to regard this sum as a value for willingness to pay to avoid risk. Finally, some have suggested that typical values of court awards in cases of accidental deaths are an appropriate measure for the VOSL. These are possibly a candidate for the extent to which society dislikes risk. But it seems more likely that these payments, too, reflect the needs of the dependents rather than an individual's willingness to pay to avoid risk.

The Department of Transport has now adopted willingness to pay measures of the value of a statistical life in place of its former reliance on gross output measures. Finding out how people behave with regard to risk enables researchers to calculate the willingness to pay to reduce risk, from which the VOSL can be deduced. There are three widely used techniques to calculate the implicit value of safety. Studies aimed at estimating this figure (Boxes 7.4 and 7.5) have been made in the context of industrial risks by considering the element of compensation in the wages paid to those employed in dangerous occupations (the Hedonic/Compensating Wage Differential approach). Other things being equal, jobs with higher risks of accident attached to them will require greater wages to compensate for this risk. This approach has the advantage of dealing with actual rather than with hypothetical choices. On the other hand it could be argued that the results from such studies owe as much to the intervention of regulatory bodies such as the Health and Safety Executive as to the rational choices made by individuals. Compensating wage-differential-type studies also suffer from the deficiency that, when questioned, workers' perceptions of the risks present in their own industry seem to be rather poor. There are also variables such as unionisation and sex or race discrimination which also affect wages and have to be included in the analysis as explanations of relative wage rates. A related method, revealed preference techniques, are based on trade-offs and tend to rely on a number of assumptions. Revealed preference techniques have, for example, been used to determine the value of life from the decision to purchase a smoke detector, to fit seat belts in the time before they were compulsory or when to fit a new set of tyres to one's car.

Box 7.6 VOSL BASED ON CONTINGENT VALUATION STUDIES (All figures based on 1993 prices)			
Study	Date	Country	VOSL (£m)
Jones-Lee	1985	UK	2.60
Persson	1989	Sweden	1.9–2.3
Maier	1989	Austria	2.44
Average			2.30

Source: Jones-Lee, 1992

Other studies question people directly regarding their willingness to pay to avoid hypothetical changes in the risk of an accident (Box 7.6). The values for a statistical life are then approximated by dividing the willingness to pay for the change by the corresponding variation in probability. For example, if the average respondent is willing to contribute £1 to reduce a risk of death by 1 in 1,000,000 then the implied value of a statistical life is £1,000,000. Although these changes are hypothetical rather than based on observed behaviour the directness of the approach is attractive. The questionnaire approach enables one to make estimates of the extent to which socio-economic variables such as income, age and social class determine the answers given. Willingness to pay for safety is shown to be an increasing function of income. The approach does, however, require checks on the consistency of answers and the ability of individuals to handle elementary probability-type concepts. Values for non-fatal injuries are calculated in a similar manner: respondents are invited to state their willingness to pay for a small change in the probability that they will be involved in an accident leaving them in a particular stated condition, for example, paralysed.

Box 7.7
APPROVED VALUE FOR ACCIDENTS IN SEVERAL
EUROPEAN COUNTRIES
(All figures in 1993 prices)

Country	Year	Evaluation/£	Method
Belgium	1983	323,000	Value of gross earnings
Germany	1988	673,800	Value of gross earnings
Finland	1989	1,708,000	Willingness to pay
France	1985	274,200	Value of lost years
Great Britain	1988	948,100	Willingness to pay
Luxembourg	1978	351,500	Value of net earnings
Netherlands	1983	90,600	Value of net earnings
Norway	1988	362,800	Value of gross earnings
Austria	1983	584,300	Value of gross earnings
Portugal	1976	13,100	Value of gross earnings
Sweden	1990	2,102,300	Willingness to pay
Switzerland	1988	1,781,100	Willingness to pay
Spain	1984	153,800	National product

Source: Hannson and Markham, 1992

The average VOSL derived from studies done in the UK is remarkably similar to the average VOSL from those conducted in the US. Both are considerably higher than the £635,180 willingness to pay used by the Department of Transport (as measured in 1991 prices). A survey of 21 other studies of various methodologies and from different OECD countries conducted by Jones-Lee (1992) reveals an average of £1.72m per statistical life. From all these studies it is possible to argue that the VOSL is really closer to £2m, several times higher than the figure used by the Department of Transport. For how these values compare with what public bodies actually use around the world see Box 7.7. Note that all the countries (except France) include direct financial costs as well as human costs associated with a fatality which makes their uniformly low values even more surprising. The reason appears to be the general reliance on output-based measures of the value of a statistical life. It is apparent that although the values employed in the United Kingdom are among the highest, the Department of Transport still fails to use a value commensurate with that emerging from the empirical evidence. The reason is presumably a preference for particular types of infrastructure investments at the expense of road safety or a simple desire to control overall expenditure.

Such a policy costs lives. As an illustration Jones-Lee (1989) crudely estimates the effects of increasing the Department of Transport's then estimated value of a statistical life to a figure somewhat more in line with the empirical evidence. This is done to determine the extra outlays that would be implied by using such a figure in project appraisal and the number of additional lives which could be saved. Such an exercise requires a UK marginal cost function for road safety which unfortunately does not exist (Box 7.8). Jones-Lee, however, takes an OECD report which details the cost of 37 road safety countermeasures in the US and applies it to the UK. He then examines the consequences of a move from the Department of Transport's old value for a statistical life to a value which he regards as the lowest defensible. A rough estimate would be that the additional implied measures would save 600 lives annually at a cost of 10 per cent of the central and local government annual budget for road building. Using a yet higher estimate for the value of a statistical life would save an additional 900 lives at an additional cost of 22 per cent of the budget. It certainly is notable that those countries employing the highest value for the VOSL often seem to enjoy the best traffic accident records. The Netherlands is an exception. Erik Verhoef, however, has noted in a private communication to the authors that the Netherlands operates a target-based system for saving lives rather than one based upon the figure in the table. A further measure of the extent to which altering the value of a statistical life used in public investment appraisals is given by the Leitch Committee Report On Trunk Road Assessment (1977). The committee took 25 road appraisal projects and examined the extent to which the ranking of these projects in terms of their perceived net benefit to society was affected by changes in the value of a statistical life. The effects proved to be substantial, suggesting that failing to value statistical lives properly can result in a drastic misallocation of resources.

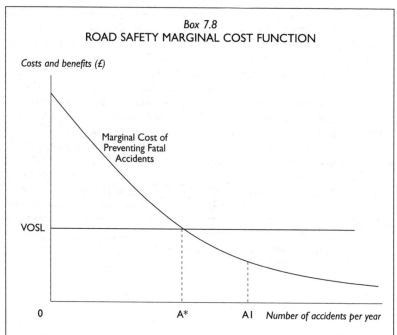

Box 7.8
ROAD SAFETY MARGINAL COST FUNCTION

The marginal cost function traces out the cost of all the different measures that can be undertaken to prevent loss of life. Public policy clearly does not devote all national resources to preventing loss of life and so some level, A1, is currently implicitly accepted by policy makers. An economist would argue that the intersection between the VOSL, measured via a WTP approach, and the marginal cost function is the best for society. Current Department of Transport VOSL may be too low, and this implies that perhaps people at the margin would benefit from a further reduction in the number of accidents.

THE EXTERNAL COSTS OF ACCIDENTS IN GREAT BRITAIN

As the preceding sections have shown it is possible to reach radically different conclusions regarding the external costs of accidents depending on the assumptions which are made and in some cases there is precious little evidence to suggest what the most appropriate assumptions might be. This section attempts to calculate the external costs of accidents in Great Britain. In the ensuing calculations it is assumed that road users perfectly perceive the risks to which they expose themselves and that γ takes a value between 0 and 0.5. For accidents involving unprotected road users it is assumed that there exists a linear relationship between the number of accidents and vehicle flow. The average private cost of an accident involving an unprotected road user involves only material damage costs. A sensitivity analysis using different estimates of human values is employed since, as discussed, the figures used by the Department of Transport are too low in relation to almost all empirical research. All the medical and ambulance costs associated with the treatment of the accident victims are external costs as given by the Department of Transport (1993) but updated to 1993 prices. Accident administration and medical damage costs are given on a per accident basis rather than a per casualty basis. Note that the number of accidents is somewhat less than the number of casualties. This is because some accidents involve injuries to more than one individual. These costs are allocated pro rata to casualties. All physical damage is paid for by the motorists involved through mandatory insurance. All calculations refer to the year 1993 and consider only accidents in Great Britain.

It is also worthwhile noting that while the official statistics are taken at face value there is a literature on the under-reporting of accidents which might be used to justify inflating the casualty statistics. This has not been done in order to avoid the charge that the authors are valuing accidents which have not occurred in reality. Nevertheless some authorities see under-reporting as a problem of some significance. Based on a survey of six hospital-based studies James (no date), for example, states that a large number of non-fatal injuries go unreported (Box 7.9).

Box 7.9
PERCENTAGE OF INJURIES REPORTED IN THE UK BASED ON HOSPITAL STUDIES

Severity	Percentage reported
Fatal	100
Serious	76
Slight	62
All injuries	62

Source: James, no date

Box 7.10 tabulates the injuries and fatalities suffered by unprotected road users (pedestrians and cyclists) and protected road users (everybody else). In the next Box these casualties are valued using the official values for grief, pain and suffering as well as net output losses and medical and ambulance costs (Box 7.11). Two distinct values are used for the human value element; the official value of £685,359 (in 1993 prices) and a more realistic value of £2,000,000 taken from Jones-Lee's (1985) survey work. Note that the willingness to pay component should include consumption (because it is assumed that the consumption of goods and services is part of the enjoyment of life and would therefore be taken into consideration

Box 7.10
INJURIES TO ROAD USERS IN GB 1993

	Killed	Serious injury	Slight injury
Protected road users	2,392	30,201	202,968
Unprotected road users	1,422	14,808	54,229
Total	3,814	45,009	257,197

Source: Department of Transport, 1994

when respondents to willingness to pay surveys give a willingness to pay value for the avoidance of an accident). Box 7.12 looks at the costs associated with accidents (rather than casualties) of varying degrees of severity. As was argued above, police and administration costs are all external to road users whereas material damage costs are paid for in full.

The total social cost of accidents befalling unprotected road users is calculated by multiplying the number of casualties by the corresponding casualty cost and adding allocable accident costs. The resulting costs are £2,652m or £4,521m depending on the values used for a statistical life. Of these costs only material damage is paid for by those who inflict the injuries. These damages amount to £107m so that the remainder (£2.5bn–£4.4bn) are the externality charges which can alternatively be expressed in terms of being between 0.6 pence and 1.1 pence per vehicle kilometre.

Box 7.11
OFFICIAL VALUES FOR CASUALTIES OF VARIOUS SEVERITIES IN THE UK
(All figures in 1993 prices)

	Human values	Net output lost	Medical and ambulance	Total
Killed[1]	685,359	51,274	486	737,119
	(2,000,000)			(2,051,760)
Serious injury	72,185	1,834	2,805	76,826
Slight injury	5,981	259	129	6,279

Source: Department of Transport, 1993
1 The figures in parenthesis use, in our view, a more accurate VOSL

Calculating externality charges for protected road users is more difficult. The total casualty costs plus allocable accident costs for protected road users is £5,758 to £8,903 depending again on the values used for a statistical life. Taking the value 0.5 for γ implies that the marginal social cost of accidents is something like 2.1 pence per

Box 7.12
ACCIDENT COSTS IN GB 1993
(All figures in 1993 prices)

Accident	Police and administration costs/accident	Material damage/ accident	Total costs/ accident
Fatal	547	3,233	3,780
Serious	438	2,559	2,997
Slight	328	1,805	2,133

Source: Department of Transport, 1992

vehicle kilometre with the low value for a human life and 3.3 pence per vehicle kilometre in the high value case. The average private cost of accidents however is just 1.3 pence in the low value case and 2.1 pence in the high value case. The difference between marginal social cost and average private cost ranges from 0.8 pence to 1.2 pence per vehicle kilometre. The marginal externality charge is therefore £3.3bn in the low value case and £4.9bn in the high value case. Taking the value 0 for γ implies that the marginal social cost of accidents is something like 1.4 pence per vehicle kilometre with the low value for a human life and 2.2 pence per vehicle kilometre in the high value case. The difference between the marginal social cost and the average private cost in this case is just 0.1 pence, resulting in a marginal externality charge of just £0.4bn. The importance of selecting the correct value for γ should now be apparent.

Box 7.13
MARGINAL EXTERNALITY COST OF ROAD TRAFFIC
ACCIDENTS IN GB 1993
(All figures are in 1993 prices)

Victim	External cost/ £ billion	External cost per kilometre/pence
Unprotected road users	2.5–4.4	0.6–1.1
Protected road users	0.4–4.9	0.1–1.2
Total	*2.9–9.4*	*0.7–2.3*

Source: See text

The total charge per vehicle kilometre for the case of the protected and unprotected road users combined should therefore be no lower than 0.7 pence and perhaps as high as 2.3 pence. The revenue associated with such charges is £2.9bn and £9.4bn respectively (Box 7.13).

AVERTIVE BEHAVIOUR AND THE ECONOMICS OF THE BARRIER EFFECT

As discussed earlier, the number of traffic accidents involving cyclists and pedestrians in Britain has been falling steadily. But in spite of this fact there is a feeling that one sort of cost has been partially offset by another: the cost of restricting the individual freedom of movement of unprotected road users. Hillman (1988) argues that: 'Preferred patterns of behaviour are altered and an increasing burden of responsibility is imposed on all road users, especially pedestrians, to reduce their exposure to risk. This is a social cost which has hardly been acknowledged and which certainly is not reflected in government transport or road safety policies.' Whitelegg (1993) states that: 'Fear...encourages parents to take their children off the streets to protect them producing the spurious result of lowered accident and injury rates and increasing the amount of traffic as children are driven to destinations (eg schools) that they would formerly have reached on foot...' The Royal Commission on Environmental Pollution (1994) also states that: '...pedestrian deaths may have fallen for a different reason, namely that there are fewer pedestrians. In London there was a 26% reduction in pedestrian casualties between 1981-85 and 1993, but the number of trips made on foot also seems to have fallen. The implications are that the accident risk for pedestrians may have remained much the same, and that the disruptive effect of road traffic on social contacts and community life may have intensified.' Several other authors (eg Appleyard, 1981, Hillman et al, 1990) have noted significant changes in behaviour and referred to these changes as being the result of the 'barrier effect'. As traffic levels increase the roadway appears like a barrier. Pedestrians no longer move around freely and social interactions begin to suffer.

Although seemingly compelling, these statements can be criticised because they lack a theoretical basis which explains exactly why the traditional method of multiplying the number of accidents by the value of the accident is inadequate. Recently, however, Maddison (1996) has developed a theoretical model of the 'barrier effect' and has defined the term more exactly. His paper demonstrates that if avertive actions are possible, the procedure of valuing the impact of road transport by the number of accidents multiplied by the value of a statistical life is incorrect and that the direction of bias involved is always downwards.

To support his contention Maddison presents two different models of avertive behaviour. In the first model, avertive actions are undertaken not because they are desirable for their own sake but purely because they reduce the risk of an accident. Confronted with an increase in traffic the individual rationally decides to engage in more avertive activity and to accept a residual increase in risk. Thus the marginal willingness to pay to reduce the flow of traffic to its original level is the value of the change in risk (which is what is traditionally measured) plus the additional avertive expenditures (the barrier effect). In the second model Maddison deals with the case in which some avertive actions are desirable for their own sake quite independently of their effect on risk. As before, the marginal willingness to pay is the measured increase in risk multiplied by the cost of an accident and the change in expenditure on the avertive activity. But now a deduction is required because of the activity's direct contribution to welfare. But these deductions are never sufficient to outweigh the disutility arising from the extra expenditures on the avertive activity; the intuition is that, provided that individuals optimise their response to the heightened risk, then those activities are already pushed beyond the point where they are desired for their own sake. So in both cases the practice of multiplying the number of accidents by the value of an accident results in an underestimate of the true cost.

Somewhat surprisingly, documented evidence of adjustments to the physical danger of road traffic is hard to find. Most probably this is because actions to reduce the risk of being the victim of a road traffic accident are so obvious and partly because it has not been realised what implications avoiding actions have for measures of the human cost of traffic flows based purely on accident statistics. A study aimed specifically at establishing that a range of actions are undertaken at least partly (if not wholly) because they reduced the risk of an accident, would be valuable. This is because many actions have alternative explanations besides a desire to reduce risk, enabling road-lobbyists to suggest that certain actions (such as driving children to school) are increasing solely because of their direct effect on utility rather than for any other purpose such as a desire to reduce risk. But if it can be empirically demonstrated that a wide range of actions are motivated at least in part due to a desire to reduce the risk of being the victim of an accident, then the theoretical results of Maddison prove that there must be some additional cost involved to road transport which is not captured by the practice of multiplying accident numbers by their cost.

Even so, empirical evidence in the form of reductions in the number of miles walked or cycled is highly suggestive of averting action. Since 1975-76 the average number of miles walked per person per year has fallen by 15 per cent and the number of miles cycled by 24 per cent (Department of Transport, 1994). But adaptation to the increased volume of traffic extends far beyond changing the number of miles walked or cycled. Many individuals deliberately wear reflective clothing to help drivers see them or protective head gear or have bought such things for a child under their guardianship. Journeys by foot or by bicycle are significantly lengthened because of waiting to cross busy roads. Individuals may avoid visiting certain places (eg particular shops or people who live across the street) because the traffic was too heavy. Appleyard (1981) notes a change in the quality and quantity of social interaction in those streets of San Francisco suffering from high levels of traffic. As the flow of traffic in the street increases from 2,000 vehicles per day to 16,000 vehicles per day the number of 'friends per person' drops from 3.0 to 0.9, and the number of 'acquaintances per person' drops from 6.3 to 3.1. Places where pedestrians can no longer visit with ease are being abandoned. We leave it to the reader to decide for themselves the extent to which fear of traffic changes their own behaviour.

What little research there has been on averting activities has focused on the need to supervise children more closely or restrict their activities simply through fear of traffic. Hillman et al (1990) examine how the independent mobility of children has changed over time. In 1971 nearly three-quarters of all children were permitted to cross the road on their own but by 1990 this proportion had fallen to a half. Nearly four times as many children were driven to school in 1990 compared to 1971, and a steep rise was recorded in the number being escorted on foot by an older person. Of course there may be some other explanation for this change in behaviour, for example, the greater comfort of travel by car, the fear of molestation, the closure of local schools or a desire to prevent the child playing truant. But Hillman et al find that the main reason for taking children to school by car, and the one stated by 43 per cent of parents, was fear of traffic.

Turning to the matter of calculating the monetary cost of the barrier effect of road traffic, the only feasible approach seems to involve the use of the contingent valuation method and even then formidable problems present themselves, such as the problem of embedding. Only Soguel (1994) has attempted to implement the theoretically correct measure of the physical impact of road transport on the community (ie including both a valuation of the change in the physical risk plus the value of the induced change in averting activities) for the town of Neuchatel in Switzerland. He uses the contingent valuation method to calculate the total willingness to pay for the elimination of traffic flow in a defined area of the city. Unfortunately it seems probable that the study also included something of the willingness of the residents to pay for a reduction in other transport-related disamenities and furthermore the estimated willingness to pay is quite specific to the area in which all traffic was to be eliminated. Obviously it cannot be transferred outside the context of the study. Citing some Scandinavian literature based on observable changes in behaviour Litman (1994) argues that the barrier effect is likely to be of the same order of magnitude as noise costs.

The astute reader will now be wondering whether avertive behaviour to the threat of air pollution also means that estimates of the cost of air pollution presented earlier in this book understate the true cost. The answer is that they probably do, but evidence of avertive behaviour with regards to air pollution, other than that of an anecdotal variety, is virtually impossible to find. Kirkby (1972) conducted a survey of individuals living in three British cities (Exeter, Sheffield and Edinburgh) and asked them a series of questions relating to activities undertaken specifically to avoid exposure to air pollution. Exact details of the study are not available but the question posed was this: 'When air pollution is particularly bad, what can a person do?' The results of the questionnaire suggest that individuals, even as far back as 1972, had at least considered a range of possible avertive actions including wearing a smog mask or personal air filter, deciding to stay indoors, closing the windows, complaining, or even temporarily moving out of the area. Note, however, that these results refer to changes which the respondents imagined were possible rather than actions which the respondents had themselves actually resorted to. There appears to be no more recent evidence on the prevalence of avertive actions with regards to air pollution in Britain than this. But casual observation suggests that people do indeed take avertive action: for example, bicycle couriers in London often wear smog masks and people do avoid jogging in the park on high pollution days.

POLICIES TO REDUCE ROAD TRAFFIC ACCIDENTS

The use of market based instruments to tackle external costs related to traffic accidents is severely constrained. The problem is that the expected external costs of an accident depend upon when, where and how a vehicle is driven as well as the skills of the individual driver. Clearly the government cannot observe all these things so there is little potential for the use of market based instruments. Consequently policy makers have relied upon a range of regulatory policy instruments most of which have been in use for at least 25 years. These include driver testing prior to licensing, drink–drive programmes, vehicle design, road design, provision of emergency services, separation of cars and pedestrians, compulsory use of seat belts, speed humps, etc. One perennial suggestion involves using speed restrictions to cut the number of road traffic accidents, given the relationship between speed and the number and severity of any accidents. Calculating the optimal speed involves equating the marginal value of the time losses imposed on road users with the marginal benefits in terms of the reduction in the number of accidents plus the fuel savings from driving more slowly and then solving for speed (see for example Haight, 1994, and for an early example to calculate optimal speeds on motorways in the United Kingdom a paper by Ghosh et al, 1975). The available evidence suggests that optimal speeds are quite sensitive to the value of a statistical life and it might be interesting to see what impact choosing a more realistic value for this along with the new fuel prices might have on the optimal speed limit. Most countries operate a system of variable speed limits. Minimum standards for vehicle safety and the compulsory use of seat belts have both been justified in terms of the occupants not bearing the full costs of any accident in which they might be involved. There is, however, a view that these regulations have led to some form of risk compensation whereby road users feel that they can now drive faster and take more risks because they are better protected. The true impact of these measures on the number of accidents is therefore uncertain.

Reducing the amount of travel or changing the mode of travel are also means of reducing accidents but are seldom considered. This is because planners typically take the desire for mobility as given and seek to reduce the number of accidents within that constraint. Taxing different road users on the basis of their mileage via road pricing as outlined in the earlier section would help to confront road users with the risks that they pose to others. As explained, this also encourages a change in the mode of transport to safer forms. But it is apparent that before using taxes to correct for traffic accident externalities it is necessary to know considerably more about the relationship between traffic flow and accident rates as well as the extent to which road users incorrectly perceive the risks to which they expose themselves. These questions deserve a high research priority. The reader may question whether such a policy is fair. Why should skilled road users pay as much as the young and rash? The answer is that they probably should not but this is a policy which operates on an aggregate level. The Government simply cannot observe differences in the level of skill of different road users. Instead, it should do the best it can which is a flat rate fee per kilometre.

It is interesting to ask what would happen if courts awarded an appropriate sum for accidental death irrespective of blame (strict liability) without compensation. Would this eventually filter through into changes of behaviour through motor vehicle insurance premiums and would this effect the desired changes in behaviour and internalise the external costs of accidents? There is a view which states that insurance would diminish the care taken by drivers. The argument is that drivers in some sense are divorced from the financial responsibility for the accidents in which they are involved. This is not in general true because it ignores the profit incentives of the insurers to strike bad risks from their books or make poor risks pay more. Any change in the behaviour of law courts would certainly be reflected in the behaviour of insurers. Insurance companies would be more careful in screening the identity of the drivers they insure and learning as much about them as possible as well as refusing to give cover to bad risks. This would certainly have a beneficial effect on the accident rate. Inevitably, however, those whose premiums rise most (the young and the irresponsible) would be tempted to drive without insurance.

Apart from using road pricing to reduce particular types of traffic and the use of speed limits, the other policy is clearly to increase the value of statistical life used in public policy appraisal to a more realistic figure. This will result in a change in the nature of road projects away from those based on the desire to save time and instead towards those projects intended to promote safety.

Chapter 8

Aggregate Externality Charges and the Taxation of Road Transport

INTRODUCTION

The purpose of this chapter is to draw together the various estimates of the marginal external costs associated with road transport and to compare them with the taxes paid. As was pointed out earlier, these taxes should not include elements such as Value Added Tax (VAT) which are charged purely for the purposes of raising revenue. These cost estimates are then compared with estimates drawn from other sources on a category-by-category basis and differences between them highlighted. The subsequent section discusses policies for a sustainable transport system and the final section concludes.

AGGREGATE EXTERNALITY CHARGES

The marginal external costs associated with road transport are listed in the boxes below. These estimates show the aggregate marginal external costs to be £45.9bn–£52.9bn (Box 8.1). These costs outweigh the taxes paid by road transport by a factor of three (Box 8.2). It is important to understand that these figures (£45.9bn–£52.9bn) are not to be interpreted as the total external costs imposed by road users on the rest of society. If this amount were transferred from road users to non-road-users the latter would certainly be overcompensated for any ill effects that they suffered as a result of road transportation. Nor is it the amount which ought to be extracted from road users (the revenue raised by the optimal tax) since if such taxes were ever raised the number of journeys and the marginal external costs associated with them would certainly fall (Boxes 8.3 and 8.4). Any interpretation of these figures as a suggestion on the part of the authors that taxes on road transport should rise by 200 per cent is therefore wrong. The proper interpretation of these figures is merely that, on average, the marginal road user pays only about one-third of the marginal external costs of his or her journey whereas an efficient allocation of resources would demand that they pay all of it. There must accordingly be many journeys for which the private benefits are outweighed by the wider costs to society. Either some contraction of road transport is merited or alternatively some attempt must be made to reduce the environmental impact of these journeys.

Box 8.1
UK ROAD TRANSPORT MARGINAL EXTERNAL COST 1993
(All figures are in 1993 prices)

Externality	Cost (£bn)
Global warming	0.1
Air pollution	19.7
Noise	2.6–3.1
Congestion costs	19.1
Road damage	1.5
Accidents	2.9–9.4
Total	45.9–52.9

Source: See text

Another way of thinking about these figures is in terms of a cost per vehicle kilometre. On average, the external costs inflicted by the last road user amount to between 11.2 pence and 12.9 pence. The tax paid per kilometre is on average only 4 pence. Furthermore, since Vehicle Excise Duty is a fixed cost which does not vary with mileage the marginal tax paid is probably more like 3.1 pence per kilometre. If the road transport sector was operating efficiently, these amounts would be equal and the fact that they differ to the extent that they do is indicative of great inefficiencies in road transport. It is very important that the reader is aware that these figures are averaged across all journeys and mask profound differences for different types of journeys (eg urban–rural, peak–off peak, etc) and different classes of road users. For example, urban journeys contribute 97 per cent of the congestion costs but account for only 41 per cent of traffic (Newbery, 1995). It is further possible to normalise these costs with respect to passenger kilometres or tonne kilometres in order to provide a consistent basis for comparisons of the external costs of different modes. The allocation of these costs between different journeys would constitute a most interesting exercise, if it could be reliably performed, since it would pinpoint those journeys inflicting the greatest marginal external costs on

Box 8.2
MARGINAL EXTERNAL COST AND ROAD TAXES COMPARED 1993
(All figures are in 1993 prices)

Road taxes	£16.4 bn
Marginal external cost	£45.9 bn–£52.9 bn
Taxes as percentage of external cost	31%–36%

Source: Department of Transport, 1993, and authors' calculations

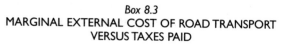

Box 8.3
MARGINAL EXTERNAL COST OF ROAD TRANSPORT
VERSUS TAXES PAID

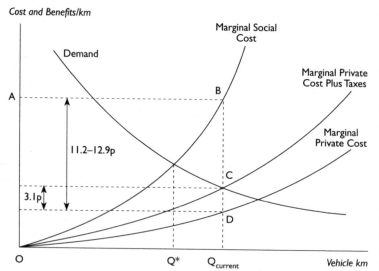

This part of the book has estimated the marginal external costs imposed by the currrent number of road journeys on the UK economy. This equates to distance BD, and is estimated at 11.2 to 12.9 pence per kilometre. Current taxes paid equal distance CD or 3.1 pence per kilometre. Benefits to society as a whole could be improved by reducing the number of vehicle kilometres driven per year from $Q_{current}$ to Q^* at which point the benefit from the journey exactly equals the cost imposed on society.
Source: See text

society. It must be realised, however, that the assumptions required to allocate these costs to different journey types are onerous and that the probable compounding of errors tends to diminish the attractiveness of any such exercise. Estimates of how these external costs vary by type of journey are therefore not provided here.

It is interesting to compare these figures with the authors' own previous work (Pearce et al, 1993) and the work of Newbery (1995) in order to draw attention to the disagreements and similarities between them. Pearce et al suggested considerably lower marginal external costs for road transport although still greatly in excess of road taxes (Box 8.5). But it must be noted that these estimates refer to different years: 1991 in the case of the previous work and 1993 in the case of the present study. The main differences occur in the case of air pollution. The current study is based upon a series of dose–response functions which detail the effects of particulates on

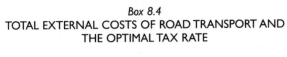

Box 8.4
TOTAL EXTERNAL COSTS OF ROAD TRANSPORT AND
THE OPTIMAL TAX RATE

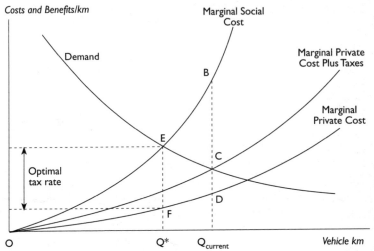

The optimal tax rate is not the same as the marginal external costs derived above to be 11.2–12.9 pence per km. It is distance EF rather than BD: the authors' are not advocating a total tax rate of 11.2–12.9 pence on UK vehicles. The total external costs from road transport is shown by the area OBDO. This has not been estimated either.

mortality and morbidity. These are seen to be of the utmost importance as well as the fact that vehicle emissions are much more likely to contribute to the dose received than any other source.

The noise cost estimates are based upon a survey of Hedonic house prices studies whereas in the previous work the estimates were based upon an assumption that noise damage costs amounted to 0.1 per cent of GNP. The authors no longer wish to defend the lower estimate for noise damages based, as it was, predominantly on the flawed avoidance cost technique. The other figure that has changed significantly is the accident cost figure. This is largely because it includes an element of uncertainty to illustrate the effects of different assumptions concerning whether accidents involving occupants of motor vehicles are externalities or not. The work of Newbery (1995) also refers to 1993 and takes a number of estimates from the earlier work of Pearce et al (1993) for global warming and noise damages. His figure for air pollution is a combination of the earlier estimates of Pearce et al (1993) and later work by Pearce and Crowards (1995) focusing exclusively on particulates. He reaches conclusions similar to, though not quite as extreme as, the findings of this study.

Box 8.5
COMPARISON OF UK ROAD TRANSPORT MARGINAL
EXTERNAL COST ESTIMATES

Externality	Cost (£bn): this study	Cost (£bn): Newbery, 1995	Cost (£bn): Pearce et al, 1993
Global warming	0.1	0.4	0.4
Air pollution	19.7	2.8–7.4	2.4
Noise	2.6–3.1	0.6	0.6
Congestion costs	19.1	19.1	13.5
Road damage	1.5	1.5	1.3
Accidents	2.9–9.4	4.5–7.5	4.7–7.5
Total	45.9–52.9	29.3–36.9	22.9–25.7

Source: See text
Note: Pearce et al, 1993, refers to the year 1991

These figures can also be compared to the estimates of the environmental costs of road transport contained within the Royal Commission on Environmental Pollution (1994) report. But as previously mentioned, the Royal Commission's exercise appears to be of the 'unpaid bill' variety whereby the expenditures on roads and the taxes paid by road users are compared to the environmental costs imposed on the rest of society. The Royal Commission therefore includes expenditures on road building, taxes on the purchase of vehicles and excludes congestion costs. As such their exercise is of a radically different nature to the exercise undertaken here. Nonetheless it is interesting to compare the two sets of figures which appear to be drawn from consideration of a variety of international studies (Box 8.6). Even allowing for the absence of congestion costs the total quantified external costs are much lower than the estimates suggested here, mainly because of the air pollution estimates. The climate change damages on the other hand are much higher. At the lower end of the range for the environmental costs suggested by the Royal Commission on Environmental Pollution, the revenue from road transport exceeds the quantified external costs.

Finally, it is appropriate at this point to reiterate some of the main sources of uncertainty concerning the current estimates. These remarks are offered in order to inspire caution on the part of those who may wish to use these figures. The figures for global warming are the least secure. The impact of climate change on the global economy of 50 years hence is hardly well understood and neither are the linkages by which carbon emissions increase atmospheric stocks of greenhouse gases (GHGs) which translate into changed climate and higher sea levels. These uncertainties could lead to a major revision of the shadow price of GHGs in future years. At the current time it is not even possible to give a range of uncertainty around the best guess

```
┌─────────────────────────────────────────────────────────────────────────┐
│                              Box 8.6
```

Box 8.6
ROYAL COMMISSION ESTIMATES OF THE ENVIRONMENTAL COSTS OF THE TRANSPORT SYSTEM (1994/1995)
(All figures are in £ billion per year. Costs attributable to road transport alone are shown in parentheses)

Cost	Lower end of range	Upper end of range
Air pollution	2.4	6.0
Climate change	1.8	3.6
Noise and vibration	1.2	5.4
Accidents	5.5 (5.4)	5.5 (5.4)
Total cost	*10.9 (10.0)*	*20.5 (18.3)*

Source: Royal Commission on Environmental Pollution, 1994, Table 7.2

figures. The figures for air pollution are also deficient in a large number of respects. Reliable dose–response functions do not exist for a large number of pollutants. The functional form of these dose–response functions is assumed to be linear and the extent of any 'harvesting effect' is unknown. The cumulative effects of long-term exposure to pollutants is not well understood and the transferability of the dose–response functions used is hardly straightforward. The monitoring of key pollutants such as PM_{10} is deficient in that the rural concentrations are not known and have to be inferred. The extent to which vehicle emissions contribute to the dose received by the general public is not at all well understood but is hardly likely to be the same as the fraction of national emissions emanating from road transport. The non-health impacts are even less well understood and have been ignored even though they are most unlikely to be zero.

Noise damages are similarly deficient. While the link between house prices and ambient noise levels has been securely established what is unclear is the willingness of the public to pay for noise reduction measures outside the context of the home. The marginal valuation of per decibel noise reductions is typically assumed to be linear and the aversion to night-time noise is not well researched. Congestion costs are dependent on an estimated speed flow relationship which is allegedly too simplistic. There is an inability to determine what fraction of accidents involving motorised road users are external and finally nothing is known regarding the extent to which flows of motor vehicles impede the objectives of cyclists and pedestrians and these costs are consequently omitted. Considerably smaller and considerably greater effects are therefore possible compared to the overall marginal external cost estimate which has been given. Together, these numerous uncertainties form the agenda for future research. There is a lot to do.

POLICIES FOR A SUSTAINABLE TRANSPORT SYSTEM

Having a sustainable road transport system means making each road user pay at least the full marginal cost of his or her journey. At the moment users of the road network pay only a fraction of these costs and even then these costs are not properly allocated between different road users and different journeys. As a result the external costs of road transport have grown out of control. The authors do not however think that the transition to a sustainable transport system necessarily involves an abrupt change in lifestyle. There is no obvious need to reduce mobility and no need to limit private ownership of motor vehicles. The important point is that the desire for mobility should evince itself in particular forms.

An important principle is that polluting should be taxed or licensed rather than the activity with which it is associated (motoring). By focusing on pollution rather than on motoring *per se* an incentive is given to avoid the financial consequences of the tax by a range of responses including reducing the polluting per mile driven, reducing total mileage and for the victims to engage in defensive activities. It also provides incentives for the development of new low-cost pollution controlling devices. It is easy to show that, compared to market based instruments for pollution control, the traditional standards based approach is inefficient in both a static and a dynamic sense (standards are capable of inflicting very high economic costs on some individuals). The impact on lifestyles of a transition to a sustainable transport system therefore depends intimately upon the particular choice of policy instruments.

Despite their advantages, market based instruments can be applied only in situations in which the polluting activity can be monitored. Unfortunately, the external effects of road transport are often ephemeral in nature, specific to the time of travel, the route taken, the vehicle used and the manner in which it is being driven. In order to calculate and then levy the appropriate tax equal to the marginal external cost the Government must be capable of monitoring the movements and emissions levels of individual vehicles. This, it clearly cannot do – at least not at the present. The best long-term strategy for a Government is to enhance its ability to monitor the activities of all road users more fully in preparation for charging them for their environmental impacts. In the shorter term the appropriate policies involve adaptation of the existing fiscal system rather than command and control policies relating to vehicle construction and use. And it is here that much more could be done than is being done at the present. It is apparent that the two main taxes currently imposed upon road transport almost totally fail to confront road users with the marginal external costs of their journeys. There are at present virtually no incentives for individuals to reduce the environmental impact of their motoring. It is indeed a very poor proxy to use the existing tax system of fuel duty and Vehicle Excise Duty

(VED) to charge for congestion costs and road damage costs. Neither tax is highly correlated with noise, accident, urban air pollution or congestion costs because these vary with the road on which the vehicle is travelling, the time, the maintenance of the vehicle and whether it is fitted with a catalytic converter. The Royal Commission's proposal to increase the price of a gallon of petrol to £5 would therefore do extraordinarily little to tackle the majority of the environmental problems associated with road transport. The only pollutant which is closely connected with fuel use is carbon dioxide. And it could well be argued that reductions in GHG emissions required to meet the UK's obligations towards the Framework Convention on Climate Change could be taken from elsewhere. VED in particular has no power whatsoever to confront the road user with the full costs of their journey. In effect once the VED is paid then the cost of all subsequent journeys is zero. The VED tax could be retained as a purely revenue-raising measure if it is thought desirable on distributive grounds. But it would be far more imaginative to differentiate the tax on grounds of the emissions characteristics of the vehicles, in particular noise, and the efficacy of the exhaust purification technology of the vehicle.

While it is in principle preferable that each mode of transport is charged according to its full marginal external costs it should be noted, however, that there are at least two good arguments for the subsidisation of public transport. First, if for political or technological reasons it proves impossible to charge the full costs to road users then it may be advisable to dispense with the full marginal cost rule for other modes, too, in order to decrease the disturbances from the true price relations the individuals face. Subsidising public transport is therefore not wrong in principle while governments fail to tax motorists for the external costs of their journeys. Second, public transport systems are generally characterized by increasing returns to scale (the cost per passenger falls as the number of passengers using a service increases) and decreasing marginal costs. Setting the price equal to the marginal cost actually implies a subsidy. It is thus in general optimal to subsidise public transport systems even in the case where we could charge other road users optimally. If Governments cannot charge them fully the arguments for subsidies of course becomes even stronger. Furthermore, if it would be possible to charge private road users the full marginal costs of their journeys, the demand for mass transportation systems would increase which in turn would increase the supply, decrease the price and probably also increase the financial viability of these systems.

Throughout the preceding chapters various policy recommendations have been made in order to confront road users with the environmental costs of their activities and to present them with financial incentives to change their behaviour. It seems appropriate to summarise the 13 main policy conclusions at this point (Box 8.7).

Box 8.7
POLICY MEASURES RECOMMENDED FOR A SUSTAINABLE
TRANSPORT SYSTEM

- The appropriate policy to deal with carbon emissions contributing to climate change is not to set sector specific targets but rather to set a uniform tax on carbon emissions throughout the entire economy. This presents the least-cost way of tackling carbon emissions since the marginal costs of abatement are equalised across different sectors of the economy.

- Fuel prices should be based on the environmental damage each fuel causes; and price differentials should reflect the environmental advantages of one fuel over another. It must be made clear that such a policy will be consistently applied to non-conventional fuels. This policy will encourage the emergence of cleaner fuels and their penetration into the market. Such differentials appear to be more important than the absolute price of fuels. A good policy might be to create a tax differential in favour of 'city diesel'.

- In order to facilitate the proper pricing of motor fuels there has to be considerably greater work done in first monitoring emissions and then using these records to conduct panel data analyses of their possible impact on excess mortality in urban areas. These studies should attempt to avoid the mistakes of existing work by looking at many different pollutants simultaneously as well as looking at the lagged impact of high pollution incidents for the possible existence of any harvesting effect. There needs to be more work on the cumulative impact of exposure to pollution.

- Purchase or ownership taxes need to be differentiated in order to reflect the emissions characteristics of the vehicle. In particular, financial incentives should exist for the purchase of vehicles which surpass currently agreed emissions standards. This will improve the characteristics of the vehicle fleet overall and provide motor manufacturers with incentives to improve the characteristics of their vehicles.

- Some means must be found of catching gross polluters. The emissions tests which form part of the MOT are unlikely to achieve this simply because they are anticipated. A more effective deterrent is either to have road-side testing of emissions or in the longer term to use pollution cameras to catch gross polluters who are then instructed to present their vehicle for testing at an approved test centre.

- It is desirable to possess real-time monitoring of air pollution. These monitors are placed in main streets so that the citizens of major metropolitan centres can see the quality of the air that they breathe and how it compares to the standards suggested by various institutions. This information assists those with breathing difficulties to decide when it may be prudent to go indoors. It is clear that at the present time some of these monitors would, if placed in central London, regularly register levels exceeding health guidelines. Such instances would generate (warranted) concern and ease the passage of otherwise politically difficult measures designed to address the problem. This may in the end prove to be the greatest benefit such monitors yield.

- The means for controlling noise pollution are similar to those for controlling air pollution. There need to be financial incentives for the purchase of vehicles which meet noise standards not currently required of new vehicles coupled with road-side spot checks for noisy vehicles as well as a noise test as part of the MOT. There are no studies on the willingness of the British public to pay for reductions in noise levels and this needs to be rectified in order to form a basis for the extent of any tax differentiation. Noise costs per kilometre might also be reflected in road pricing for congestion.

- Open access to the urban central road network must cease: the resultant congestion is extremely wasteful and the increase in pollution levels from lower speeds and stop–start driving conditions is highly significant. Expanding capacity is not really an option for dealing with congestion in urban central areas and some means of rationing demand must be implemented. There are overwhelming arguments in favour of electronic distance charging but this is an option which is likely to be a long time coming. In the short term the best option is probably an area licensing system which requires motorists to possess a licence to drive in a certain area.

- These area licences might be differentiated according to whether they are likely to be revoked in times of air pollution crises caused by particular weather patterns over the UK. The precise number of permits to be revoked and the exact trigger points clearly need to be calculated by cost–benefit analysis. This system of dealing with air pollution crises is both efficient and effective (quite unlike moral persuasion).

- Any charge made for road damage must be related to the distance which a vehicle travels since those travelling greater distances cause more damage (although it also depends on the nature of the roads on which particular types of vehicles will travel). Only one kind of tax appears to give a fair reflection of the variable costs of HGV road traffic (ie the noise and axle weight): the kilometre tax. Odometers have been successfully used in some countries and given the dominance of HGVs in causing road damage the kilometre tax might be confined to this class of vehicle. This tax should be related to the weight of the vehicle and to the number of axles it possess.

- The chief means of reducing the external costs of accidents is to charge road users on the basis of their mileage a fee representing the additional costs they impose on others. This charge will need to be differentiated with respect to different classes of road users and requires improved knowledge of the relationship between traffic flow and accidents, and the extent of public misperceptions concerning accident rates. Such a measure might favourably alter the composition of traffic.

- The vexed question of speed restrictions on roads need to be revisited in an attempt to balance the advantages from time savings with lower numbers of accidents and fuel savings.

- The other chief means of reducing accidents is clearly to use a value for life which is commensurate with virtually all the empirical evidence. This will change the composition of road investments away from those intended to relieve congestion and promote time savings to those intended to reduce accidents by various schemes.

CONCLUSIONS

Road transport is one sector of the UK economy in which almost everything has gone wrong. Previous transport policy has resulted in too much pollution, too much noise, too much congestion, too much investment in 'profitable' roads, too many accidents, too little investment in public transport, and planning decisions being taken on the basis of misleading price signals. Without a fundamental shift in policy it is inevitable that the transport sector will continue to impose large and growing costs on the natural environment, human health and the competitiveness of the British economy.

At the root of these problems lies the free access nature of the roads and the atmosphere, enabling motorists to impose costs on others which they do not bear themselves. In the absence of a correct price signal for using the roads and the atmosphere, car drivers need not pay either for the congestion costs which they inflict upon other road users or the pollution which their journeys create. This has encouraged an excessive reliance upon private transport. In other words, the benefits from the UK's extensive road network are being dissipated. Any policy to tackle these problems must involve confronting motorists with the true cost of their journeys. Higher taxes would close the gap between private costs and social costs and curtail these socially wasteful journeys. Their absence distorts price signals which are used as the basis for investment in infrastructure and public transport systems. If motorists had always paid the full cost of their journeys, urban geography and commuting patterns might be very different to those observed today.

This first part of the book has attempted to quantify the marginal external costs of road transport in the United Kingdom for which road users should be made to pay as well as suggesting the means by which this could be done. In order to put such a system into operation it is essential that society starts to measure the damage caused by emissions of various kinds in terms of money values and load these costs on to different modes in accordance with their environmental impact. Only through these means can we hope to achieve an economically efficient outcome. But it is quite apparent that society is very far from knowing the environmental costs of pollution and thereby runs the risk of setting pollution standards at far too stringent levels or alternatively at harmful levels. This would clearly be to impose a loss on society. Given the huge prevailing uncertainties in our figures and the overall probable scale of the pollution problem this leads us to the view that the value of improved information regarding these problems is very high indeed.

PART III

International Case Studies

Chapter 9

The External Costs of Road Transport in Sweden

INTRODUCTION

It is widely known that road transport creates many different kinds of 'externalities', affecting human health, regional and global climates, congestion, road wear and tear, accidents, noise, soiling and the so-called 'barrier effect'. The aim of this chapter is to present order of magnitudes estimates of these costs for Sweden and to discuss the policy response. Chapter 2 has presented the case that it is the marginal external costs that matter from an efficiency point of view, and yet a comprehensive picture of these costs is almost impossible to give, since these costs vary dramatically in different circumstances. Therefore, in addition to some examples of estimated marginal external costs, the total tax-relevant external costs will also be presented since these give an indication of the severity of the problems. These costs are defined as the total amount of tax paid that would occur if the road charge system were designed in an economically optimal way. Finally, these costs are compared with the actual tax paid in order to see whether road users as a group are 'over-charged' or not.

AN EFFICIENT ALLOCATION IN THE TRANSPORT MARKET

An economically efficient market is characterised by the fact that the economic surplus, or net benefit, ie total benefit minus total costs for the society, is maximised (Chapter 2). In a market without any external costs, this will occur when the marginal benefit, ie the benefit from consuming one unit more of a specific good (such as a vehicle kilometre), exactly equals the marginal cost, ie the cost of producing the last unit. In a competitive market with lots of buyers and sellers, this will be the spontaneous result without any influence from government. In the presence of external costs, however, this will not be the case, and typically the market left to itself will consume too much of the good in question. 'External costs' refer to the negative direct influence on the well-being of others which is not paid for by the individual him or herself. One such example is pollution by cars, which obviously will affect people other than the driver.

It is, however, possible to rectify this position, or 'internalise' the external costs through an imposition of a tax equal to the marginal external cost (so-called 'Pigouvian tax'). With such a tax, consumption will spontaneously move to the optimal level. It is important to stress that the optimal charge should equal the marginal external cost and not the average external cost. The concepts would coincide only when the marginal external cost is constant. An example when this is not the case might be where marginal external cost is an increasing function of the emission (or flow of traffic), or where the eco-system can handle low pollution levels quite well but breaks down for sufficiently high levels. Thus, it is not generally correct, from an economic efficiency point of view, to say that the total amount of tax paid should necessarily equal the total amount of damage done. Furthermore, many of the external marginal costs from traffic will vary considerably with respect to geographical location, type of vehicle, and time, which ideally should be reflected in the charge structure.

In principle, external benefits should be internalised in a similar manner through subsidies. However, the benefits from the transportation sector are almost entirely internal and if there exist any external benefits, these are generally believed to be small (Chapter 2).

AIR POLLUTION

Air pollution from road transport consists of many different chemical substances with very different consequences for human beings and the total environment. The problems arising from pollution may roughly be divided into three sub-categories: global, regional, and local problems. The first category includes emissions of carbon dioxide, since it does not matter where the emissions occur. Acidification is a typical example of a regional environmental problem. The effects (and thus the costs) differ somewhat with respect to where the emissions occur since both the current pollution pressure and sensibility of the regional nature may vary. It is, however, not likely that the effects vary much with respect to the timing of the emission even though problems related to tropospheric ozone are higher during the summer period. Local environmental problems, such as human health effects, vary with respect to both the time and the location of the emission. The environmental costs are therefore, naturally, much larger in a highly populated city centre during rush hour, particularly on a day with a severe temperature inversion problem, than in the surrounding countryside at the same time. The varying characteristics of different pollutants suggest that alternative policy instruments and methods of quantifying the environmental costs are advisable.

Emission factors

In order to measure the external costs related to air pollution from road transport, the first step is to find out the amount of different pollutants that are emitted from exhaust pipes. This is by no means a trivial task, and the values differ dramatically with respect to type and age of vehicle, control equipment, traffic conditions, driving behaviour and the current weather situation. Car producers have been set sufficiently rigid emissions targets that, in practice, catalytic converters have been fitted to petrol passenger cars in Sweden since 1989. During a transition period in 1987–88, there was a subsidy (or rather decreased tax) on cars with catalytic converters, which corresponded approximately to the additional production costs. The fraction of diesel cars in the car stock is quite low, although it has begun recently to increase due to more favourable tax regulations, especially for cars with a high annual driving distance. Since 1993 there have been three different environmental 'classes' for new cars in Sweden, where Class 3 has the lowest emission requirements corresponding to the 1989–92 rules. The fraction of somewhat cleaner Class 1 and 2 cars in the car stock is still very small, but the share of new passenger cars sold in 1994, for class 1 and 2 together, was 32 per cent, according to the Swedish Department of the Environment (SDE, 1995). Class 1 vehicles are entitled to a reduction of SKr4,000 (£1=SKr11.5) on sales tax, and while Class 2 pay the standard rate, Class 3 car owners pay an additional SKr2,000 tax (SDE, 1994). Similar tax differentiations exist for heavy vehicles. However, these differentiations have been less successful and no heavy vehicle in Class 1 or 2 exist yet on the market, largely due to problems over the design of the reliability guarantee. Actual emissions may differ dramatically from laboratory tests (Small and Kazimi, 1995). Some recent estimates of typical on-road emissions are shown in Box 9.1.

It should, however, be stressed that not all of the differences between the reported values for cars with, and without, catalytic converters are related to the difference in control technique *per se*, since the average age of the cars without catalytic converters is considerably higher than those with them. Typical values of the reduction in emission levels as a car ages are shown in Box 9.2 below. For example, every additional 10,000 km a car is driven, the VOC emissions (per km) will increase by 10 per cent, according to Hassel and Weber (1993).

The driving conditions are very important. According to a Danish study (Crawack, 1993) the emissions of carbon monoxide (CO) and volatile organic compounds (VOCs) from catalyst-equipped passenger cars in urban traffic will be about 100 per cent higher per kilometre, at an average speed of 20 km/h (rush-hour), than off-peak, at an average speed of 40 km/h. Nitrogen oxide (NO_x) emissions are 50 per cent higher during rush hour. The correspond-

Box 9.1
EMISSION FACTORS IN G/KM WITH AND WITHOUT
A CATALYTIC CONVERTER

Reference	VOCs	CO	NO$_x$	Conditions
Lenner, VTI, 1993	0.04/1.0	0.48/11.3	0.16/1.9	Long trips, Sweden
Lenner, VTI, 1993	0.41/4.4	3.4/52.5	0.35/2.1	Short trips, Sweden
Metz, 1993	0.2/2.0–3.0	1.5/15–32	0.27/1.7–2.0	Urban, Europe
Metz, 1993	0.1/0.8–2.2	1.2/10–21	0.24/2.1–2.5	Rural, Europe
Metz, 1993	0.1/1.0–2.3	1.3/12–22	0.32/2.6–3.0	Highway, Europe
Hassel, Weber, 1993	0.81/2.6	6.27/17.8	0.59/1.3	ETK-cycle, ECE urban with cold start, Germany
Hassel, Weber, 1993	0.10/1.0	1.28/6.8	0.35/2.3	EUDC, urban, Germany
Hassel, Weber, 1993	0.27/1.8	3.02/12.1	0.39/1.6	US-total, Germany
Hassel, Weber, 1993	0.14/0.9	5.13/12.8	0.75/3.2	Motorway, Germany
Barrefors, 1994	0.85/3.9	7/46.4	0.4/2.0	Short trips, 10 km, Sweden
Michaelis, 1993	0.13/1.27	0.87/6.1	0.13/2.7	Weighted cycles, UK

Box 9.2
INCREASE IN EMISSIONS WITH VEHICLE MILEAGE
Percentage increase in emissions per km per 10,000 km for cars with
catalytic converters

Reference	VOCs	CO	NO$_x$	Conditions
Hammarström, 1992	7.8	2.2	5.3	Exponential estimation, urban cycle
Hassel, Weber, 1993	10%	8%	11%	Mean value from different cycles

Source: Authors' calculation from references shown

ing emission increase for non-catalyst-equipped cars is somewhat lower. A Swedish model proposes a more than 100 per cent increase of CO emissions and almost 100 per cent increase of the NO_x emissions at these speed changes (non-specified type of car) according to Trivector (1992). It is interesting to note that if the emissions double per kilometre when the speed is halved, the overall emissions per time unit are constant. The emissions on a set length of road would then increase in the rush hour, but only in relation to the increased density of cars, ie in relation to the number of cars per km.

The fuel consumption will also increase as speed decreases in congestion. Fwa and Ang (1992) list several estimated relations of the type: Litre per km = $C1 + C2/v$, where C and $C2$ are constants and v is the average speed. A decrease from 40 km/h to 20 km/h implies an increase in fuel consumption by between 26–45 per cent with an average of 37 per cent for 10 different estimated relations.

Box 9.3
EMISSION FACTORS IN G/KM AT DIFFERENT OUTSIDE TEMPERATURES

Reference	VOCs	CO	NO_x	Conditions
Laurikko et al, 1995	2.6	21.0		Urban, Class 3, 1km, 22°C temp.–
Laurikko et al, 1995	15.7	123.1		Urban, Class 3, 1km, –7°C temp.
Laurikko et al, 1995	0.07	0.16		Urban, Class 3, 2nd km, 22°C
Laurikko et al, 1995	1.38	11.0		Urban, Class 3, 2nd km, –7°C
Laurikko et al, 1995	1.2	6.2		Urban, Class 1, 1 km, 22°C temp.
Laurikko et al, 1995	5.6	42.9		Urban, Class 1, 1 km, –7°C temp.
Holman et al,	10	72.9	1.0	Urban, 1 km trip, 0°C temp.
Holman et al,	1.2	9.2	0.2	Urban, 10 km trip, 0°C temp.
Holman et al,	4.2	43.4	1.1	Urban, 1 km trip, 10°C temp.
Holman et al,	0.6	6.0	0.2	Urban, 10 km trip, 10°C temp.

The temperature has also been shown to have significant impacts on emissions. The average temperature in Sweden is lower than in most European countries, which increases the impact of emissions from all cars, but especially from petrol cars equipped with catalytic converters. Emissions from such cars at different temperatures are shown in Box 9.3. As can be seen, the emissions in the first kilometre are generally many times higher than the next kilometre. The tests reported in Laurikko et al (1995) were conducted by the Swedish engine test centre (MTC) and were based on a sample of only a few quite new cars. The tested cars in environmental Class 1 and 3 were not otherwise identical. The test by Holman et al (1993) was conducted in the UK.

Emissions will also vary with the size of the cars. Metz (1993) shows the passenger car emissions for three different sizes of cylinder volume: less than 1.4 litres; 1.4 to 2 litres; and, more than 2 litres. For VOCs and CO, the emissions are about 7–10 per cent higher for the biggest cars compared with the smallest. For NO_x the corresponding relation is about 15 per cent. Thus, the emissions tend to increase with the size of the vehicle, although the magnitude of increase seems to be somewhat smaller than the corresponding increase with respect to fuel consumption.

Global climate change

The most important greenhouse gas is carbon dioxide, CO_2 (IPCC, 1990). The emissions from Swedish road transport were 15.7 million tonnes of CO_2 in 1990, of which 70 per cent were due to passenger cars (Swedish EPA, 1993a). Sweden was one of the first countries to introduce carbon-related tax, which was introduced in 1990 at 0.25 SEK/kg CO_2, which has subsequently been increased to 0.33 SEK/kg CO_2 in 1994 for households. Industry has a much lower rate of tax, in order not to disadvantage exporters. The household value is often used as an implicit valuation of the greenhouse effect damage by carbon dioxide. The corresponding cost would then be 5.2 billion SEK or about 0.36 per cent of GDP in 1992. The CO_2 cost for a passenger car with a specific fuel consumption of 0.1 litre/km would then be about 0.08 SEK/km. The CO_2 emissions have increased somewhat since then.

Besides CO_2 emissions, nitrous oxide (N_2O) is also a very aggressive greenhouse gas emitted primarily from cars with catalytic converters. The emission levels of N_2O are, however, very uncertain. Michaelis (1993) mentions that the order of magnitudes might be 0.01 g/km for non-catalyst cars and 0.03–0.05 for catalyst cars. The total distance driven by passenger cars in 1992 was about 53 billion km which implies a figure not far from the estimate by the Swedish EPA (1993) of emissions of 1.2 kton N_2O annually from the road transport sector. The global warming potential (per kg emission) for N_2O is assumed to be about 250–270 times that of CO_2 (IPCC, 1990). Hence, if we use the same valuation figure as above, the climate change costs by nitrous oxides are in the magnitude of 75–100 million SEK, which is small compared to the costs of CO_2. The same seems to hold also for emissions of methane and other gases.

The tax level in Sweden is high compared to most existing esti-mates of CO_2 damage. According to Fankhauser (1995), for instance, damage costs are between 0.0125 to 0.09 SEK/kg CO_2 which, of course, implies correspondingly much lower overall total values of 0.2 to 1.4 billion SEK or about 0.014 to 0.1 per cent of GDP. These estimations are, however, very sensitive to the particular assump-tions made, as discussed by Cline (1992) among others. Azar (1994) shows with explicit calculations that the discount rate chosen will affect the result tremendously. On the other hand, the tax level is probably quite far from what would be needed in order to obtain 'sufficient' reductions in the long run (reduction levels of 50-80 per cent compared to the 1990 level are often mentioned in the debate). According to the Swedish Department of Communication (SDC, 1994a) a price increase to about 20 SEK/litre is needed in order to reach a 10 per cent reduction in CO_2 emissions by the year 2020 com-pared to 1990 (see Sterner, 1994, for similar calculations explained in detail). An even higher tax may be needed if the economy grows particularly fast, or people do not respond very much to the higher prices of carbon-intensive goods by cutting consumption. If the dif-ferential from the current price was solely a result of an increased carbon tax, this rate would have to be higher than 6 SEK/kg CO_2. The corresponding total external cost from CO_2, based on the emis-sion level of 1990, would then be about 100 billion SEK/year! However, the abatement costs for the society in order to reach this level would, of course, be considerably lower. It should furthermore be noted that other sectors of the society might be much more price sensitive to an increase in the carbon tax level. Therefore, a lower CO_2 tax increase might be sufficient to reach the target level.

Regional air pollution

There are different methods of valuing regional environmental effects of air pollution. However, the valuation of almost all of the different elements of this damage are very uncertain due to the extreme com-plexity of the ecological system. ECOPLAN (1992) carried out a survey on existing estimates as a background report to the Transport and Environment (T&E) study on the external costs of transport (Kågeson, 1992, 1993). The results from most of these studies indicate rather low cost estimates. Furthermore, the variations between dif-ferent studies are huge. Many of the studies are focusing on some specific aspect or phenomenon such as future decreased harvest in agriculture. An alternative strategy, recommended by T&E and oth-ers, is to use the concept of critical loads, ie levels of emissions which the eco-system in the long run can 'handle'. There exist different def-initions of critical loads of which some are specific and stringently based purely on natural science and some are broader concepts.

Since the cost of reducing emissions from vehicles might exceed those from, for instance, large power plants, it is not necessarily cost-efficient to assume an equal percentage reduction of NO_x from the transportation sector as from the energy sector. It is most cost-efficient to abate a tonne of pollutant from the cheapest source, regardless of which sector it is in. The critical load study must then include more than the transportation sector. Kågeson (1993) concluded that a NO_x charge of 43 SEK/kg NO_x would be reasonable with respect to the critical load and the costs of better technology. Although there is no consensus on either the correct or appropriate definition, or the values of the critical loads, the order of magnitudes seem to be similar for most presented studies. The Swedish EPA (1993a) states that a 60 per cent reduction of NO_x deposition is needed to reach the critical loads in the southern part of Sweden, and somewhat lower reductions in the rest of Sweden. In a situation where most of the substances which cause regional environmental problems might be reduced quite drastically, at a rather modest cost, and the possibilities of finding reliable estimates from a damage–cost approach seem very limited, the use of critical loads seems to be a reasonable strategy.

Since 1992 there is a NO_x charge, 40 SEK/kg NO_x (close to the Kågeson suggestion), on major power plants in Sweden which has had a profound effect on emissions (Sterner, 1994). However, total NOx emissions have not decreased very much, since these emissions constitute only a small fraction of total NO_x emissions in Sweden. The same number (40 SEK/kg) is often used as an indicator of the social value of the regional environmental damage from NO_x emissions, although the charge originally was constructed on the basis of estimations of how much more expensive 'cleaner' technology is compared with the traditional technologies used. If it is impossible to tax NO_x emissions directly then it is necessary to rely on a proxy such as the fuel price instrument. But it may be necessary to raise fuel prices by considerably more in order to meet the constraint. On the other hand, policy measures related to health effects or global change will help to reach the critical load, too.

Therefore, as a rough approximation, we use the figure of 40 SEK/kg. Correspondingly we use the Swedish tax on sulphur of 30 SEK/kg S ($\approx$15 SEK/kg SO_2). SO_2 emissions from road transport have decreased substantially due to better fuel quality and are now about 3,000 tons per year or about 3 per cent of the total SO_2 emissions in Sweden, primarily from heavy traffic, which corresponds to 45 millions SEK. Several authors, such as Leksell and Löfgren (1995), Hansson (1993) and Lindberg (1995), have assumed a corresponding valuation of VOC to be 50 per cent of the NO_x value, ie 20 SEK/kg VOC. The costs from sulphur is then small compared with the costs from NO_x and VOC as shown in Box 9.4.

This corresponds to 0.16 SEK/km on average for motor vehicles. Road transport is responsible for about 40 per cent of both the total NO_x (Swedish EPA, 1993a) and VOCs (Swedish EPA, 1993b) emissions in Sweden. According to Hansson (1993) a typical average

Box 9.4
COSTS OF NO$_x$ AND VOCs EMISSIONS FROM
SWEDISH ROAD TRANSPORT
All costs in 1993 prices

	NO$_x$ '000 tons 1992	VOC '000 tons 1992	Regional environmental costs, '000 SEK
Passenger cars	86	133	6,100
Trucks, buses and others	73	25	3,420
Total	159	158	9,520
Regional environmental costs 1000 SEK	6,360	3,160	9,520=0.7% of GDP

Source: Authors' calculation

emission factor for a big truck with a trailer in Sweden 1993 is 1.48 g VOC/km and 18.13 g NO$_x$/km, which implies a marginal regional environmental cost of 0.75 SEK/km. On the other hand, a car equipped with a catalytic converter would optimally pay about 0.02 SEK/km (at 0.3 and 0.4 g/km for VOCs and NO$_x$ respectively).

Local air pollution

Leksell and Löfgren (1995) have developed a new method for monetary valuation of the human health effects of exhaust emissions in urban areas. They start from a given emission and calculate the resulting concentration levels in different areas with the help of dispersion models, wind and climate data. Then they calculate population doses, in terms of the amount inhaled by the population, using population data on the number of residents and road users in different areas. In principle, one can then go on and calculate the effects through dose–response relations and the economic value of the effects through some valuation method. However, the authors found that the dose–response relationships were particularly uncertain. Therefore, they instead chose to rely primarily on survey-based methods for valuing reductions of traffic-related concentrations in urban areas. They use the result from a Norwegian study by Slensminde and Hammer (1994) and to some extent the Swedish study by Transek (1993).

As shown in Box 9.5, NO$_x$ and VOCs constitute a large fraction of the health effects from road vehicle emissions in Göteborg. Presumably, these relations are representative for other Swedish cities, too. On the basis of the willingness to pay figure from Slensminde and Hammer (1994), Leksell and Löfgren calculate the economic valuation of the inhaled dose to 4 SEK/mg NO$_x$ and correspondingly 4 SEK/mg VOC and 40 SEK/mg particles (they consider the contributions by CO and SO$_2$ as sufficiently small to drop).

Box 9.5
ROAD TRANSPORT EMISSIONS AND NO_x EQUIVALENT EMISSIONS
IN GÖTEBORG[1] 1991

Substance	Emissions (tons/year)	Risk-factor relative to NO_x	NO_x-equivalent emissions (tons/year)	Fraction of equivalent emissions
NO_x	8,400	1	8,400	38%
VOCs	8,000	1	8,000	36%
CO	51,000	0.02	1,000	5%
SO_2	400	2	800	4%
Particulate	400	10	4000	18%
Total			22,200	100%

Source: Leksell and Löfgren, 1995, and Göteborgsregionen, 1993
1 Sweden's second town, population about 450,000

Leksell and Löfgren assume a constant marginal health cost with respect to the dose. This is by no means necessarily 'correct', since there exist threshold values or at least marginally increasing effects for some health effects, such as problems for asthmatic people as a result of high NO_x concentrations. Nevertheless, the assumption seems reasonable in order to keep the degree of complexity at a lucid level and the strategy is supported in the recent article by Small and Kazimi (1995). Furthermore, some effects, such as the number of cancers, are generally assumed to be linear in dose. The implication is that the marginal health cost, ie the health cost for one additional unit of a substance, and hence the optimal charge, will be independent of the current dose.

However, the optimal charge will vary with respect to population density in the neighbourhood, geographical conditions, car characteristics, driving behaviour, and climate. Ideally, one would like to differentiate the 'health charge' with respect to all of these variables. The health charge on a catalytic-equipped car driving at constant speed in the countryside would then be almost negligible, whereas the health charge on a typical large truck somewhere in the city centre of Göteborg might be 15 SEK/km if the climatological conditions are not favourable. It is interesting to note that a non-negligible share, about one-third, of the total dose (and hence health costs) will be inhaled by the road users themselves, and correspondingly two-thirds will be inhaled by people other than road users, but this fact will not affect the optimal charge.

Aggregate values for the total health costs from road traffic emissions are extrapolated from the calculations for Göteborg (Box 9.6). The result is about 6–7 billion SEK for Sweden, 0.45 per cent of GDP. The average health cost in Göteborg would be 48 SEK/kg NO_x

equivalent. However, during unfavourable weather conditions on a central street the dose contribution per emission unit, and hence the health costs, might be more than 15 times as high.

Since a large number of simplifying assumptions are used in each step, the results are rather uncertain. However, there exists no method at present (and probably never will) which can measure such a complicated thing as the monetary value of the health effects from air pollution, with a high degree of precision. Except for these health costs there might exist significant health costs related to particulate emissions from the road surface, tyres and brakes. Moreover, the emissions will also affect health indirectly, through agriculture and food production. We have, however, not been able to quantify these costs. Currently, there is an ongoing evaluation of the values used in social cost–benefit analysis done by the Swedish Road Administration. The report by Leksell and Löfgren (1995) will probably constitute the primary background material for valuation of the health effects.

Box 9.6
APPROXIMATE HEALTH COSTS FROM ROAD TRAFFIC
(All costs in 1993 prices)

Condition	Marginal external health cost
Passenger car, catalytic converter, average Göteborg	0.06 SEK/km (1.2 NO_x eq.g/km)
Passenger car, catalytic converter, 0°C, 1 km trip, central street, light NE 1m/s breeze, poor atmospheric conditions	8.6 SEK/km (12 NO_x eq.g/km)
Passenger car, catalytic converter, countryside	≈0
Big truck with trailer, average Göteborg	1.0 SEK/km (20 NO_x eq.g/km)
Big truck with trailer, central street, light NE 1m/s breeze	15 SEK/km (20 NO_x eq.g/km)

Source: Authors' calculation

CONGESTION

Since Sweden has a rather low population density and no really big cities (on an international scale), congestion problems are correspondingly modest compared to those of other countries. However, even though congestion at an aggregate level is not a very serious problem, in particular stretches of road in the major cities, primarily Stockholm, the time delays due to congestion are considerable. Congestion costs vary probably more than any other external costs with respect to location and time of the day. If demand shifts through the day, but the policy maker simply fixes an average tax rate throughout the day, this situation can be improved. An average charge may be better than no charge at all, but there is some 'deadweight loss' that could be removed by using a multiple price throughout the day scheme. Consider, for instance, the following situation (Box 9.7) where the demand is shifting during the day. During high demand, congestion increases and the optimal congestion charge should increase correspondingly and be equal to the difference between the marginal social cost (MSC) and the marginal private cost (MPC). If instead average congestion pricing during the day is used, the traffic level would be Q_{Lt} instead of $Q_{L,opt}$ during low demand, hence a non-optimal too low flow, and Q_{Ht} instead of $Q_{H,opt}$ during rush hour which is a non-optimal too high flow. The corresponding welfare costs related to this non-optimal pricing are shown as the 'deadweight loss' areas in the diagram.

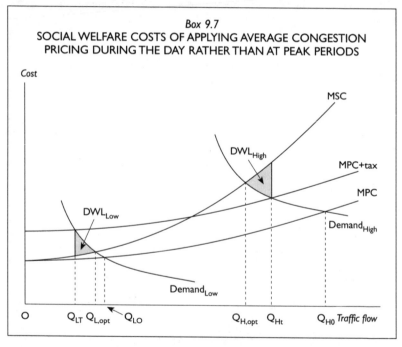

Box 9.7
SOCIAL WELFARE COSTS OF APPLYING AVERAGE CONGESTION
PRICING DURING THE DAY RATHER THAN AT PEAK PERIODS

In order to calculate the optimal congestion charge one has to know how the congestion varies with the flow on a certain stretch of road or across the whole network. As discussed in Chapter 5, it is usually assumed that speed is a linear function of flow. This allows an optimal charge per kilometre to be calculated (Newbery, 1988b, 1992), based on the speed of the traffic compared to uncongested roads, the addition to congestion from the road user above and beyond that of an average road user, and the weighted average of all other road users' value of time. According to the Swedish Road Administration the value of time on Swedish roads is on average 72.50 SEK per hour (SRA 1993, p 13.4). By assuming that the uncongested average speed in a network is about 40 km/h (including effects from traffic lights, etc) we may plot the optimal charge for a representative passenger car and a small truck at different speed levels (Box 9.8). As can be seen, the optimal congestion price increases drastically when the speed decreases.

Lindberg (1995) states that the relevant congestion prices vary between 0 and 0.1 SEK/km on the inter-urban network, with a weighted average of 0.001 SEK/km. The aggregated charge would then be less than 40 million SEK/year which is a rather small number compared to the other external costs. It is clear that the congestion costs outside the major cities are rather small. A frequently cited Swedish study (Bång et al, 1989) is based on a survey on Swedish road carriers. Their result is a total congestion cost, ie value of time lost for trucks due to congestion, of about 2.2 billion SEK (1989 monetary value) for the three biggest cities in Sweden. This is distributed as follows: Stockholm 1.725 billion SEK, Göteborg 0.270 billion SEK, and Malmö 0.215 billion SEK. These values do seem to be on the high side given that they do not include passenger cars. Those who carried out the survey seemed surprised and thought that the results should be viewed as very rough, and perhaps also a bit tendentious. One can therefore not reject the possibility of strategic bias in the result.

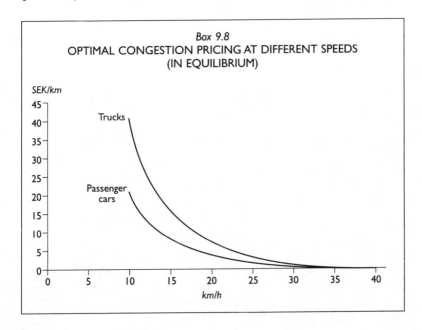

Box 9.8
OPTIMAL CONGESTION PRICING AT DIFFERENT SPEEDS
(IN EQUILIBRIUM)

Perhaps the most comprehensive study has been done by a firm of consultants, Transek (1990). They have, based on flow statistics, calculated the marginal congestion cost in different regions. Not surprisingly, they concluded that most of the costs are located in the big cities and that the congestion cost within the cities varies tremendously. They calculate the average congestion cost per kilometre driven in Sweden to be 0.13 SEK/km for passenger cars and about twice as much for buses and light trucks and four times as much for heavy trucks. No details about the calculations are shown, however. It is not correct to multiply this value with the total distance driven, respectively, in order to come up with the total costs of congestion. This is because marginal congestion costs are generally larger than average congestion costs. If one assumes a linear relation between speed and flow as discussed above, one can show that the relation between marginal and average congestion costs equals the relation between the uncongested speed and the actual speed. The aggregate relation is certainly not clear from this, but it seems reasonable that it might be in the order of 50 per cent. The overall congestion costs in Sweden, measured as the value of the time delay at the actual flow, would then be about 5 billion SEK (1993 monetary value) of which about 1 billion SEK are due to the heavy traffic. This corresponds to about 0.35 per cent of GDP. Correspondingly, the tax-relevant costs, ie the amount of tax the road users would pay with an ideal congestion pricing system at the current traffic flow, is then optimally about 10 billion SEK annually or 0.7 per cent of GDP (1992). We have then not included the external cost related to the increased fuel cost and maintenance cost for other road users. It should be emphasised that the values used are very uncertain.

NOISE POLLUTION

Noise from traffic is an external effect which is often considered to be the most serious one by people. Traffic noise consists basically of low-speed noise where the engine noise dominates, and high-speed noise where noise from the tyres dominates almost entirely. There has been significant reduction in the noise level from cars during the last 15 years. However, almost all of the improvements are from low-speed noise. High-speed noise has typically increased, since speed has generally increased, and high-speed low-profile tyres make more noise than 'traditional' ones (Swedish Department of the Environment, 1993).

Apart from decreased 'quality of life', transport noise is also responsible for productivity losses caused by an inability to concentrate at work or disrupted sleep resulting in tiredness. The external 'noise costs' are typically estimated by Hedonic prices or by some survey-based Contingent Valuation Method (CVM) methodology (Soguel, 1995).

Box 9.9
NOISE COSTS FROM ROAD TRANSPORT
(Calculated as number of annoyed people (1990) times a value per annoyed person in 1993 prices)

Noise level dBA	No. of individuals exposed	Percentage annoyed	Implicit value/exposed SEK/year	Aggregate value million 1993 SEK/year
55-60	840,000	5%	400	336
60-65	405,000	20%	1,600	648
65-70	271,000	50%	4,000	1,084
>70	65,000	100%	8,000	520
Total	1,581,000			2,588=0.18% of GDP

Source: Hansson, 1993, SDE, 1993, and SRA, 1992

The values used by the Swedish Road Administration are 8,000 SEK per disturbed individual per year, where the fraction disturbed at different (outside) noise levels are shown in Box 9.9. The Swedish figures are originally based on an early Swedish Hedonic price study (Hammar 1974). These values have then been adjusted upwards considerably (in excess of inflation) by the Swedish Road Administration. Multiplying these values by the number of individuals exposed at different noise levels implies a total noise cost of about 2.6 billion SEK/year. Ignoring one implausibly large estimate, the average value of 15 different studies listed in Verhoef (1994) is 0.39 per cent of GDP. Some of these studies only consider part of total noise costs. Hence, this estimate may be an underestimate. Since Sweden is a relatively low-density country, the order of magnitudes of the above estimated costs seems reasonable.

Although it is rather difficult to estimate the appropriate noise costs per additional km driven it has to be done in order to calculate the optimal traffic noise charge. If we first divide the estimation for the total noise costs with total number of kilometres driven we end up with an average noise cost per kilometre. The relationship between average costs and marginal costs along a certain road is not obvious, however. In Box 9.10, the official Swedish valuations are shown together with Hammar (1974) and a Dutch Hedonic price study by Infraconsult (1992) which are used as a basis for further calculations by GVF (1993) and Hansson (1995). It seems likely that the marginal cost for an additional dBA in general is higher than the average cost, ie the marginal cost increases with the noise level, as in Box 9.10. On the other hand the noise level (measured as dBA) is not a linear function of the traffic intensity, but logarithmic. Hence a doubling of the noise intensity will in general cause a relatively

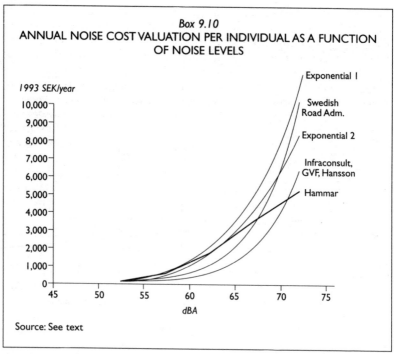

Box 9.10
ANNUAL NOISE COST VALUATION PER INDIVIDUAL AS A FUNCTION
OF NOISE LEVELS

Source: See text

much smaller change in the noise level of around 3 dBA. However, for the special case where the noise cost is a certain exponential function of the noise level, such as the ones shown in the diagram, it turns out that the total (external) noise cost is proportional to the traffic intensity. Hence, the marginal noise cost (and the optimal noise charge) is constant with respect to the traffic intensity (everything else assumed equal). As seen in the diagram, it seems that the 'real' progression is not as high as for these exponential functions in the range between 52–72 dBA. On the other hand, the 'real' marginal noise cost at levels below 52 dBA are most likely not zero. It also seems reasonable that the noise cost at very high levels increases quite dramatically. Therefore, the exponential assumption does not seem too bad, even though it is not correct in an absolute sense.

If so, the average noise cost would exactly equal the marginal noise cost and an additional vehicle kilometre would cause the same noise costs independent of the present traffic flow. As opposed to some other external costs (notably congestion), the optimal noise charge should then not change during rush hour (or whenever the traffic intensity changes), provided that the noise level from the car does not change (if anything, the noise charge should probably be lower during rush hour).

The noise cost varies, however, considerably with respect to where (and to some extent when) the car is driven, as well as how it is driven. It is self-evident that the noise cost caused by a lorry is much higher when driven in the middle of the night, at a high speed, close to a residential area, as compared to that in the remote countryside. According to van Gent and Rietveld (1993) the noise of one freight truck is comparable to the noise of 10–25 passenger cars whereas Mayeres (1993) mentions the relation to be 10 to 1 between trucks and cars, and also between motorcycles and cars. About 88 per cent of the vehicle kilometres driven in Sweden relate to passenger cars, 10 per cent to heavy vehicles (trucks and buses) and slightly more than 1 per cent to motorcycles. Heavy vehicles will be driven less in densely populated areas than passenger cars (about 25 per cent rather than 40 per cent). If we assume, very roughly, that there is no noise costs (or a negligible level) associated with driving in the countryside, we can conclude that the average noise cost for a passenger car (when it causes some noise cost at all) is about 0.06 SEK/km and the corresponding cost for a lorry or a motorcycle is about 0.6-1.5 SEK/km. Since these are average numbers, it is clear that this cost might be quite large under some unfavourable circumstances, such as through a housing area at night.

ACCIDENTS

It is not very obvious how to calculate external costs of accidents. Some of the costs associated with traffic accidents are not external. The risk of an accident that a road user exposes him or herself to is hardly external because, if the individual acts rationally, he or she will adapt their behaviour in order to take account of the cost associated with the risk of an accident. A similar logic applies to the potential damage cost of your own car. It can, of course, be argued that this cost in reality is external since the insurance company generally would have to pay the cost of any damage to the car. On the other hand, the road user has already paid the insurance company a fee which ideally should reflect the cost for the expected damage. What about the damage cost to the other road user? A road user will of course not adapt his behaviour in order to decrease the risk of damaging other road users' cars, but since all road users in most western countries are paying a compulsory insurance to cover such damage costs, it can be seen as a second-best strategy in absence of more detailed information on driving behaviour. For that reason, those costs should be treated as internal and, provided the insurance is constructed in an optimal way, they are not tax-relevant costs.

More obvious external costs seem to be the medical care costs that a road user on average causes. This is because the health care is paid for through the public budget and road users do not pay more than others. There is no reason to believe that a road user would adopt safer behaviour to save medical costs for society! Similarly, costs for rehabilitation after an accident, as well as different kinds of socially paid costs for disabled persons and administration costs, are external, unless these costs are covered by insurance.

Some costs, however, are more difficult to define as either external or internal. The loss of net output to the society, ie the difference between the future individual production value and the individual's own consumption, is commonly argued to represent an external cost (Jones-Lee, 1990). However, on average, people seem to cost the society a corresponding amount by not paying tax as a result of invalidity and health costs. For this reason, this cost should not be added to the other external costs for fatal accidents. It is, however, likely that the society will have to pay a corresponding amount of money for disabled persons after a non-fatal accident, to cover the living expenditures for the individual.

The most important (possibly external) accident cost associated with traffic seems to be the risk cost imposed on others. To what extent this cost actually is external is not totally clear. At first, it seems obvious that a road user poses a risk to all other road users since he or she could collide with any of them. It is fairly easy to show that if the number of collisions is proportional to the number of intersections, the total number of collisions will increase as a square of the traffic flow. This is so because the probability of each car colliding with another car, per kilometre driven, will increase linearly with the traffic flow and the total number of accidents is the product of risk per kilometre per car and the traffic flow. If the road users do not adapt their behaviour to the increased risk when traffic intensity increases, the total number of collisions will probably increase as a square of the traffic flow and the total number of single accidents will increase linearly with traffic. However, most recent empirical studies claim that this is not the case in reality. Vitaliano and Held (1991) for instance, claim that the total number of accidents increases only linearly with traffic, suggesting that the probability of an accident per car kilometre would be independent of the traffic flow. This is also the official view of the UK Department of Transport (1987) among others. If this is the case, it has been argued, no such externality exists.

Even though this relation might be true, ie the risk level might be independent of the traffic intensity, this phenomenon needs an economic explanation. The most obvious one, pointed out by different authors such as Newbery (1988, p 170) and Vitaliano and Held themselves, is that individuals adapt their behaviour in response to the changed flow. They will, for instance, lower their speed or concentrate harder and be more watchful when the traffic flow increases. The number of collisions per kilometre would then increase but the single accident rate would decrease. Moreover, the adaptation of the road users is in itself an external cost. As shown in Johansson (1995), the optimal charge would then be somewhat higher than 50 per cent of the optimal accident charge without this adaptation. On the other hand the optimal charge with respect to the risk of hurting a pedestrian or another unprotected road user would also be lower than would have been the case without this adaptation, since an adaptation of the speed at a higher vehicle flow would affect the safety of the unprotected road users too.

As a simple, and perhaps a bit conservative, estimate we will assume that the costs associated with the willingness to pay for risk reduction are internal costs for accidents between different motorized road users (except for motorcycles) but external costs with respect to the unprotected road users. The other components will be treated as discussed above. In order to calculate the tax-relevant external costs we need monetary valuations of the different components and accident statistics. The official cost values used by the Swedish Road Administration (1993) are shown in Box 9.11.

Box 9.11
OFFICIAL MONETARY VALUATIONS USED BY THE SWEDISH ROAD
ADMINISTRATION
(All figures are in '000 SEK, 1993 prices)

	Killed	Severely injured	Lightly injured
WTP for risk reduction			
(human value)	11,000	1,800	45
Loss of net output	798	228	12
Medical care	25	161	8
Admin costs	46	11	5
Property values	231	50	25
Total	12,100	2,250	95

Source: See text

The willingness to pay (WTP) measure for risk reduction is dominating the figures for the more serious accidents. See Persson (1992) for the calculations of the WTP values (based on CVM), Cedervall and Persson (1988) for estimations of loss of net output and medical costs, and Hort and Persson (1985) for administration costs and property values. Of course, there are large uncertainties in these kinds of measures. The numbers are, however, of the same magnitudes as in most other serious studies in the field, see for instance Jones-Lee (1990) and Viscusi (1993) for surveys. By combining these values with the accident statistics we are able to calculate the total social costs of road accidents as well as the tax-relevant part.

As can be seen from Box 9.12, the tax-relevant external costs in densely populated areas are larger than in the countryside, even though the latter traffic flow is larger than the former. The total tax-relevant external cost from road transport would then be equal to

Box 9.12
POLICE-REPORTED ROAD TRAFFIC ACCIDENTS IN SWEDEN 1992
(Costs all in billion SEK)

Accident type	Killed	Severely injured	Lightly injured	Total costs reported accidents[1]	Total costs	External costs
Densely populated areas:						
Single accident	64	436	1,419	1.9	3.5	0.51
Collision between motor vehicles	39	631	4,520	2.3	4.9	0.88
Collision between motor vehicle and other road user[2]	119	948	2,411	3.8	7.1	6.72
Other	26	193	544	0.8	1.5	0.22
Total	248	2,208	8,894	8.8	17.0	8.33
Rural areas:						
Single accident	192	1,152	3,125	5.2	9.3	1.3
Collision between motor vehicles	218	1,091	3,566	5.4	9.6	1.28
Collision between motor vehicle and other road user	79	190	263	1.4	2.0	1.07
Other	22	64	174	0.4	0.7	0.07
Total	511	2,497	7,128	12.5	21.5	3.72

Source: Statistics Sweden, 1993

Note: Total costs calculated using Box 9.11

1 The numbers differ since not all 'real' accidents are reported to the police. Furthermore, some of those accidents which first are categorised as lightly injured by the police will be re-classified to seriously injured (SRA 1992)

2 includes moped, bicycle, or pedestrian

8.3+3.7 = 12 billion SEK or 0.83 per cent of GDP. This corresponds to 0.2 SEK/km on average. According to the figures by Persson and Ødegaard (1993) the marginal cost per kilometre should be about four times as high for trucks and buses as for passenger cars. Then the marginal costs (on average) for passenger cars in densely populated areas should be about 0.3 SEK/km and 1.2 SEK/km for trucks and buses. In the countryside, the corresponding values are 0.075 SEK/km for passenger cars and 0.3 SEK/km for trucks and buses. These relations between densely populated areas and the countryside depend, however, quite heavily on our simplifying assumptions about which costs should be treated as external, which is not totally clear. For that reason, the optimal relation between the charges in different areas might be a bit lower.

The risk a single road user imposes on others is dependent, needless to say, on the actual behaviour and characteristics of the driver, such as speed chosen, driving ability in general, influence of drugs and cautiousness. The possibility of taxing with respect to these characteristics as closely as possible is important. There might exist some external costs also for accidents without any injured persons (police costs, etc). We have not tried to calculate those. They are probably quite small compared to the others, although perhaps not negligible.

ROAD DAMAGE

Road damage caused primarily by heavy vehicles is an external effect. The latest comprehensive study of the social costs connected with heavy vehicles in Sweden is done by the Swedish Department of Communication (SDC) (1987). Damage costs and other variable costs strongly related to the axle weight were about 1 billion SEK in 1985 (about 7 per cent of the total road expenditures in 1985), which corresponds to about 1.5 billion SEK in 1993 monetary value, or about 0.1 per cent of GDP. This corresponds to about 0.2 SEK per kilometre for the heavy traffic, which might seem to be a surprisingly low value. We have, however, not included any costs related to the increased construction cost for new roads in order to handle the higher pressure from heavy vehicles or similar costs. The wear and tear of the road surface is also external. According to the SDC (1987 p9) this cost should be about 35 per cent of the damage costs, or about 0.5 billion SEK. Note that passenger cars, too, are responsible for this cost.

Apart from the costs relating to repairing the roads, there are also costs relating to the fact that the comfort of other road users will be lower when the road is damaged. Furthermore, the maintenance costs of the cars might also increase. However, Newbery (1988a) in his 'Fundamental Theorem' shows that these costs should not be counted as 'tax-relevant' costs. The reason, in short, is that if the road is restored to its original state whenever the roughness, or some other quality indicator, reaches a predetermined level, the average quality of the road will not be lower if the traffic flow is high. This is because the road will then be restored in shorter time intervals.

CORROSION

According to Kågeson (1993) the external costs related to corrosion might be in the magnitude of 0.05–0.15 per cent of GDP. The sulphur emissions from the transport sector in Sweden, however, are very small. According to a recent Swedish study, Andersson (1994), the corrosion costs from SO_2 emissions are in the order of 5 SEK/kg SO_2 which would imply a tax-relevant cost of less than 20 million SEK/year. There might be some synergetic effect of NO_x and SO_2, but that effect is not clear. Presumably, the corrosion costs from the road transport sector in Sweden are therefore quite small.

POLICY INSTRUMENTS

According to economic theory the optimal traffic charge is equal to the short-run external marginal cost. Even if government has to use tax to raise revenue, this result holds (Sandmo, 1976). An ideal set of policy instruments would therefore differentiate the charge perfectly with respect to type of vehicle (emission profile, noise characteristics, and congestion factor), geographic location, time, weather conditions, driving behaviour, traffic conditions and other variables. Until recently, one might have thought that it would be totally impossible to create something like this. Of course this is true in an absolute sense. It will always be impossible to differentiate the charge perfectly with respect to all of these variables. However, the technical development in the field of information technology in the traffic sector, so-called RTI (Road Traffic Informatics) -technology, has been rapid. For instance, there are currently tests of road pricing in Germany, based on a combination of two different technologies; the digital mobile phone system GSM and the satellite system GPS (Global Positioning System). With such a system, it would be possible for the car to know where and when it is located, and hence what charge per kilometre it currently should face. It would not be too difficult to supplement such a system with variations in the weather, the speed of the car, etc. Needless to say, there are many practical, ethical, judicial and political problems, in addition to the technological ones, to overcome with such an advanced system. See Johansson and Mattsson (1995), Lewis (1993) and Blair and Worsford (1994) for recent surveys of road pricing.

The introduction of advanced information technology might in itself have profound effects on travel behaviour, and the congestion costs might be reduced. The effects on air pollution from cars, however, are generally assumed to be small (if not combined with road pricing), although in Chapter 5 it was argued that this may not be the case. There might also be some negative effects on noise, as pointed out by SDE (1994), since the traffic will be spread out to other areas, which are not planned to accommodate large traffic flows.

In the meantime, one has to rely on some imperfect strategy. Since the fuel consumed is not very highly correlated with many of these external costs, a fuel tax is not an ideal policy instrument to deal with these externalities. Different toll systems are proposed in the two major cities, Stockholm and Göteborg. However, as in many other places, these systems are not proposed primarily to deal with the external costs from transport in an efficient way, but to raise revenue for new infrastructure investments. As a consequence, the systems have so far not been very efficient from a socio-economic point of view (SDC 1994), although there exist alternative solutions in the debate (Eriksson, 1994).

Sweden used to have an odometer-based system for charging trucks per distance driven. The charge was quite heavily differentiated with respect to axle weight and other variables (SDC 1987, Hansson 1993). This system was, however, abandoned in 1993, as an adaptation to the rules within the European Community (Swedish Department of Finance, 1992). As a result, the correspondence between the short-run external marginal costs and the variable charge has decreased drastically. Furthermore, the overall taxation on the use of heavy vehicles has also decreased substantially.

Emission standards will probably still play an important role in the foreseeable future. Since 1993, Sweden has had an environmental classification for new cars, both for passenger cars and heavy vehicles. Even though these differentiations have been less successful for heavy vehicles, the introduction of environmental classes for diesel fuel has been rather successful. The tax is differentiated in three classes here as well, with respect to the contents of sulphur, aromatics, polycyclic aromatics and cetane indices (Sterner, 1994). In 1993, the market shares were 20 per cent for Class 1 and 57 per cent for Class 2 (Swedish Petroleum Institute). The former tax differentiation between leaded and unleaded gasoline (16 per cent higher tax on leaded gasoline) has contributed to the fact that leaded gasoline has been entirely out of the market since the second half of 1994 (lead has been forbidden in petrol since 1 January 1995). However, there is still a tax differentiation between three classes of petrol. The tax levels in February 1995 was 3.81 SEK/litre for Class 3 (for older cars) and 3.28 and 3.22 SEK/litre for the two better classes respectively.

AGGREGATE EXTERNALITY CHARGES

The different elements of the tax-relevant external costs from road transport are valued using different methodologies. Sometimes there exist direct market prices which one can use, but sometimes one has to find out the willingness to pay measure with a survey technique Contingent Valuation Method (CVM) or observe price changes on related goods (Hedonic techniques). The relative validity of these techniques for measuring different external costs are still disputed by economists. In Box 9.13 the valuation methods used in this study for Sweden are listed.

By 'tax-relevant external costs', we simply mean the amount of tax that the road users would pay if the road taxes were constructed in an economically optimal way, with the current traffic flow. If we compare this value with the amount of road taxes that the road users actually pay, we will clearly have an indication of whether road users as a group are 'overcharged' or not. If we sum up our findings of the tax-relevant external costs so far, we end up with a figure of almost 50 billion SEK per year, or 3–3.5 per cent of GDP. We have not then calculated the costs related to the barrier effects, which might be considerable. Nor have we included any monetary value on the possible corrosion costs or soiling. Still, as can be seen in the figure below, the tax-relevant external costs seem to be in the order of 15 billion SEK/year larger than the actual amount of tax paid. As pointed out several times, however, all of these monetary valuations are quite uncertain. This is especially true for the valuation of the global warming effects which has an uncertainty range corresponding to at least a factor 20, so that the 'true' value may lie between 5 and 2,000 per cent of the estimate given!

Box 9.13
METHODS USED TO VALUE EXTERNAL COSTS OF ROAD
TRANSPORT IN SWEDEN

	Market prices	Willingness to pay CVM or Hedonic techniques	Avoidance costs/ political valuations
Greenhouse effect			x
Regional environment effects			x
Health effects		x	
Congestion	(x)	x	
Noise		x	(x)
Accidents			
Risk reduction		x	
Medical care	x		
Administration	x		
Property values	x		
Loss of net output	x		
Road wear and tear	x		

Source: See text
Note: Crosses in parentheses denote that the methodology has been used to some (minor) extent

---

Furthermore, it should be emphasised, again, that it is not a sufficient condition for economic efficiency, that the tax-relevant external costs from road transport equal the tax collected from that sector. It is not sufficient that the road users pay the same amount in tax as they would do if the road tax system were optimally constructed. Instead, what matters is that the (short-run) marginal external cost should come as close as possible to the actual variable charge paid. Clearly, the potential for a significant improvement by only using rather blunt policy instruments such as fuel taxes, annual taxes and vehicle sales taxes is limited.

As can be seen from Box 9.14, accident costs are the largest single tax-relevant external cost component. If one instead adds the three different air pollution costs together, this component would clearly dominate the others. There is little support for the proposition that road users are being 'overcharged', which is often argued by motor organisations and others.

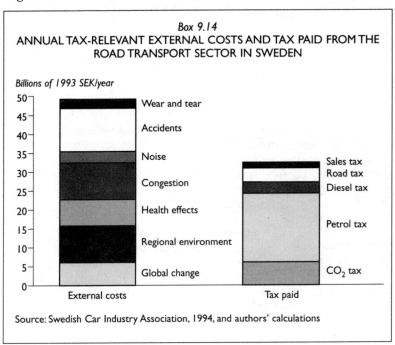

Box 9.14
ANNUAL TAX-RELEVANT EXTERNAL COSTS AND TAX PAID FROM THE ROAD TRANSPORT SECTOR IN SWEDEN

Source: Swedish Car Industry Association, 1994, and authors' calculations

Chapter 10

The External Costs of Road Transport in North America

INTRODUCTION

Imagine how your community would be affected if tomorrow motor vehicle use were to double. This would impose many problems, or 'costs' to use the language of economics, including increased traffic and parking congestion, air and noise pollution, and traffic accidents. Road maintenance and traffic law enforcement costs would also increase. There would be pressure to widen roads and build more parking facilities, imposing financial and environmental costs. Over time, urban sprawl would probably increase and mobility for non-drivers decline.

In fact, this is exactly what is happening in North America (the United States and Canada), as in other parts of the world, although gradually, over the course of a few decades. A number of factors encourage motor vehicle use in North America. Transportation investment and land use policies favour automobiles over other forms of transport. Low prices also encourage driving. Although owning a motor vehicle is expensive (typically costing thousands of dollars per year in purchase, residential parking, insurance and registration costs), operating costs are low. Fuel is cheap and non-residential parking is normally provided free, due to generous tax and zoning laws. The variable price drivers pay is well below the marginal costs they impose. During the 1920s and 1930s, underpricing motor vehicle use may have been justified in order to capture economies of scale in vehicle and road production and to make driving affordable to lower-income users. Increasing external costs and diminishing returns have negated these benefits, but the policies continue.

The implications of transportation underpricing in North America was once only an academic concern of a few transport economists, such as the work of Keeler et al (1975). In recent years this issue has attracted wider attention. A number of recent studies have examined various external costs, and a few have attempted to summarise the total costs of transportation (MacKenzie et al, 1992; PMSK, 1993; Miller and Moffet, 1993; Apogee Research, 1994; Office of Technology Assessment (OTA), 1994; Litman, 1995a). These studies show that current policies underprice motor vehicle use. Transportation professionals are beginning to acknowledge that external costs are significant and are gradually developing tools to incorporate these costs into decision making. Changes are occurring, particularly in terms of growing support for Transportation Demand Management (TDM) programs.

COST CATEGORIES

Costs can be categorized according to whether they are internal or external, fixed or variable, market or non-market, direct or indirect. These distinctions indicate how a cost affects private and public decisions. Consumers tend to be most affected by costs that are internal, variable and short term. Public agencies tend to focus on market costs since they are easiest to measure. External, fixed, long-term, non-market and indirect costs tend to be undervalued. Many costs of driving have these features, which skews both users' and society's transportation decisions, resulting in economic inefficiency and inequity (Box 10.1).

Box 10.1
MOTOR VEHICLE TRANSPORTATION COST CATEGORIES
Italics = Non-market

	Variable	Fixed
Internal (user)	Fuel	Vehicle purchase
	Short-term parking	Vehicle registration
	Vehicle maintenance (part)	Insurance payments
	User time	Long-term parking
	User accident risk	Facilities
	Stress	Vehicle maintenance (part)
External (social)	Road maintenance	Road construction
	Traffic law enforcement	'Free' or subsidised parking
	Insurance disbursements	Traffic planning
	Congestion delays	Street lighting
	Environmental impacts	Land use impacts
	Uncompensated accident risk	Social inequity

There is sometimes debate over what constitutes an external cost. One issue is whether externalities should be defined at the individual or the sector level. Congestion, accident losses, and some other costs are borne largely by drivers. Beshers (1994) argues that even parking subsidies are internal costs at the sector level since most households own an automobile and so both pay for and benefit from this subsidy. Whether externalities should be defined at the individual or sector level depends on the goal of the analysis. If the concern about externalities is equity ('*It's not fair that somebody else benefits at my expense*') then sector-level analysis is sufficient. But if the concern is inefficient consumption patterns ('If prices are low consumers use resources wastefully') then externalities must be defined at the individual level. This reiterates the point made in Chapter 2.

Additional debate occurs as to whether a particular indirect cost should be charged to transportation. For example, although automobile use is a contributing factor in urban sprawl some people argue that this is a land use issue, not a transportation cost. The proper conceptual measure of such an impact is the with-and-without test: the difference between what would occur *with and without* a particular transport program or policy (van Kooten, 1993). If building a road would cause additional urban sprawl, costs of that incremental increase in sprawl should be charged to the road project.

COST DEFINITIONS AND ESTIMATES

Vehicle ownership and operating costs

Vehicle ownership costs include depreciation, insurance, registration, and taxes. Vehicle operating costs, the costs that vary with vehicle use, include fuel and oil, tolls, short-term parking, maintenance and repairs. Fixed costs for a typical car are approximately US$2,500 per year, averaging about $0.20 per mile (Jack Faucett Associates, 1992), and variable costs average approximately $0.12 per mile, although users often fail to perceive irregular costs such as vehicle repairs as a variable cost.

Travel time

Vehicle travel time is a cost to employers who pay drivers' wages and for individuals who forgo other activities. This cost has been widely studied and a number of standard values are used to calculate the value of travel time savings (Waters, 1992).

Box 10.2
ACCIDENT COST DISTRIBUTION

Allocation	Market	Non-Market
Internal	Vehicle damage deductible	Pain and grief to driver causing accident
External at the individual level, internal at the sector level	Uncompensated expenses to other automobile users, and insurance companies	Uncompensated pain and grief to other automobile users
External	Uncompensated expenses to non-drivers, including financial costs borne by society	Uncompensated pain and grief to non-drivers

---

Accidents

Each year tens of thousands of North Americans die, millions are injured, and millions more experience financial losses from automobile accidents. Two approaches are used to monetise these costs (Miller, 1991; Haight, 1994). The human capital method focuses on market costs, including medical expenses and lost productivity. This typically places the cost of a statistical death at about $0.5 million, with lesser values for various injuries. The comprehensive approach also includes non-market costs (pain, grief, and reduced quality of life) as reflected in people's willingness to pay. This approach typically places the value of a death at $2–$5 million, with comparable values for injuries.

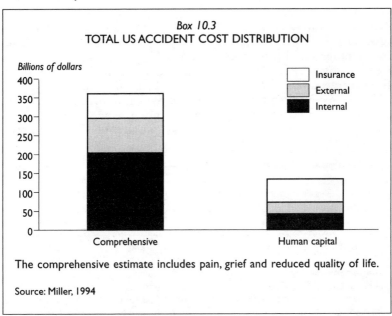

Box 10.3
TOTAL US ACCIDENT COST DISTRIBUTION

The comprehensive estimate includes pain, grief and reduced quality of life.

Source: Miller, 1994

Some accident costs are completely internal, others are external to individual drivers but internal at the sector level, and some are completely external (Elvik, 1994), as shown in Box 10.2. Box 10.3 illustrates the distribution of costs according to Miller. Both Miller and Elvik estimate that approximately 40 per cent of costs are external at the individual level. Miller's estimates can also be broken down by mode of transport (Box 10.4).

Parking

Motor vehicles typically spend 95 per cent of their time parked. A typical car requires one residential and one employee parking space, plus a share of parking at various other destinations. Most North

---

Box 10.4
TOTAL ACCIDENT COST ESTIMATES BY MODE

Vehicle type	1994 $/Vehicle mile
Automobile, overall	0.12
Automobile, drunk driver	5.50
Automobile, sober driver	0.06
Motorcycle	1.50
Bus	0.32
Commercial aircraft	0.28

Source: Miller, 1994

American zoning codes require generous amounts of parking, as illustrated in Box 10.5, which Willson (1995) indicates often result in oversupply even during peak demand periods. US motorists receive free parking at approximately 99 per cent of destinations away from their residence (National Personal Transportation Survey (NPTS), 1992), an external cost borne by businesses and local government. Subsidised employee parking is tax exempt in the US, making it an attractive benefit that significantly increases automobile commuting (Shoup, 1994).

Box 10.5
TYPICAL OFF-STREET PARKING REQUIREMENTS

Building type	Unit	Spaces
Office buildings	per 1,000 sq ft.	2.5
Retail	per 1,000 sq ft.	5
Single family dwellings	house	1–2
Apartments	unit	1
Public services (museums, libraries)	per 1,000 sq ft.	3.3
Hospitals	per 1,000 sq ft.	10
Theatres	per seat	0.25

Source: Homberger et al, 1992
Note: Local zoning laws require property owners to provide abundant parking. This oversupply causes most parking to be provided free, effectively subsidising driving.

Parking facilities also impose non-market costs including environmental degradation, increased urban sprawl and automobile oriented land use patterns (Willson, 1995). Current parking regulations are unfair and regressive since non-drivers receive no comparable subsidy, and because lower-income households own fewer automobiles and pay a larger portion of income for residential parking than

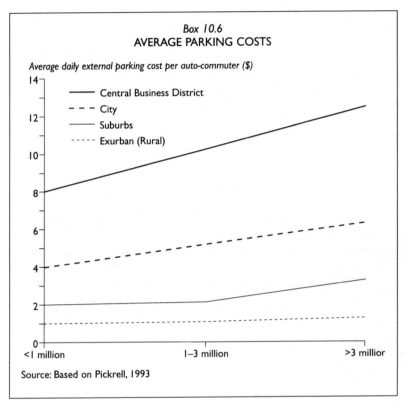

Box 10.6
AVERAGE PARKING COSTS

Average daily external parking cost per auto-commuter ($)

Central Business District
City
Suburbs
Exurban (Rural)

<1 million   1–3 million   >3 million

Source: Based on Pickrell, 1993

wealthier households (Litman, 1995b). The average daily external parking costs per auto commuter are shown in Box 10.6.

Congestion

Traffic congestion is the additional cost (travel delay, vehicle operating expenses and driver stress) resulting from interactions among road users. Congestion occurs primarily during peak-period travel, but a number of North American cities experience congestion all day long. Congestion is external at the individual level, causing economic inefficiency. It also imposes costs that are external at the sector level by delaying transit riders, bicyclists and pedestrians, and by increasing noise and air pollution. Note that buses and bicycles also contribute to congestion but at a lower rate per passenger than automobiles.

There are several ways to calculate congestion externalities (Miller and Li, 1994). An analytically correct but difficult approach is to compute marginal delay costs from an additional vehicle, taking into account the speed–flow relationship for each road segment (Downs, 1992), and this was the approach followed in Chapter 6. Another approach is to determine the price drivers must be charged to reduce demand to roadway design capacity. A third approach is based on the cost of increasing road capacity to an optimal level. In theory these estimates should converge, assuming that roadway capacity is expanded based on vehicle delay costs as reflected in vehicle users' willingness to pay, but in practice they often provide different results (Moore and Thorsnes, 1993). A common but crude method for calculating congestion costs is to sum the additional travel time over free-flowing conditions.

A problem with modelling congestion costs is the effect of generated traffic (also called induced travel). If travel demand were fixed, each additional vehicle would impose a specific cost and each vehicle less would provide a specific saving. But congestion often maintains a self-limiting equilibrium (Small, 1992). As Wardrop observed: 'The amount of traffic adjusts itself to a barely tolerable speed' (Holden, 1989, p 239). Congestion delays cause drivers to use other routes, travel at other times, shift modes, and avoid some trips. Uncongested roads attract traffic and encourage increased driving.

Generated traffic has three implications for assessing congestion costs (Litman, 1995c). First, generated travel has relatively low value because these are trips that users don't make unless traffic conditions are favourable. Second, generated traffic reduces the congestion relief benefits of increased road capacity. A recent study found that the ranking of preferred transportation investments nearly reversed after generated traffic 'feedback' was incorporated into conventional traffic modelling, due to overestimated congestion reduction benefits (Johnston and Ceerla, 1994). Third, generated traffic increases total motor vehicle external costs.

Various studies estimate urban congestion external costs to average $0.05 to $0.20 per vehicle mile (Cameron, 1991; Small, 1992; Miller and Moffet, 1993; OTA, 1994; Levinson, 1995), with higher values in some conditions.

Roadway facilities

Vehicles impose costs by using road space and wearing the road surface (Small et al, 1989). Several cost allocation studies have estimated this cost by vehicle class. Box 10.7 shows the result of one such study. These costs vary depending on when and where driving occurs. Box 10.8 illustrates one estimate of roadway facility costs by type of vehicle and location.

Many people assume incorrectly that fuel and vehicle taxes pay all roadway facility costs. Although user charges cover most highway costs in North America, a major portion of local road costs is funded by general taxes. The deficit between roadway facility costs and revenues averages about $0.015 per vehicle mile. In addition to these financial costs roads require significant land resources. The annualised opportunity cost of land used for road rights-of-way is estimated to total $75 billion or more (Lee, 1995) in the US. An automobile-oriented road system increases roadway land requirements by 50–75 per cent (Dimitriou, 1993), the additional cost of which should be allocated to motor vehicle use. This is estimated to average $0.025 per vehicle mile (Litman, 1995a). External roadway financial and land costs therefore total approximately $0.04 per automobile mile, with higher costs for larger vehicles.

Box 10.7
CALTRANS 1987 HIGHWAY COST ALLOCATION VALUES (PER VEHICLE)

Vehicle class	Capital costs ($ million)	Maintenance costs ($ million)	Total costs ($ million)	Annual miles (billion)	Unit costs ($/mile)
Automobile	1,035	1,150	2,186	158	0.014
Motorcycles	8.2	12.3	20.5	1.5	0.008
Pickups and vans	263.2	376	639.2	36.3	0.018
Recreation vehicles	48.4	59.1	107.5	4.4	0.024
Buses	11.3	11.1	22.4	0.9	0.025
Trucks	613.7	490.4	1,104.1	13.9	0.079
All vehicles	1,980.2	2,099	4,079.2	215	0.019

Source: Californian Department of Transportation

Box 10.8
ROADWAY MAINTENANCE COST ESTIMATES

Road class	Urban car $/mile	Urban truck $/ESAL	Rural car $/mile	Rural truck $/mile
Interstate	0.014	0.29	0.005	0.10
Arterial	0.038	0.76	0.012	0.24
Collector	0.037	0.74	0.016	0.32
Local	0.046	0.92	0.029	0.58
Average	0.033	0.677	0.015	0.31

Source: Miller and Moffet, 1993
Note: ESAL= Equivalent Standard Axle Load of 18,000 lbs

Transportation services

In addition to the cost of roadway facilities, motor vehicles impose costs on various public services including law enforcement (police and courts), emergency response (police, fire and emergency medical services), traffic planning, and street lighting. These costs vary depending on location, with higher costs per mile in urban areas.

Studies indicate that these costs average $0.01–0.02 per vehicle mile (California Energy Commission (CEC), 1994; OTA, 1994).

Equity and option value

Society benefits from a diverse transportation system that provides mobility to economically, socially and physically disadvantaged people ('Equity Value'), and gives everybody travel options that are occasionally useful ('Option Value') (Johnson, 1993; American Public Transport Association (APTA), 1992). Subsidies for public transit, special mobility services (which provide transportation for disabled people), and public surveys demonstrate that these values are significant (Hamburg et al, 1995). Activities that increase automobile dependency impose a cost in terms of reduced equity and option value.

Air pollution

Motor vehicles are major contributors of air pollutants, as illustrated in Box 10.9. Air pollution is a serious problem in many parts of North America, causing human illness and death, reduced agricultural productivity and environmental damage. Increasingly strict vehicle emission standards have resulted in sophisticated control technologies, including catalytic converters and alternative fuels, and further emission reductions are required under the 1990 US Clean Air Act.

Although these controls reduce emissions per vehicle mile, they

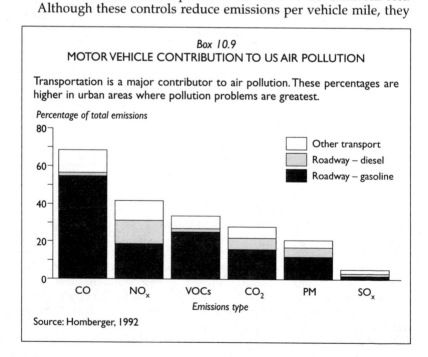

Box 10.9
MOTOR VEHICLE CONTRIBUTION TO US AIR POLLUTION

Transportation is a major contributor to air pollution. These percentages are higher in urban areas where pollution problems are greatest.

Source: Homberger, 1992

have technical limitations. Significant emissions occur during cold starts, after vehicle operation ('hot soaks'), and during petroleum processing. Increased motor vehicle use is diminishing many of the pollution reduction gains. Recent research indicates that small particulates (PM_{10}) are the most significant air pollution human health hazard. Particulate emissions result from tyre and brake lining wear, and from road dust, indicating that any motor vehicle use (including electric vehicles) produces significant air pollution costs (United States Environmental Protection Agency (USEPA), 1994).

Air pollution costs have been monetised for utility and industrial policy analysis (indicating the maximum amount that should be spent per tonne of emission reduction). Box 10.10 summarizes unit emission costs used by 37 government, utility and research agencies.

Motor vehicle air pollution cost estimates range from about $0.01 to $0.10 per vehicle mile (OTA, 1994; Litman, 1995a; Small and Kazimi, 1995), with higher costs in some urban areas. Large diesel trucks impose costs an order of magnitude larger.

Box 10.10
SUMMARY OF AIR EMISSION UNIT VALUES USED BY 37 AGENCIES
(All values in US$)

1990 $/ton	CH_4	CO	CO_2	H_2S	N_2O	NO_x	SO_x	TSP	VOCs/ ROG
Minimum	100	500	2	1,800	3,700	42	405	167	340
Maximum	740	1,000	84	1,800	4,158	40,000	21,185	8,780	21,175
Average value	326	842	25	1,800	3,880	8,212	4,011	3,401	5,986
Median value	375	907	20	1,800	3,700	4,209	1,793	2,496	3,300
Count	9	6	26	1	5	36	34	20	15

Source: Bell, 1994

Noise

Motor vehicle traffic noise is a significant cost of motor vehicle traffic. Traffic noise costs are measured using Hedonic pricing methods (the difference in value of residential property exposed to traffic noise compared with homes in quieter locations). However, this method cannot capture total noise costs due to the imprecision of estimating noise exposure for large numbers of houses, and because people experience disamenity from traffic noise away from their residence (at work, when walking or bicycling along a street, at a park, etc). Verhoef (1994) states that Hedonic estimates of traffic noise represent only one-eighth of total costs, and Bein (1994) reaches a similar conclusion based on Slensminde's research.

Several North American studies place average automobile noise costs at $0.001 to $0.005 per vehicle mile, with higher costs for larger vehicles (Keeler et al, 1975; Miller and Moffet, 1993; Apogee Research, 1994). However, these studies underestimate this cost as described above, so total noise costs are probably about $0.02 or more per mile in urban areas and $0.005 for rural driving. More research is needed to improve these estimates.

Resource externalities

Motor vehicle production and use consume many raw materials including metals, aggregates and energy. Although North America is a leading petroleum producer, voracious energy appetite also makes it one of the largest petroleum importers. The US currently imports almost 50 per cent of its petroleum, and this percentage is increasing.

Consumption of these resources imposes external costs, including economic subsidies, environmental degradation, international conflicts, and balance of payments deficits. The existence of these external costs is indicated by the broad support that exists for resource recycling and energy conservation. There is little agreement as to the total monetary value of energy externalities, but most estimates indicate that it is significant, probably equal to several cents per gallon of fuel (Hubbard, 1991; CEC, 1994; OTA, 1994)

Barrier effect

The barrier effect, also called 'severance', is the disamenity motor vehicle traffic imposes on other road users. It has direct costs (time delays and discomfort to pedestrians and bicyclists) and indirect costs (increased automobile use and dependency). It is also inequitable because pedestrians and bicyclists include a large portion of economically, socially and physically disadvantaged people. Recent North American studies have demonstrated negative impacts on pedestrian travel by motor vehicle traffic and automobile oriented street designs (1000 Friends of Oregon, 1993; Handy, 1995). Efforts to monetise this cost are currently limited to Scandinavian research (Slensminde, 1992; Swedish National Road Administration, 1986; Danish Road Directorate, 1992). Applying these models to North American conditions indicates a cost averaging approximately $0.01 per vehicle mile, with higher costs in urban areas and lower costs in rural areas.

Land use impacts

Roads and parking facilities consume significant amounts of land directly, and encourage urban sprawl that increases per capita land use. This imposes external costs resulting from loss of undeveloped land, including farms, forests, wetlands termed by planners and landscape architects as 'greenspace', which provide a variety of

external benefits including wildlife habitat, air and water regenera-
tion, aesthetic enhancement, biological diversity and social benefits
of agriculture. Roads also increase municipal service costs (fresh
water, sewage, power, roads, etc) as illustrated in Box 10.11, and
increase automobile dependency. Automobile oriented land use also
has negative impacts on neighbourhoods and communities
(Crowhurst Lennard and Lennard, 1995; Appleyard, 1981).

Land use impacts are varied and complex, and charging them as
costs to motor vehicle use is controversial. It is relatively easy, however, to demonstrate that these impacts include significant costs and
that motor vehicle use is a major contributor. For instance, the with-
and-without test can be used to determine how much a particular
transportation decision contributes to land use changes and imposes these costs. Several studies and surveys support the hypothesis
that sprawl resulting from automobile use imposes significant external cost, and results in part from an automobile oriented
transportation system (Litman, 1995a). There are few monetised estimates of this cost, but it appears to rank in magnitude between noise
and air pollution, although perhaps higher when the external costs
resulting from increased automobile dependency are included.
Some people argue that low-density land use (sprawl) provides benefits that compensate for these costs. The benefits of sprawl are
almost entirely internalised, so the best test of this argument would

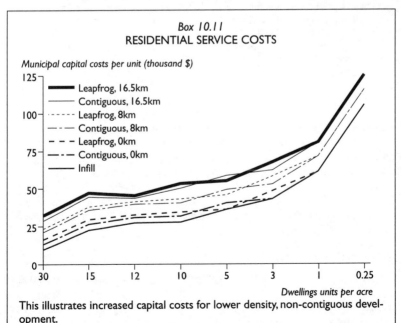

Box 10.11
RESIDENTIAL SERVICE COSTS

Municipal capital costs per unit (thousand $)

— Leapfrog, 16.5km
— Contiguous, 16.5km
····· Leapfrog, 8km
—·— Contiguous, 8km
— — Leapfrog, 0km
—··— Contiguous, 0km
— Infill

Dwellings units per acre

This illustrates increased capital costs for lower density, non-contiguous development.
Source: Summarised from Frank, 1989

be to charge users for all external costs and see whether they are willing to pay. There is no reason for society to subsidise these benefits.

Water pollution and hydrologic impacts

Automobiles contribute to water pollution and hydrologic problems as listed in Box 10.12. Quantifying these costs is challenging. First, it is difficult to determine exactly how much roads and motor vehicle use contribute to water pollution problems since impacts are diffuse and cumulative. Second, it is difficult to place a dollar value on water quality and flow. Even if we know the quantity of pollutants originating from roads and automobile traffic and their environmental impacts, we face the problem of monetising costs such as loss of wildlife habitat, reduced wild fish populations, and contaminated groundwater.

Despite these difficulties, several studies have quantified portions of this cost (Miller and Moffet, 1993; OTA, 1994). The Washington State Department of Transportation estimates that meeting water-quality

---

Box 10.12
TYPICAL WATER AND HYDROLOGIC IMPACTS

Water pollution	Hydrological impacts
Drips and disposal of vehicle fluids	Increased impervious surfaces
Road de-icing (salt) damage	Flooding and siltation
Roadside herbicides	Loss of wetlands
Leaking underground storage tanks	Shoreline modifications
Air pollution settlement	Construction activities along the shoreline

---

and flood-control requirements for state highway storm-water runoff will cost $75 to $220 million a year in capital and operating costs, or $0.002 to $0.005 per vehicle mile (Entranco, 1992). This estimate only covers about 10 per cent of total lane miles in the state (carrying about 50 per cent of total motor vehicle travel), excludes parking surfaces, and does not include residual impacts, so an estimate of $0.01 per vehicle mile probably represents a lower bound of this cost (Litman, 1995a)

Waste disposal

Disposal of junked vehicles, used tyres, old batteries and other semi-hazardous materials resulting from motor vehicle production and use imposes some external disposal costs on society, although current recycling and special disposal programmes funded by user charges are internalising many of these costs.

Summary

Box 10.13 summarises the distribution of the costs described above, while Boxes 10.14–16 illustrate these costs for different travel conditions and modes.

	Box 10.13		
	TRANSPORTATION COST CATEGORIES		
Cost	Internal/External	Fixed/Variable	Market/ Non-market
Vehicle ownership	Internal	Fixed	Market
Vehicle operating	Internal	Variable	Market
Operating subsidies	External	Fixed	Market
User travel time	Internal	Variable	Non-mkt
Internal accident	Internal	Variable	Non-mkt
External accident	External	Variable	Non-mkt
Internal parking	Internal	Fixed	Market
External parking	External	Fixed	Market
Congestion	External	Variable	Non-mkt
Road facilities	External	Variable	Market
Roadway land value	External	Variable	Non-mkt
Transportation services	External	Variable	Market
Equity & option value	External	Variable	Non-mkt
Air pollution	External	Variable	Non-mkt
Noise	External	Variable	Non-mkt
Resource consumption	External	Variable	Non-mkt
Barrier effect	External	Variable	Non-mkt
Land use impacts	External	Variable	Non-mkt
Water pollution	External	Variable	Non-mkt
Waste disposal	External	Variable	Non-mkt

Source: See text

Transportation elasticities and generated traffic

A key question in this discussion is how much effect underpricing has on motor vehicle use. Economists use elasticities to quantify the change in consumption (in this case travel) caused by a change in price. A high elasticity means that consumption is sensitive to price, indicating a 'luxury' good. A low elasticity means that consumption is insensitive to price, indicating a 'necessity'.

The elasticity of motor vehicle use has been widely studied, usually with respect to gasoline price (Oum et al, 1992). Typical results indicate that each 10 per cent increase in fuel prices reduces total vehicle travel (mileage) by only 1–2 per cent in the short term, and 3–4 per cent over the long term (long-term elasticities tend to be higher because consumers have more time to adjust durable factors,

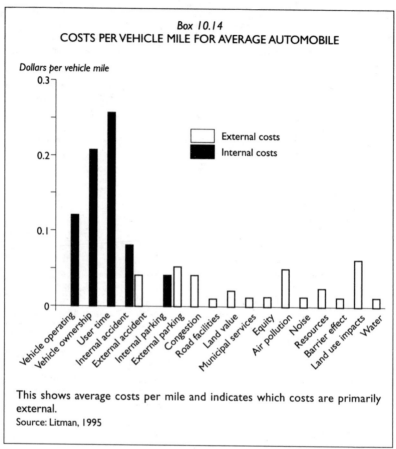

Box 10.14
COSTS PER VEHICLE MILE FOR AVERAGE AUTOMOBILE

This shows average costs per mile and indicates which costs are primarily external.

Source: Litman, 1995

such as where they live and work). These estimates are often used to argue that driving is an inelastic good, and therefore a necessity. That may be an incorrect conclusion, however, since fuel only represents about 20 per cent of total motor vehicle costs. This indicates an elasticity of driving with respect to total cost of –0.5 to –1.0 in the short term, and –1.5 to –2.0 in the long term, implying that a significant portion of motor vehicle use is 'luxury' travel. This hypothesis is supported by Shoup's (1994) research on the elasticity of driving with respect to parking price.

Motor vehicle use is also elastic with respect to travel speed and ease. Roadway improvements that reduce traffic congestion and travel time result in generated traffic. Hansen et al (1993) calculated the elasticity of generated traffic with respect to road capacity. This has significant implications for transportation planning because the generated traffic captures many of the roadway improvement benefits (Litman, 1995c).

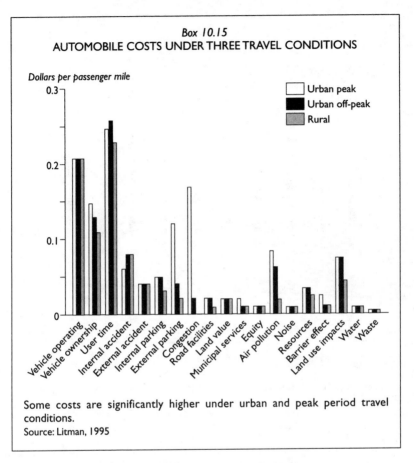

Box 10.15
AUTOMOBILE COSTS UNDER THREE TRAVEL CONDITIONS

Some costs are significantly higher under urban and peak period travel conditions.
Source: Litman, 1995

IMPLICATIONS OF UNDERPRICING

Now that we have defined, estimated and categorised the distribution of transportation we have the tools to investigate the implications of current cost distributions.

Economic efficiency

A basic tenet of market theory is that economic efficiency is maximised when marginal user prices (defined as perceived variable internal costs) reflect total marginal costs. We can see from the estimates cited above that motor vehicle use is significantly underpriced compared with the total costs it imposes on society. External costs are estimated to average 33 per cent or more of total costs. In other words, user costs would need to increase 50 per cent or more to incorporate all costs. Box 10.17 summarizes these costs.

Externalised costs are not the only cause of underpricing. Many

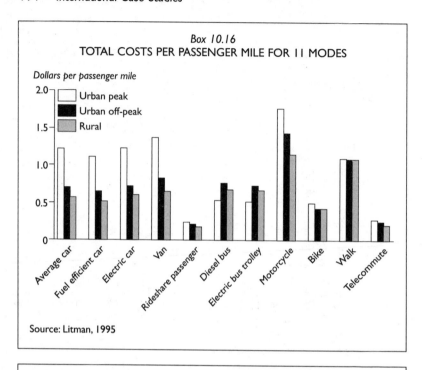

Box 10.16
TOTAL COSTS PER PASSENGER MILE FOR 11 MODES

Source: Litman, 1995

Box 10.17
AVERAGE AUTOMOBILE COSTS AS A PERCENTAGE OF TOTAL COSTS

	Total costs per mile	Internal costs: per mile	percentage of total	External costs: per mile	percentage of total
Urban peak	$1.32	$0.71	54%	$0.61	46%
Urban off-peak	$1.05	$0.71	68%	$0.34	32%
Rural	$0.84	$0.64	76%	$0.20	24%
Weighted average	$0.99	$0.67	68%	$0.32	32%

vehicle costs are fixed, which further reduces the ratio between prices and total costs. Operating costs (variable financial costs) are only about 35 per cent of users' financial costs, and only about 13 per cent of the total cost of driving. External costs equal 180 per cent to 380 per cent of vehicle operating costs; each dollar spent on gas, maintenance, and short-term parking incurs on average $2.60 worth of external costs. Car owners are 'captive' to most of these costs. We pay fixed and external costs no matter how much or little we drive, which reduces the incentive to limit driving to high value trips. To put this another way, automobile owners who drive less or more efficiently receive only a small portion of the savings they produce.

Although underpricing of such a common consumer good may appear beneficial from a narrow perspective (and indeed benefits many individuals in the short term), mispricing reduces overall economic efficiency. External costs are not eliminated, they simply show up elsewhere, as higher prices for commercial goods (for parking subsidies), increased local taxes (to pay for road services), increased illness and medical costs (from pollution and accidents), and lower residential property values (from urban traffic). Underpricing increases consumption of transport over other goods, and driving over other travel modes. Low prices cause per capita mileage to increase, forcing other constraints, such as congestion, pollution, and resource depletion to limit growth. Another effect of under-priced driving is that the efficiency of non-automotive modes declines. Since walking, bicycling, transit and rail transport receive little capital investment, land use patterns and social habits develop which conflict with these travel options.

This is not to say that driving would cease if costs were inter-nalised and marginalised. Consumers would be willing to pay more for some trips. However, some driving has relatively low value to the user, either because the trip itself provides little net benefit or because alternative modes exist. Increasing prices to reflect a greater portion of total costs would reduce low value driving, improving the transportation system's overall efficiency.

Underpricing increases total transportation costs by encouraging inefficient travel habits and automobile dependency. Hook (1993) argues that this gives the US an economic disadvantage compared with countries such as Japan which devote a much smaller portion of GNP to transport. Lower expenditures on transportation reduce Japanese industrial and employment costs, increase productivity and frees funds for capital investment.

A variety of strategies have been proposed for internalising costs. A common suggestion is to increase fuel taxes. This, howev-er, is not an optimal charge since fuel prices do not directly affect when or where driving takes place, or provide incentives to buy a low-polluting car. Over the long run drivers would buy more fuel-efficient cars, which does not reduce congestion, accidents, park-ing costs, noise or most other environmental impacts. Recently there has been increased interest in congestion pricing as a method of internalising costs. This could reduce congestion but not other externalities such as pollution and parking subsidies.

User charges should be applied as closely as possible to the source of an externality to optimise economic efficiency, although econo-mists and policy makers recognize that in practice a 'second best' solution is often necessary. No single mechanism can capture all external costs due to their diverse nature. Komanoff (1995) identifies several price changes needed: weight–distance charges, fuel taxes, congestion pricing, smog fees, parking fees, marginalised insurance, and higher fines for violators for optimal efficiency. He estimates that no charge should raise more than 33 per cent of total user revenue for maximum economic efficiency. OTA (1994) reaches a similar conclusion.

Environmental impacts

Shoup (1994) finds that automobile commuting declines by 20–40 per cent if employees can choose between free parking or a cash payment of equal value. Making automobile insurance a variable cost would reduce driving 5–14 per cent in the short term and 16–41 per cent over the long term (El-Gasseir, 1990). Additional reductions in travel would result from internalising other economic, environmental and social costs. A conservative estimate is that eliminating transportation underpricing could reduce total motor vehicle use by 33 per cent or more, and environmental impacts (air pollution, noise, resource consumption and negative land use impacts) by comparable amounts, with no new technologies. Targeted strategies and significant investments in alternative travel modes could reduce impacts further.

Social equity

An argument frequently used to justify underpricing is that any increase in the price of driving is inequitable. This is only true based on a narrow perspective. Although underpricing benefits low-income drivers directly in the short term, it incurs numerous indirect costs and creates automobile-dependent transportation systems and land use patterns in the long term. As land use becomes more automobile oriented, destinations become more dispersed so individuals are forced to travel more in order to access the same activities (Moore and Thorsnes, 1994). Thus it is not clear that low-income drivers benefit overall from underpricing when total impacts are considered. Non-drivers are certainly worse off by underpricing since they pay costs (market and non-market), receive few direct benefits, and are increasingly disadvantaged relative to drivers. There are more effective ways to benefit disadvantaged people than underpricing motor vehicle use, including targeted subsidies and improving alternative travel modes.

Individual choice

A frequent argument used by pro-highway advocates is that underpricing increases travel choice and personal freedom (Cox and Love, 1994). The truth, of course, is just the opposite. Under current policies, home owners and renters must typically pay for two or more parking spaces per unit, whether they need them or not. Drivers receive free parking, but non-drivers receive no comparable subsidy, reflecting a lack of choice in available benefits. Non-drivers in an automobile-dependent community have few transportation choices and little freedom. Individuals have no choice but to suffer the financial, accident risk and environmental costs of automobile use. These examples illustrate the absurdity of assuming that underpricing increases choice or freedom.

POLICY RECOMMENDATIONS

Economic efficiency and environmental quality would increase if prices more closely reflected marginal costs. Specific strategies include:

- Charge insurance and vehicle registration taxes proportionally to vehicle mileage.
- Increase parking charges to reflect costs and 'cashing out' free parking. This must be matched by more flexible parking requirements that reduce oversupply to capture full benefits. Charge users for only the parking they use.
- Establish a mileage tax or increase fuel taxes to cover roadway system costs.
- Use congestion pricing to internalise congestion externalities.
- Use pollution taxes to internalise environmental costs.
- Reduce subsidies to urban sprawl by pricing public services at their cost.

Tax and price increases should be gradual and predictable to allow individuals and firms to adjust when making long-term decisions. Transportation and land use policies should reduce automobile dependency by improving alternative travel modes (walking, bicycling, public transit, telecommuting) and by locating activity centres (schools, shops, play areas) where they are most accessible. It is a good policy to insist that decision makers (planners, engineers, politicians) make a habit of using the transportation systems they develop, and that they live at least a few weeks each year without use of a private automobile in order to experience the problems and pleasures of being dependent on other modes.

SUMMARY

Motor vehicle use is significantly underpriced in North America. Driving imposes external economic, environmental and social costs. These costs show up as higher consumer prices to pay for 'free' parking, higher taxes to pay for roads and related services, and increased health costs. Many of the internal costs of driving are fixed; vehicle owners must pay the same amount no matter how much they drive.

Average vehicle costs per mile decline with increased use, so vehicle owners have an incentive to maximise driving in order to 'get their money's worth', and those who drive less than average subsidise those who drive more. Drivers have no incentive to limit their driving to trips in which total benefits exceed total costs. Negative effects of underpriced driving include:

- Increased overall transportation costs. Low marginal prices for driving encourage individuals to spend a greater portion of their budget on driving and incur greater external costs.
- Increased automobile dependency and reduced transportation choices. Walking, bicycling, public transit and rail facilities and service receive less investment than would otherwise occur. Land use patterns develop that are suitable for driving and unsuitable for other travel modes.
- Increased land devoted to roads and parking facilities, leaving less land for other productive uses, and less land left as greenspace.
- Increased air, noise, and water pollution, resource consumption and traffic accidents. At one time, underpricing may have provided significant external benefits due to economies of scale by reducing average roadway and industrial development costs (which is to say that you benefit overall if your neighbours drive more), but there is no evidence that current driving provides external marginal benefits.

Underpricing is inequitable. Wealthy households drive significantly more than poor households, thereby capturing greater benefits. The short-term impacts of underpricing on lower income households are mixed; the benefits of cheap automobile use is balanced by higher costs for other goods and reduced travel options. Long-term impacts, impacts on non-drivers in general, and impacts on the most vulnerable populations (the very poor, disabled, pensioners and children) are all highly negative. The equity and economic efficiency effects of increased transport prices depend on how new prices are structured, how quickly and predictably changes occur, whether alternative travel (walking, bicycling, bus, and train) provisions are improved, and how revenues are distributed.

Chapter 11

The External Costs of Road Transport in The Netherlands

INTRODUCTION

The growing social pressures resulting from transport (in terms of environmental degradation, noise annoyance, accidents and congestion) have led to a large body of literature on the external costs of transport (Verhoef, 1994a). The extensive research efforts, however, have not yet been able to initiate the political response that is often hoped for with the publication of the research findings. Apart from an apparent lack of political priority (or perhaps courage) to engage in more stringent environmental policies regarding transport, a number of factors contribute to the fact that many of the policy recommendations have not been followed. In the first place, regulators do have to make a practically inescapable trade-off between the efficiency and social feasibility of policies (Verhoef, Nijkamp and Rietveld, 1995). Furthermore, due to differences in the interpretation of the concept of externalities and the wide range of techniques and methodologies employed in the estimation of such effects, empirical estimates of external costs of transport may differ by a factor of ten or more – whereas they often intend to measure the same thing. Next, there is still no consensus on the question of whether 'external benefits' of transport might compensate for the external costs. In addition, debates on the implications of the research findings are often further clouded by a mixing up of arguments of an allocative efficiency and of an equity nature. In this chapter, some of these issues are dealt with. The next section starts with discussing the definition of externalities. Applying this definition, it will be concluded that transport hardly yields any positive external effects. However, considerable negative externalities are involved. The section after that deals with the efficiency and equity impacts of externalities. Finally, some recent estimates of external costs of transport in the Netherlands are discussed.

DEFINITION OF EXTERNALITIES

Although the concept of external effects is widely used in economics, there seems to be some uncertainty as to its exact definition and interpretation, which justifies a short discussion of the concept itself. It is commonly recognised that externalities are an important form of market failure. Their existence leads to a deviation from the ideal neo-classical world in which the price mechanism takes care of socially optimal resource allocation (Pareto efficiency). In the presence of externalities, market prices do not reflect full social costs (or benefits), and additional taxes (or subsidies) are called for in order to restore the efficient workings of the market mechanism. Furthermore, it is generally accepted that the source of externalities is typically to be found in the absence of property rights (see Baumol and Oates (1988), p.26). Hence, the theory of externalities is often applied in environmental economics. Environmental quality is a typical 'good' for which property rights are not defined and no market exists.

These commonplaces may clearly indicate the causes and consequences of external effects, but still leave the definition unclear. Still, an exact definition is necessary in order to identify transport's external effects. Such a definition might be as follows: an external effect exists when an actor's (the receptor's) utility (or production) function contains a real variable whose actual value depends on the behaviour of another actor (the supplier), who does not take this effect of his behaviour into account in his decision making process. This definition is in line with, for instance, Mishan (1971). In the terminology proposed by Bator (1958), such externalities concern his concept of 'ownership externalities', as opposed to the 'technical externalities' (increasing returns to scale or indivisibilities in production) and 'public good' externalities he distinguishes. In the terminology of Viner (1931) and Scitovsky (1954), the above definition concerns 'technological' externalities, as opposed to 'pecuniary externalities'. Note that Bator's 'technical externalities' are something completely different from Viner's and Scitovsky's 'technological externalities'! Pecuniary externalities, which are ruled out by considering real variables only (that is, excluding monetary variables), do not lead to shifts of production and utility functions, but merely to movements along these functions.

Consequently, in the terminology of Buchanan and Stubblebine (1962), externalities as defined above are potentially 'Pareto-relevant', whereas pecuniary externalities are not (see also Mishan, 1971). The final condition in the definition distinguishes externalities from other types of unpriced interactions, such as barter, violence, jealousy, altruism or goodwill-promoting activities. Such phenomena differ fundamentally from external effects, both in a theoretical and in a policy-relevance respect. According to Mishan (1971), 'the essential feature of an external effect is that the effect produced is not a deliberate creation but an unintended or incidental by-product of some otherwise legitimate activity' (p 2). The unresolved tension between the receptor, facing a quantitative constraint on the 'consumption' of the externality, and the supplier, who has no a priori interest in the magnitude of the externality, can only persist provided there is no market on which the externality is traded. Such market failures stem from a lack of (well-defined) property rights concerning the externality, which is in turn often related to prohibitively high transaction costs. As pointed out by Coase (1960), in the absence of transaction costs, both the supplier and the receptor of the externality can benefit from negotiations on the size of the externality, and corrective Pigouvian taxation would in that case only distort the resulting Pareto-efficient outcome.

Externalities comprise both efficiency and equity aspects. The first refer to the fact that, in the presence of externalities, the competitive market outcome is not Pareto-efficient. The second relate to the fact that the receptors of a negative (positive) externality are clearly worse (better) off at any non-zero level of the effect, unless compensations take place. As pointed out below, this distinction is also important when assessing the policy implications of externalities.

The question of whether unpriced external relations are either external effects or other types of unpriced external relations involves important policy consequences. This is demonstrated in Box 11.1 for a certain activity Q. The standard case in Figure 1A shows the optimal workings of the market mechanism in absence of external effects. In this case, no government intervention is called for: Adam Smith's invisible hand secures social welfare maximisation (the bold triangle) at the market equilibrium Q_0 where marginal private cost (MPC) equals marginal private benefits (MPB). MPB and MPC can be interpreted as the benefits and costs as experienced by one actor. They can also be thought of as being the demand and supply curves for a marketed good, in which case P_0 is the market clearing (efficient) price.

The existence of (marginal) external costs (MEC) in Figure 1B drives a wedge between marginal social cost (MSC) and marginal private cost. The market outcome Q_0, where private welfare is maximised, is not optimal from a social point of view. The resulting level of the externality (A+B+C) is excessively large. Social welfare maximisation requires the activity to be restricted to a level of Q^*, where the marginal social cost is equal to the marginal benefits and the deadweight welfare loss C is avoided. This optimum can, for instance, be accomplished by means of a quantitative restriction (Q^*) or a Pigouvian tax (t^*) on the activity. The triangle gives the optimal level of the external cost. The bold triangle again represents maximum social welfare.

Figure 1C shows the reverse case, where (marginal) external benefits (MEB) exist. Marginal social benefits (MSB) now exceed the marginal private benefits. In this case, social welfare maximisation requires encouragement of the activity up to Q^*, for instance by means of Pigouvian subsidisation (s^*). Finally, Figure 1D illustrates the case of pecuniary benefits. We take Figure 1B as a starting point, assuming that the activity gives rise to external costs. Then, suppose

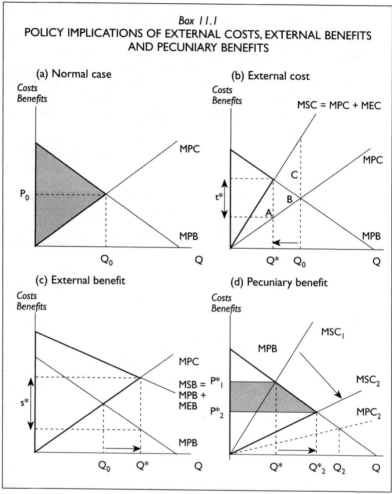

Box 11.1
POLICY IMPLICATIONS OF EXTERNAL COSTS, EXTERNAL BENEFITS
AND PECUNIARY BENEFITS

(a) Normal case

(b) External cost

(c) External benefit

(d) Pecuniary benefit

the private cost curve of the activity shifts downwards, perhaps due to technological developments or lower input prices. Assuming unaltered external costs, MSC will fall as well. A new social optimum Q_2^*, with a higher social welfare arises: the bold triangle is increased in comparison with Figure 1B. Moreover, if Q is a traded good and MPB reflects market demand, the consumer surplus increases by the shaded area. This results from the lower market price P_2^* and the larger quantity sold Q_2^*. This benefit, however, is not external but pecuniary: it results from a movement along – not a shift in – the MPB curve. For the attainment of the new social optimum (the move from Q_1^* to Q_2^*), market forces can be relied upon, and there is no reason for stimulating the activity, unlike the case of external benefits. Also, the pecuniary benefits do not 'compensate' for the external costs: social welfare maximisation still requires a restriction from the new market outcome Q_2 to the new social optimum Q_2^*.

Consequently, the question of whether unpriced costs and benefits of road transport are either external or pecuniary in nature, is crucial from a policy point of view. The next section therefore discusses the important question of whether road transport gives rise to external costs and/or benefits.

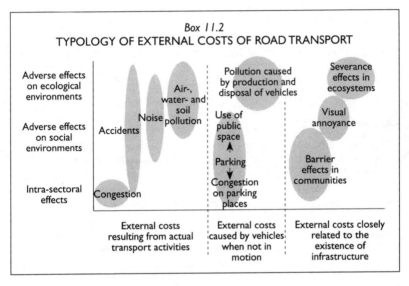

Box 11.2
TYPOLOGY OF EXTERNAL COSTS OF ROAD TRANSPORT

EXTERNAL EFFECTS OF TRANSPORT

External costs

The existence of external costs of transport is beyond dispute. In Box 11.2, the main external costs of road transport are roughly classified along two dimensions. Along the vertical axis, a distinction is made between external costs that road users impose upon each other: intra-sectoral external costs; and external costs which are imposed upon the rest of the society: environmental or inter-sectoral externalities. A further distinction is made between environmental externalities in the ecological sense (ie harming natural environments) and, in a somewhat different sense, concerning social environments. On the horizontal axis, the external costs are divided into effects that arise from actual transport activities, external costs that arise when vehicles are not in motion and external costs that are closely related (but not solely attributable) to the existence of infrastructure. This chapter does not consider the externalities arising from the mere presence of infrastructure.

The shaded areas indicate the first-order incidence of the external costs. Some external costs exhibit both intra-sectoral and environmental properties. For instance, external accident costs are to a certain extent imposed upon fellow car users (the intra-sectoral incidence); partly upon people outside this population (the social environmental incidence) and may finally have an ecological environmental incidence when transport of hazardous substances is involved. The second-order incidence of the externalities can occur at different scale levels. For example, congestion usually increases emissions per vehicle–kilometre. The severity of these external costs will to a large extent be time and place sensitive. Box 11.2 indicates that road traffic indeed causes a wide range of external costs. Box 11.3 gives an impression of the sizes and some current trends in some of the external costs associated with actual road transport activities in the Netherlands.

External benefits?

There seems to be some confusion on the question of whether transport yields important external benefits. Representatives of the automobile industry and related sectors in particular often claim that the external benefits of road transport largely exceed its external costs, thus casting doubt on the need to restrict car use. For instance, according to Diekmann (1991, p 39), (auto-)mobility 'contributes towards the quality of life... and... the overall growth in prosperity and leisure time since World War II could never have been accomplished without mass-motorisation'.

However important the contribution of transport to general well-being may be, the crucial question is, of course, whether such benefits are indeed external. If so, Pareto-efficiency might require encouragement of mobility by means of Pigouvian subsidies, or through the creation of Coasian markets where the non-paying profiteers could compensate the mobile people in order to seduce them to increase their mobility. External benefits would at least to a certain extent compensate for the external costs of transport. Therefore, it is important to examine the suggested external benefits of transport.

First, transport obviously plays a vital role in modern economies. However, the interrelations of the transport sector with other actors and sectors generally take place in well-defined markets. Often claimed 'external benefits' of growing transport volumes like lower production costs and consumer prices, greater variability in product choice, and faster delivery are actually pecuniary benefits. These benefits (the realisation of the increase in the consumer surplus in Box 11.1 – Figure 1D due to cheaper and hence more transport) require no government intervention. As pointed out above, these effects do not compensate for transport's external costs. Related to this type of argument is the sort of proposition stating that most

Box 11.3
EXTERNAL EFFECTS OF ROAD TRANSPORT IN THE NETHERLANDS

		1970	1985	1990	1991	1992
Emissions[1]	CO_2	13,340	20,720	23,790	24,370	25,330
	CO	1,662	923	675	601	587
	NO_x	143	262	273	274	272
	SO_2	16	11	13	13	14
	VOCs	317	225	191	172	167
Noise[2]			54			
Fatalities				1,241	1,155	1,177
Congestion	No. of traffic jams		5,640	6,088	7,482	9,850

Sources: CBS, 1995; RIVM, 1993; AVV, 1994; OECD, 1993
1 In million kilograms
2 Percentage of population with noise annoyance from road transport of 55 dB(A) or more (1987)

modern economies would collapse without transport. This is obviously true; however, the conclusion that therefore a large share of GNP is actually an external benefit of transport is equally obviously false. The same sort of reasoning could be applied to the food industry, the energy sector, various raw materials sectors, and (in the long term) maternity care (be it commercial, public, or supplied within the household). With such reasoning, one could explain a multiple of GNP as 'external benefits' of various activities. Clearly, these are simply market internal interdependencies.

Second, spin-off effects of transport in terms of value added or employment in related economic sectors (vehicle manufacturing and maintenance, oil industry, etc) do not provide a sound economic reason for not restricting transport to its optimal levels. Insofar as these effects result from excessively high levels of transport, such general economic goals should preferably be aimed at by means of less distorting instruments. Third, there is a large group of unpriced external relations associated with transport which do not qualify as external benefits. Such effects, for instance, occur when people receiving guests derive benefit from the visit, but do not actually compensate for the associated travel costs. Usually, however, this involves either barter behaviour or altruistic behaviour. In the first case, the travelling person expects a counter-visit in the (near) future, and therefore both parties do – implicitly – agree not to pay for each others' travel costs. Alternatively, the visitor takes the utility of the receiving person into account. Insofar as the receiving person finds that he is not being paid enough visits, he may be expected to be able to reveal his willingness to pay for more visits directly to the visitor. Neither form of individual utility maximising behaviour is inconsistent with Pareto optimality, and social welfare can therefore – again – not be increased by encouraging such behaviour.

Furthermore, the benefits of infrastructure are often mistaken for external benefits of transport itself. Such benefits concern, for instance, the effects of infrastructure on (regional) economic development and employment levels. Rietveld (1989) asserts that, according to the theory, the economic effects of the building of new infrastructure will be moderately positive (if infrastructure was initially lacking), neutral (if infrastructure already exists) or even negative (redistributional effects between regions). Consideration of such effects may very well play an important role in decisions on infrastructure investments (for instance in cost–benefit analyses), but should be clearly separated from the actual use of the infrastructure. This point can again be clarified with the aid of Figure 1D. Apart from showing the pecuniary benefits of transport as such, this diagram can also be used to demonstrate lower costs for users resulting from infrastructural investments. The (shaded) increase in the consumer surplus now reflects the benefits of infrastructural improvements as enjoyed by its users, for instance in terms of gains in travel times. However, these gains do of course by no means compensate for transport's external costs. Here, the investment in additional infrastructure is socially desirable only if the increase in the bold triangle (ie the increase in the social surplus) is large enough to cover the investment's social costs, provided the infrastructure will be used at the socially optimal level. Any investment in infrastructure will of course only yield maximum benefits when it is used at, and not beyond, the socially optimal level of transport. A comparable category of often-claimed external benefits of transport is the increased security resulting from better accessibility for fire-engines, police cars, ambulances, etc. However, the increased accessibility for such services is to be attributed to the infrastructure only, and certainly not to the actual transport activities. On the contrary, the higher the mobility, the more such services will suffer from congestion. Consequently, if there is any form of an external effect of transport in this respect, it is an external cost rather than a benefit.

In summary, we are not able to detect any significant external benefits of transport activities (apart perhaps from the sort of benefits enjoyed by 'car-, boat-, train- or plane-spotters'). Since, on the other hand, considerable external costs are involved, transport may be expected to be beyond its socially optimal level. Transport indeed puts an excessive burden on our societies, and government intervention which aims at reducing the external costs of transport will therefore generally increase social welfare. Empirical work towards the external effects of transport can therefore be restricted to its external costs. In the next section, we discuss the efficiency and equity aspects of externalities in more detail.

EFFICIENCY AND EQUITY IMPACTS OF EXTERNALITIES

As already mentioned, externalities comprise both equity and alloca-tive efficiency aspects. These two elements are often confused in debates on environmental regulation. Unfortunately, there is no straightforward mapping of the two goals of efficient allocation and 'equitable distribution', however defined. This means that one could arrive at rather different policy recommendations on the regulation of externalities, depending on which viewpoint is taken. First of all, let us consider the welfare of the receptors of an external cost. It seems reasonable at first sight that, from an equity point of view, Pigouvian tax revenues should be used to compensate the receptors of the external cost for the remaining (if all is well, optimal) level of the externality. However, this turns out to be problematic as soon as a more realistic model is constructed, in which a receptor of an exter-nality is able to protect him or herself by means of defensive measures. Such defensive measures can take the form of physical investments (for instance, double glazing in case of noise annoy-ance), or relocation in case of localised externalities. In Verhoef (1994b), this problem is investigated in several settings, and a main conclusion is that it is in general not in line with overall efficient allocation to compensate receptors for the external cost suffered, nor for any defensive measures undertaken (in some cases, efficient allo-cation even requires taxation of receptors in order to secure the optimal number of receptors of an external cost!). Compensations would prevent receptors of external costs from undertaking the opti-mal level of defensive measures. Hence, for the optimal efficient allocation, one might end up in a situation which is not very attrac-tive from the equity point of view, namely where receptors of an external cost not only remain uncompensated for the externality they suffer, but should also be (financially) responsible for their own defensive measures.

Related to this issue is, from a distributional point of view, the unattractive property of externalities because their valuation should be based on the receptors' willingness to pay for their avoidance. It is not difficult to show that this value, apart from being directly relat-ed to the marginal disutility of the effect itself, is inversely related to the marginal utility of income. This means that, other things being equal, the same exposure to a negative external effect implies a high-er external cost for higher income receptors (see Verhoef, 1994b). The inequitable implications of this property are evident: an externality-generating activity should then, from the allocative efficiency point of view, be located near low-income rather than near high-income receptors.

Focusing on the generators of externalities now, also in this case there is often a tension between allocative efficiency and what seems to be just from the equity point of view. For instance, consider the well-known Polluter Pays principle. Taking the case of Figure 1B as an example, optimal Pigouvian taxation implies a total tax sum Q^*t^*, which is in the sketched case exactly twice as large as the optimal level of the external cost (area). Hence, the question of whether the polluter should pay the total external cost, or whether marginal tax rules should be used, may often lead to different outcomes in terms of both allocative efficiency and equity – unless of course marginal external costs are constant and therefore equal to average external costs. Given such tensions between efficiency and equity considerations, it is no surprise that the mixing up of equity and allocative efficiency arguments may often lead to rather fuzzy discussions about the policy implications of research findings on external costs of transport. Box 11.4, focusing again on road transport, gives an overview of the most important characteristics and implications of taking these two perspectives, demonstrating the absence of a direct mapping between the two and hence identifying some sources of confusion in the above-mentioned discussions.

First of all, the ultimate research goal is different. From the efficiency perspective, one would ultimately like to arrive at an assessment of optimal levels of road transport, preferably to be realized with first-best optimal Pigouvian taxation. This means that each road user should be taxed according to his or her marginal external costs, implying that the appropriate level of analysis is the individual level. Consequently, intra-sectoral externalities (such as congestion) as well as inter-sectoral environmental externalities should play a role, and hence also the full (expected) marginal external costs of accidents call for regulatory taxation.

From the equity point of view on the other hand, road transport's 'unpaid bill' is presumably the relevant research goal, and this is also what people often have in mind when confronted with empirical results on the external costs of road transport. This bill amounts to the sum of total external costs plus the induced defensive measures undertaken by the receptors of the external costs. In this case, a sectoral perspective is the most natural one. Intra-sectoral externalities (congestion as well as a certain part of the accident costs) are no part of this burden that road transport imposes upon the rest of society, and should therefore not be included in the 'unpaid bill'.

In the bottom rows of Box 11.4, the relevance of some existing financial transfers for the interpretation of external cost estimates according to both perspectives are indicated. For instance, whereas defensive outlays by receptors of the externalities are part of the 'unpaid bill', they should not be accounted for in optimal Pigouvian taxes. These should simply be based on marginal external costs, given the level of protection chosen by the receptors of the externality. It is clear, however, that defensive outlays can be used to assess the marginal external costs. The household production function val-

Box 11.4
ALLOCATIVE EFFICIENCY VERSUS THE EQUITY PERSPECTIVE

	Allocative efficiency perspective	*Equity perspective*
Goal of the analysis	Assessment of 'optimal mobility' and optimal regulatory taxes	Assessment of the 'unpaid bill'
Relevant external cost measure	Marginal external cost	Total external cost plus induced defensive outlays by receptors
Apt level of aggregation	Individual	Sectoral
Relevant external cost categories	Intra-sectoral and inter-sectoral external costs	Inter-sectoral external costs
Relevance of some existing financial transfers:		
Defensive outlays by receptors	Should not be accounted for in optimal taxes	Should be added to 'unpaid bill'
Insurance premiums	Very limited relevance[1]	Limited relevance[2]
Car ownership taxes	Very limited relevance[1]	Relevant[3]
Indirect taxes on fuel	Potential relevance[4]	Potential relevance[5]

Source: Author
1 These transfers are usually fixed yearly payments, (largely) independent of total kilometres driven. Hence, they have no direct impact on road usage, and – if anything – only have a very distorted impact via car ownership.
2 A certain share of accident costs (including fatalities) are intra-sectoral, and hence should not play a role in the 'unpaid bill' analysis. Neither therefore should a certain share of the insurance premiums. Moreover, from the perspective of the 'unpaid bill', the relevant question is whether the payments from the insurance companies to society are enough to cover the costs imposed on the rest of the society (medical care, emergency services, legal costs, repairing damages to buildings, psychological costs of pain and suffering incurred by victims outside the road sector, etc).
3 These taxes are a relevant coverage for part of the 'unpaid bill' only if they exceed government outlays on infrastructure (depreciation, maintenance, management, police, etc).
4 Taxes on fuel will act as a substitute for Pigouvian taxation only when the rates exceed those of indirect taxes on other goods (forgetting here about the 'optimal taxation' argument for the sake of simplicity).
5 Also here, only any indirect taxes above average rates can be considered as relevant transfers from road users to society, compensating for part of the unpaid bill.

uation method of externalities is based on this assumption. More important are the following three categories: insurance premiums, car ownership taxes, and fuel tax. All of these are often mentioned as compensating financial outlays of road users, followed by the suggestion that they should therefore be subtracted from external

cost estimates before assessing any policy implications. It is especially at this point that allocative efficiency and equity arguments
are often mixed up.

As indicated in the first column, these financial transfers only
have very limited relevance from the allocative efficiency perspective. As far as the impact of insurance premiums and car ownership
taxes are concerned, they only have a very limited impact on car
mobility since they mainly involve fixed yearly payments, independent of actual mileage driven. Although a distributional impact is
therefore clearly there, the regulatory impact is minimal and strongly distorted, as these payments at best only affect car ownership. But
even the impact of fuel taxes as a substitute for optimal Pigouvian
taxation should not be overestimated. As allocative efficiency is
strongly dependent on relative prices, such an impact of fuel taxes
cannot be expected for rates below the average rate. Moreover, taking the purist stance, the theory of optimal taxation (see, for instance,
Sandmo, 1976) dictates indirect taxes to be inversely related to
demand elasticity. Clearly then, even in the absence of externalities,
and given the relative inelasticity of demand for road transport, fuel
taxes might have to be relatively high in comparison to other indirect taxes anyway when the goal of allocative efficiency is pursued.
However, even without speculation on relative demand elasticities,
it will be clear that only a modest part of the three financial transfers
discussed above can indeed be interpreted as a substitute for optimal regulatory taxes.

The relevance of these payments for the assessment of the equity
issue is larger than for allocative efficiency, but is also not as straightforward as it may seem at first sight. Starting with insurance for
accidents, it can be noted that, as far as the inter-sectoral incidence
of external accident costs is concerned, the relevant question is in
particular whether the payments from the insurance companies to
society are enough to cover the inter-sectoral costs involved (medical care, emergency services, legal costs, repairing damages to
buildings, psychological costs of pain and suffering incurred by victims outside the road sector, etc). Insurance premiums themselves
are less relevant from this perspective. Car ownership taxes, insofar
as exceeding government outlays on supplying road infrastructure
capacity in general (including costs of depreciation, maintenance,
management, police, etc), can indeed be considered as a relevant
coverage for part of the 'unpaid bill' of road transport. Finally, any
indirect fuel taxes above average rates can also be considered as relevant transfers from road users to society, compensating for part of
the unpaid bill.

It will be clear now that estimates of external costs of road transport do not lead to unambiguous policy implications unless a clear
goal for regulation is formulated. From the viewpoint of environmental quality, this should be the goal of allocative efficiency. For

this goal, one can safely state that additional Pigouvian taxation of road transport is necessary. However, representatives of the road lobby will tend to use arguments of an equity nature to point out that road users already pay a lot to society, and that additional (economic) regulation is 'unfair'. As pointed out in Verhoef, Nijkamp and Rietveld (1995), two main possibilities of escaping from this impasse are the variabilisation of existing road taxes, and application of tradeable permits rather than regulatory taxes.

SOME RECENT EMPIRICAL RESEARCH IN THE NETHERLANDS

For the valuation of external effects (that is, putting a monetary value on external effects which are by definition unpriced), a broad range of techniques have been developed over the last few decades. Box 11.5 gives a concise overview of the methods used especially for environmental externalities, including noise annoyance.

Box 11.5 VALUATION METHODS				
Valuation approaches		**Short-cut approaches**		
Behavioural		*Non-behavioural*		
Surrogate markets	*Hypothetical markets*			
*Hedonic techniques	*Contingent valuation techniques	*Damage costs: buildings, agriculture, crops, etc	*Prevention costs: potential defensive-, abatement-, or repair programmes	*Actual defensive-, abatement-, or repair outlays.
*Travel cost method *Household production functions		*Cost of illness		

On the left-hand side, methods aiming at the assessment of the actual external costs are given. It would take too long to discuss these techniques in detail here; good discussions can be found in Johansson (1987), Mitchell and Carson (1989), and Pearce and Markandya (1989). From a theoretical point of view, behavioural techniques deserve preference, as they actually aim at assessing the receptors' valuation of the effect. In contrast, a major drawback of the non-behavioural linkage techniques is that the victims' valuation of the effect is not considered at all. Mitchell and Carson (1989) observe in this respect that there is little theoretical basis for the use of these techniques in welfare economics, since the damage functions are not directly related to the consumers' utility functions. Furthermore, non-behavioural techniques result in an estimate of the user value of environmental goods at best, and are not capable of inferring non-use values. Still, non-behavioural techniques receive much support in practice, in particular since the figures produced appear to be 'harder'.

Often, however, time or money is lacking to undertake actual valuation studies. Then, short-cut approaches as mentioned on the right-hand side of Box 11.5 are usually applied, in which the costs of actual or potential defensive-, abatement- or repair programmes (instead of the external costs themselves) are assessed. Two such strategies can be distinguished, namely where either actual or potential outlays are considered. Although these techniques yield results that may be relevant for assessing the equity impacts of external costs, they are not particularly apt for the allocative efficiency type of study .

Consider for instance the most often used short-cut approach, where an external effect is valued at the theoretical cost of prevention programmes, necessary to reduce the externality to a 'reasonable' level. First of all, this approach suffers from circular reasoning, since the 'optimal' level of these programmes and hence also of the remaining externality is more or less arbitrarily chosen – whereas it should actually result from weighing of the costs of such programmes against the benefits in terms of reducing the external costs. Hence, assuming the externality not to be a very serious problem leads to considering relatively moderate programmes at relatively low costs, in turn producing a relatively low 'external cost' estimate. A particular problem for using these figures for the regulation of transport is that Pigouvian fees should be equal to the remaining marginal external costs, given the abatement- defensive- and repair programmes undertaken. Indeed, once carried out, an extremely effective but expensive abatement programme, reducing the remaining marginal external costs to zero, implies zero Pigouvian taxes, and certainly not regulatory taxes based on the excessively high costs of the programme. Clearly, however, these remaining external costs are just not measured with such methods. Therefore, only in a case where the circular reasoning happens to be undertaken for the optimal level of the external cost would it produce results that could also be used for the purpose of a marginal analysis, eventually resulting in the assessment of Pigouvian taxes.

In the second approach, actual defensive-, abatement- or repair outlays are interpreted as representing the victims' or social willingness to pay for reducing annoyance to 'acceptable' levels and therefore representing 'the' external cost. Although market data on victims' expenditures on defensive measures may indeed be used for inferring their valuation of an external cost (the household production function approach is based on that notion), this short-cut approach as such only measures the defensive outlays, and again does not say much about the total or marginal level of the remaining external cost. For that purpose, indeed a household production function study is needed, focusing on the marginal behaviour of the receptors of the externality.

The measurement of external accident costs yields some additional problems. The cost components associated with traffic accidents usually include the physical damage to vehicles, infrastructure, properties and natural environment; legal, police and emergency service costs; costs of injuries and fatalities, such as medical and funeral costs; psychological costs of pain and suffering; values of life; and production losses. In the first place, as outlined above, these costs are to a certain extent intra-sectoral. The common practice of adding accident costs to costs of air pollution and noise annoyance in order to assess the 'total external costs' of transport is therefore questionable. If anything, this is not correct for analyses from the viewpoint of equity. Secondly, the valuation of life, pain and suffering is of course a very difficult thing. On the one hand, we almost have to put a monetary value on these items, as one would otherwise run the risk of implicitly assuming a zero price. On the other hand, one could argue that for the purpose of Pigouvian taxation based on marginal external costs, it would be sufficient to work with ex ante valuations of increased risk, rather than with full values of life, pain and suffering. These latter are relevant only for the ex post assessment of total external costs.

In conclusion, before turning to empirical estimates of external costs of transport in the Netherlands, it is important to realise that the valuation of externalities is a very difficult thing to do, and that one should be very careful in interpreting the results obtained. First of all, the absolute values will be very sensitive to the methods used. Secondly, a translation of these figures into marginal measures, needed in order to study the allocative efficiency implications, is fraught with methodological difficulties, among which the estimation of the external cost function is likely to be the most important. Apart from that, figures obtained with prevention cost methods are in particular suspect for the purpose of Pigouvian tax derivation.

Empirical work towards the external costs of transport in the Netherlands is scarce. The two most important recent estimates were undertaken by Bonenschansker, Leijsen and De Groot (1995) and Bleijenberg, Van den Berg and De Wit (1994). Their main results are given in Box 11.6 and Box 11.7. It would take far too long to discuss both studies in detail. In order to give a short description of the methodologies followed, it can be noted that Bonenschansker et al (1995) have tried to estimate the external costs via assessment of damage costs, whereas Bleijenberg et al (1994) have applied a broad range of external costs estimates from the (international) literature for the Dutch situation. Both approaches obviously have their respective weaknesses; however, any approach would. In any case, the method used by Bonenschansker will certainly only give a lower bound estimate of the external costs of transport, firstly because many items are left blank due to a lack of data (for instance, no estimate of the external costs of greenhouse gas emissions has been made), and secondly because damage costs are by definition only a part of total external costs. It is therefore no surprise that the figures reported by Bonenschansker et al, especially those relating to the costs of environmental externalities, are lower than those reported by Bleijenberg et al. Given the more comprehensive measures, the estimates of external costs of air pollution of Bleijenberg et al seem more adequate than the rather low values produced by Bonenschansker et al To increase the comparability of these figures with those given in other chapters of this book, Box 11.7 gives the implied valuation of environmental externalities per kg emissions according to the more detailed study of Bleijenberg et el.

Box 11.6
ESTIMATES OF THE EXTERNAL COSTS OF TRANSPORT
IN THE NETHERLANDS (BILLION Dfl)

	Road			Rail			Water (inland)		
Bleijenberg et al (1994) Air pollution:	Low	Mid	High	Low	Mid	High	Low	Mid	High
CO_2	0.95	2.62	11.66		0.01	0.05	0.06	0.17	0.74
NO_x	0.49	2.57	3.28		0.01	0.01	0.04	0.22	0.28
SO_2	0.01	0.03	0.09						0.01
VOCs	0.23	1.80	2.64					0.01	0.01
Noise	0.20	0.64	1.09	0.01	0.02	0.03			
Fatalities	0.73	1.80	2.02					0.01	0.01
Injured	0.48	1.87	4.33						
Total	*3.09*	*11.32*	*25.09*	*0.01*	*0.04*	*0.10*	*0.11*	*0.41*	*1.05*
Bonenschansker et al (1995) Air pollution (exc. CO_2)		0.9–1.2			0.0			0.0	
Noise		0.5–1.1			0.1			0.0	
Accidents		2.3–3.8			0.0			0.0	
Congestion		0.3–0.6							
Total		*4.0–6.6*			*0.1*			*0.0–0.1*	

Source: Bleijenberg et al, 1994 and Bonenschansker et al, 1995

Box 11.7
VALUATION OF ENVIRONMENTAL EXTERNAL COSTS FOR THE MOST
IMPORTANT POLLUTANTS (Dfl/kg)

	Low	Mid	High
CO_2	0.04	0.11	0.49
NO_x	1.8	9.4	12.0
SO_2	0.8	2.0	6.9
VOCs	1.2	9.4	12.0

Source: Bleijenberg et al, 1994

Next, the most uncertain but also the most important factor in the determination of external accident costs is the value of life. The average value of life calculated by Bonenschansker et al, based on production losses, is Dfl 528,000. This is also the lower bound estimate used by Bleijenberg et al Both studies use a high variant of Dfl 1.5 million, based on international (willingness to pay) studies. Finally, concerning noise, Bleijenberg et al extract values per person–kilometre and per tonne–kilometre from the international literature. It is especially for this externality that such a procedure seems questionable, since it does not take into account country-specific characteristics such as the proximity of transport infrastructure to residential areas. Bonenschansker et al calculate external costs of noise annoyance based on value reductions of houses. For their high estimates, a zero annoyance level of 30 dB(A), a Noise Depreciation Sensitivity Index (NDSI) of 0.4 per cent and a discount rate of 3 per cent is used. For their low estimates, a more common zero annoyance level of 55 dB(A) and a NDSI of 0.8 per cent is used, comparable to the estimates for the UK provided in Chapter 5. Adapting that chapter's discount rate of 8 per cent instead of the relatively low value of 3 per cent raises the estimate from Dfl 456 million up to Dfl 1.2 million. It is noteworthy that the estimates of external costs of noise annoyance of road transport provided by Bonenschansker et al and Bleijenberg et al are rather close, notwithstanding the different approaches.

The results presented above clearly show that estimates of the external costs of transport strongly depend on the measurement methods adopted, and may therefore indeed vary by a factor of ten. An obvious research conclusion is that much more research is needed in order to identify the reliability and applicability of the various valuation techniques. The external costs of transport are high (ranging from 0.6 per cent to 5.1 per cent of GNP in the low and high estimates of Bleijenberg et al), and that – given the current policy practices – there seems to be room for considerable efficiency improvements by means of proper pricing of transport.

This point is illustrated in Box 11.8, where for the most important modalities figures are given that represent the 'social deficit'; that is, government expenditures (notably on infrastructure supply, maintenance and other services), plus external costs, minus taxes collected from these modalities (excluding VAT for reasons outlined above). These figures are taken from Bonenschansker et al (1995), where further details on the calculations can be found. Apart from passenger transport by car evaluated according to the low external cost estimate of Bonenschansker et al, all figures are positive, indicating that overall tax revenues categorically fall short of public costs plus external costs. For the more comprehensive valuations provided by Bleijenberg et al, these deficits are of course higher. It is interesting to see that, whereas the external costs of road transport by far exceed those for other modalities, other uncovered public costs of these other modes are much higher, leading to a rather balanced picture for the overall subsidisation of the various transport modes (especially for passenger transport).

Box 11.8
BALANCE OF PUBLIC EXPENDITURE, EXTERNAL COSTS, PUBLIC REVENUE AND OTHER FISCAL MEASURES FOR VARIOUS MODES IN 1990 (million Dfl)

	Passenger		Freight	
	I	II	I	II
Road	2,423	2,161	4,046	2,017
Rail	2,446	2,466	140	143
Light rail	3,961	3,212		
Inland shipping			1,075	692

Source: Bonenschansker et al, 1995
I Based on mid estimates of Bleijenberg et al, 1994
II Based on low estimates of Bonenschansker et al, 1995

Clearly, figures such as those given in Box 11.8 are more related to issues of equity than to issues of allocative efficiency. When considering the fact that for road transport only about 40 per cent of the tax revenues in the Netherlands are variable (that is, related to fuel), and that marginal external costs are likely to be rising, it will be clear that from the viewpoint of allocative efficiency, even higher variable taxes may be called for than is implied in the box. These higher variable taxes may of course be accompanied with reductions in fixed taxes for reasons of social acceptability. Concerning these marginal price policies, let us end by saying that, on basis of their results, Bleijenberg et al (1994) recommend an average increase of variable taxes of Dfl 1 per litre fuel as a benchmark for road transport policies in the Netherlands in the near future.

CONCLUSION

In this paper, some conceptual issues concerning external effects of transport were discussed. Starting with the definition of externalities, it was argued that transport does not yield any significant external benefits, whereas considerable external costs are involved. The latter have equity as well as allocative efficiency implications. Unfortunately, there is no straightforward mapping between the two, which gives rise to uncertainty and fuzzy discussions as far as the policy implications of external cost estimates for transport are concerned. A clear separation of these issues is a prerequisite for a less ambiguous interpretation of research results. Some issues related to the actual estimation of the external costs of transport were raised, and some recent empirical estimates for the Netherlands were presented, indicating that there is a clear need for further research as well as a clear need for more stringent policies regarding the environmental impacts of transport.

Annexe

A Catalogue of Existing External Cost Estimates

INTRODUCTION

Road transport and, to a lesser extent, other forms of transportation, impose social costs on the community. Those costs take varied forms: road accidents; congestion; noise nuisance; community severance (the 'barrier effect'); local pollution in the form of particulate matter, carbon monoxide, lead, volatile organic compounds, etc; transboundary pollution from sulphur oxides; global pollution from carbon dioxide. In principle, all such costs are capable of monetisation, ie of having a monetary value attached to them based on the received concepts of willingness to pay (WTP) and willingness to accept (WTA) (Freeman, 1993). This paper surveys the available estimates of these monetised social costs for various countries. Full details of new estimates for the United Kingdom have been presented in Part 2. This annexe does not report estimates for congestion costs or road maintenance costs.

AGGREGATE MEASURES OF THE EXTERNAL COST OF ROAD TRANSPORT

Estimating the social costs of road transportation is a fairly recent activity. Box A1 brings together a number of estimates produced for different countries. As methodologies vary widely, and reliability is also uneven, not too much can be learned from comparing the figures without more detailed analysis. For example, a number of pollution estimates have been based on costs of avoidance rather than costs of damage. Cost of damage, as measured by WTP to avoid that damage, or WTA to tolerate damage, is the correct concept for measurement. Costs of avoidance (costs of abatement, costs of control) are not the correct measure, although in an optimal world the marginal costs of avoiding pollution will equal the marginal damage costs. Otherwise the two are not equal and using costs of avoidance to measure costs of damage produces a tautologous link, namely that the benefit–cost ratio of avoiding pollution is always unity. This is because the costs of control must necessarily equal the costs of damage. The procedure here is to report all estimates and to indicate the nature of the valuation procedure used rather than delete estimates based on the 'wrong' theoretical foundations. Apart from varying methodologies, the studies cover different social costs. These differences are explored more in subsequent sections. Box A1 records the external costs only and does not cover market costs that may not be borne by drivers – eg road construction and repair. These are dealt with separately below. Box A1 is also confined to those studies that record an overall measure of cost, ie one covering at least the main categories of externality. Many other studies cover partial estimates for one or more effects. Finally, Box A1 excludes social costs from rail and aviation. All studies tend to agree that these are small relative to road transport. Thus, Rothengatter and Mauch (1994) ascribe 92 per cent of all transport external costs to road transport, exactly the same proportion as estimated by Kågeson (1993).

Box A1 reports aggregate estimates. Where ranges of estimates are available, only the central or 'best' estimate is shown here. The table is dominated by the major work of Rothengatter and Mauch (1994) which is the most extensive European review of transport social costs. A comparable review for North America is Litman (1995a). Leaving the US estimates to one side, Box A1 suggests a range of around 3–5 per cent of GNP for the external costs of transport. The convergence of the results is of course somewhat misleading in that one study (Rothengatter and Mauch), using a common methodology to 'transfer' social costs from single European countries to other countries, dominates the results. Nonetheless, Rothengatter and Mauch's study is the most comprehensive to date. (Rothengatter and Mauch's methodology for damage-based estimates is outlined below.) Relative outliers from this range are Portugal with a very high 9.8 per cent of GNP, and, to a marked lesser extent, Belgium and Greece with over 5 per cent GNP costs.

The figure for the US from Mackenzie et al looks comfortably in the 'ballpark' for aggregate social costs, but these include an allowance for military expenditures to secure oil supplies from the Middle East and for which the motorist does not pay. Litman's estimate is a staggering 12 per cent of US GNP. His justification for such a high number rests on the fact that the majority of the costs are in non-market form, so that expressing them as a percentage of marketed GNP exaggerates their significance. Put another way, if GNP was measured correctly, to include all non-market effects, the numerator would be larger as well, so that the fraction of 'true' GNP would be smaller. However, this is also true of the Rothengatter and Mauch study and the results there suggest GNP costs of about one-quarter those reported in Litman. In fact the explanation for Litman's high estimate lies in the extensive number of external cost categories that he estimates. These include: congestions costs, external parking costs, road maintenance costs, forgone land use values,

Box A1
ESTIMATES OF THE TOTAL EXTERNAL COSTS OF ROAD TRANSPORT
(All figures are in billion ECUs. Year prices in parentheses)

Country	Cars	Buses	M/cycles	Freight	Total	Total (percentage of GDP)	Author
Europe 17 inc. Norway (1991)	164.2	9.1	20.9	56.4	250.6	4.2	Rothengatter 1994
Belgium (1991)	6.5	0.2	0.6	1.3	8.7	5.4	Rothengatter 1994
Denmark (1991)	2.1	0.2	0.4	1.0	3.4	3.2	Rothengatter 1994
Finland (1991)	2.2	0.2	0.2	0.7	3.3	3.3	Rothengatter 1994
France (1991)	22.8	1.2	1.8	15.0	40.8	4.2	Rothengatter 1994
Germany (1991)	45.8	1.7	5.0	9.4	61.9	4.5	Rothengatter 1994.
(1994)	<8.8	to	24.6	1.9–9.9	10.7–34.5	0.8–2.5	Friedrich, 1995
Greece (1991)	1.7	0.3	0.2	1.0	3.2	5.6	Rothengatter 1994
Ireland (1991)	1.0	neg	neg	0.5	1.5	4.2	Rothengatter 1994
Italy (1991)	19.7	1.6	6.8	6.7	34.8	3.8	Rothengatter 1994
Netherlands (1991)	5.3	0.2	0.5	1.9	7.9	3.3	Rothengatter 1994
(1990)	2.9	<	0.7>	1.3	4.9	2.2	Bleijenberg 1994
(1987)						1.2	van der Kolk 1987
Norway (1991)	1.6	0.1	0.2	0.4	2.3	2.7	Rothengatter 1994
Portugal (1991)	4.2	0.3	0.5	0.4	5.4	9.8	Rothengatter 1994
Spain (1991)	11.8	1.2	1.4	6.3	20.7	4.9	Rothengatter 1994
Sweden (1991)	3.8	0.2	0.6	1.0	5.6	3.0	Rothengatter 1994
Switzerland (1991)	3.8	0.1	1.0	0.8	5.7	3.1	Rothengatter 1994
(1992)					2.0	1.1	Jeanrenaud 1992(1)
UK (1991)	26.6	1.5	1.4	9.0	38.5	4.7	Rothengatter 1994
(1991)					30.0	3.7	Pearce 1993
USA (1992?)					110	2.1	Mackenzie 1992
(1994)					778($)	12.3	Litman 1994

1 Accidents, noise and air pollution damage to buildings only. Estimate of 7.7 Swiss centimes per vehicle kilometre multiplied by 50.3 billion vehicle km = 3.87 billion Swiss Francs.

costs of emergency services, barrier effects, environmental impacts of vehicle construction, land use impacts (eg aesthetics), water pollution and waste disposal costs for used oil, vehicles etc.

The data in Box A1 can be converted to costs per passenger kilometre (pkm) and per tonne kilometre (tkm). Rothengatter and Mauch (1994) report the following estimates for 'EUR 17' (European Union plus Norway):

Road:
    cars   50 ecu per 1,000 pkm
    buses   20 ecu per 1,000 tkm
    freight 58 ecu per 1,000 tkm

Rail :
  passenger 10 ecu per 1000 pkm
  freight   7 ecu per 1000 tkm

THE MAIN FACTORS IN TRANSPORT SOCIAL COST

The Rothengatter-Mauch (R–M) study suggests that around 92 per cent of all transportation external costs in the European Union come from road transport. Cars dominate the picture, accounting for 60 per cent of external costs and freight for around 20 per cent. The passenger-freight proportions for all external costs are 77 per cent and 23 per cent respectively.

R–M compute four kinds of damage estimates:

- road accidents
- noise nuisance
- air pollution
- climate change.

As the section below suggests, R–M's climate change costings are somewhat high, while our work in Chapter 4 suggests that the omission of small particulate damage from the air pollution estimates is likely to lead to a severe underestimate of the health damages of air pollution. Taking them at their face value, the relative contribution of the above factors to overall external cost in the European Union (EUR-17) are:

  accidents = 54 per cent
  noise = 14 per cent
  air pollution = 16 per cent
  climate = 16 per cent

These proportions can be compared to those for the USA. Taking just these categories in Litman's analysis suggests 47 per cent as the contribution of accidents, 43 per cent from air pollution and climate together, and 9 per cent from noise – very similar proportions. Ignoring the estimate for 'security costs' (military expenditures to secure oil supplies) in the Mackenzie et al study, the proportions in that study would be accidents 54 per cent, noise 9 per cent, climate 26 per cent, and air pollution (health costs only) 10 per cent. Again, the similarity of proportions is reasonable. Friedrich's estimates (1995) for West Germany exclude particulate matter, ozone and benzene, although dose–response functions for these pollutants are available. Climate change is quoted at 'possibly several billions' of Deutschmarks. However, the damage costs that are reported for air pollution and noise are similar if averages are taken, again supporting the overall fractions reported above. Accident costs are put at a factor of 2.7 times those for noise, which is again similar to the studies above. Finally, Jeanrenaud (1992) reports estimates of Swiss transport costs for accidents, noise and buildings damage (air pollution) in the ratio 39:39:22 per cent, making noise of equal importance to accidents in Switzerland.

SPECIFIC ISSUES IN TRANSPORT SOCIAL COSTS

Air pollution costs

The aggregate studies suggest that air pollution (excluding climate change) may contribute 10–16 per cent of external costs. A number of other studies have estimated air pollution costs. Quinet (1990) suggests a guideline figure of 0.4 per cent of GNP as the cost of non-climate air pollution from road transport, based on a survey of a number of studies. An update of Quinet (1990) in Quinet (1994) suggests a range from 0.03–0.11 per cent for Sweden up to 0.92–1.05 per cent for Germany. In a careful and up-to-date study, Otterström (1995) estimates air pollution costs from road traffic in Finland to be some Fmk 2.88 billion, excluding any transboundary effects and excluding climate change. This amounts to some 0.6 per cent of Finnish GNP. Pearce et al (1993) estimate air pollution in the UK to have cost £2.4 billion, ie some 0.4 per cent of GNP. Friedrich's study for West Germany (1993) suggests costs in the region of 0.1 to 0.5 per cent of GNP, although these exclude damage costs for particulates and ozone.

Noise costs

Pearce (1993) surveys Hedonic property price models on the damage from noise nuisance and concludes that there is a very reasonable consensus estimate of 0.5–1.0 per cent change in property price per unit L_{eq} (equivalent continuous sound level). Swiss studies confirm the general relationship: Pommerehne (1988) found a 1.27 per cent depreciation elasticity; Iten and Maggi 0.9 per cent; Soguel (1991) 0.9 per cent, all three studies using the Hedonic property approach. Soguel (1994) used contingent valuation to obtain a WTP of SFr 56–67, or 0.9 per cent – 1.5 per cent in house price depreciation terms. Quinet (1994) surveys a rather different literature, omitting virtually all of the US studies, but does not repeat his earlier (Quinet, 1990) guideline of about 0.1 per cent of GNP as the social cost of noise. Friedrich (1995) puts noise costs in West Germany from road traffic at 0.03–0.06 per cent of GNP, indeed suggesting that noise nuisance may be on a par with the lower end of the estimate for accidents and certainly equivalent in importance with the damage from the air pollutants they estimate. Bleijenberg et al (1994) put noise nuisance costs from road traffic in the Netherlands at some

DFl 640 million, or 0.1 per cent of GNP in 1990. In a review of early estimates, which overlap those reviewed by Quinet (1990), Verhoef (1994) finds a range of 0.2-0.9 per cent of GNP, but for studies of widely varying quality. Mackenzie, Dower and Chen (1992) estimate US noise costs at $9 billion, or 0.15 per cent of US GNP.

Barrier (severance) effects

Few monetised estimates of the effects of roads as barriers to people exist. Saelensminde (1992) reports estimates for Norway at US$112 per capita (as quoted in Litman, 1995a) but the basis for this estimate is not clear. Litman converts this estimate to a US-based estimate of $0.009 per vehicle mile for an average US car by grossing up the per capita estimate to the US population and then allocating to vehicles.

Historic buildings

A further neglected area in valuation is the effect of traffic on historic buildings. Grosclaude and Soguel (1993) report a contingent valuation result for Neuchatel, Switzerland, concerning air pollution damage to historic buildings. They estimate an annual willingness to pay of SFr108 per household to protect six buildings, ie some $71 per annum. As the results are specific to the stock at risk in Neuchatel it is not possible to extrapolate these findings.

CONCLUSIONS

The available studies seeking to secure an aggregate cost measure for the externalities associated with road transport vary enormously in respect of their methodologies and coverage. The most extensive European study is that of Rothengatter and Mauch (1994) which covers accidents, air pollution, climate change and noise. Some doubts attach to the conversion methodology whereby reference cost estimates are adapted to other countries, while the climate change measures appear to be considerable overestimates. The average external cost is around 4.6 per cent of European GNP. The most comprehensive study is that of Litman (1994) for the USA. This produces a huge social cost figure of around 12 per cent of GNP but this is because the coverage of the externalities is extremely wide. Doubts exist as to the legitimacy of some of the 'damage transfer' procedures used, but the Litman study is unquestionably the most detailed available and underlines the extensive range of externalities associated with road transport.

The studies are in broad agreement as to the importance of (a) the motor car as the dominant source of external cost, and (b) accidents, noise and air pollution/climate as the dominant factors in the magnitude of external cost. However, congestion has not been included here and this would make a substantial difference. Expressed as percentages of GNP the external costs from noise and air pollution appear to be fairly consistent across studies. Areas where research is deficient remain and include barrier effects and the impact on historic buildings.

A NOTE ON THE ROTHENGATTER–MAUCH METHODOLOGY

The Rothengatter–Mauch (R–M) methodology proceeds as follows for damage-based estimates (control cost procedures are also used):

1   For noise, individual WTP studies are analysed for a reference country. This WTP per household per noise level category (eg 65–70 dBA) is then extrapolated to other countries by computing the number of households exposed to each level of noise.
2   For air pollution, the procedure is to find a reference cost, C_R and then compute a cost for each country, C_i, where
$C_i = C_R \, p_i / p_j. \, 1/2.\{\sqrt{(e_i / e_j)} + U_i / U_j\}$
p_i / p_j = ratio of price levels in country i and the reference country j;
e_i / e_j = ratio of emissions per square kilometre in each country;
U_i / U_j = ratio of urban densities, ie percentage of population urbanised in each country.
3   Set $k = 1/2.\{\sqrt{(e_i / e_j)} + U_i / U_j\}$, where k is the conversion factor.
4   Hence $C_i = k. \, C_R. \, p_i / p_j$
The objective of the equation is to transfer values from one country where WTP estimates exist to another country with differing concentrations of urban population and differing emission densities. R–M are not very clear on what is meant by 'emissions'. From the text it looks as if the measures literally are national emissions of the various pollutants. But the relevant measure should be ambient concentrations. These will differ from emissions by the extent to which emissions are transported across national boundaries. No account appears to have been taken of this in the study. A further lack of clarity arises in that the k factor is applied to C_R to obtain a unit value for the relevant country. This is then multiplied by national emissions to get an aggregate damage cost. A worked example given in R–M (Annex 3), however, records emissions which are used to calculate 'emissions density' which are wholly different from the emissions (in R–M, Table 16) used to calculate total damage.
5   For climate change R–M adopt three approaches: two based on damage estimates and one based on prevention costs. Climate change effects are valued by prevention costs alone, which is unfortunate given the availability of damage cost estimates (eg

Fankhauser, 1995). R–M give an estimate (p 122) of CO_2 emissions from road traffic transport in EUR17 as 578 million tonnes CO_2, plus 19 mtCO_2 from rail (p 118), plus 158 mtCO_2 from air (p 124), ie some 755 mtCO_2 or about 206 mt as carbon (the R–M estimates are clearly in units of CO_2). Using Fankhauser's estimate of marginal damage of \$20 tC would give a EUR17 total of US\$4.12 billion or about 3.2 billion ecu (at \$1.3 = 1 ecu), compared to R–M's prevention cost approach of 43.7 billion ecu. The difference is startling. R–M's prevention cost unit figure appears to be \$38 per tonne of CO_2, ie some \$140 per tonne carbon. This accounts for some of the discrepancy (it would, for example bring the damage based figure up to about 22 billion ecus) but, on the other hand, R–M do not apply their prevention cost figure to all CO_2 emissions, preferring to apply them to some 'targets' for emission reduction in each country. R–M's climate change costing therefore remains somewhat unsatisfactory.

The damage and prevention cost approaches are applied to air pollution. Damage cost approach I uses 'reference cost' estimates for NO_x of 1500 ecu/tonne and VOCs of 1700 ecu/tonne. R–M make no estimate for particulate emissions due to having 'no workable reference cost estimates' (p 139). These reference cost estimates are then adjusted by the k factor above. The reference costs are from a particular study and are average costs. Damage cost approach II uses an update of the first study and computes marginal costs for Switzerland. These are substantially higher. This explains the difference between approaches I and II. It would appear from Box A2 that approaches I and II are in turn averaged to obtain the final estimate.

Box A2
ROTHENGATTER–MAUCH DAMAGE COSTS
(All costs in m ecus)

Damage costs	Air	Climate
Damage approach I	15,910	–
Damage approach II	69,158	–
Prevention cost approach	17,693	43,744
Average of I and II	42,534	–

References

1000 Friends of Oregon (1993) *The Pedestrian Environment*, 1000 Friends of Oregon, Portland

Adams, J (1995) 'Traffic Congestion Already a Road User Charge', *Local Transport Today*

Adviesdienst Verkeer en Vervoer (AVV) (1994) *Verkeersgegevens; Jaarrapport 1993*, Ministerie van Verkeer en Waterstaat, The Hague

AEA Technology (1995) *Air Pollution in the UK: 1993/1994*, prepared by the Environmental Technology Centre, NETCEN, for the Department of the Environment, Harwell

Alberini et al (1994) 'Estimating an Emissions Supply Function from Accelerated Vehicle Retirement Programs', *Resources for the Future Discussion Paper 94–09 RFF*, Washington DC

Allen (1980) *Relationships between Highway Noise, Noise Mitigation and Residential Property Values*, FHWA/VA.81/1, Virginia Highways and Transportation Research Council, Charlottesville, US

American Public Transit Association (APTA) (1992) *Transit Fact Book*, APTA, Washington DC

Andersson, B (1994) *Korrossionsskadekostnader*, underlagsrapport *till Svenska miljöräkenskaper*, lägesrapport fran Konjunkturinstitutet och Statistika Centralbyran, December

Apogee Research (1994) *The Costs of Transportation*, Conservation Law Foundation, Boston

Appleyard, D (1981) *Livable Streets*, University of California Press, Berkeley

Austin, D (1995) 'Road Pricing in London for Congestion and Emissions', unpublished MSc dissertation, University College London

Azar, C (1994) 'The Marginal Cost of CO_2 Emissions', *Energy – The International Journal* 19(12) pp 1255–61

Ball, D J, R S Hamilton and R M Harrison (1991) 'The Influence of Highway Related Pollutants on Environmental Quality' in R S Hamilton and R M Harrison (eds) *Highway Pollution*, Elsevier, Amsterdam

Bang, K L, A Lindqvist, L Tiliander and B Ljungström (1989) 'Varutransporter i storstadsregionerna', *Storstadstrafik 2, Bakgrundsmaterial*, Statens Offentliga Utredningrir 1989:15

Barde, J-P and K Button (1990) *Transport Policy and the Environment*, Earthscan, London

Bateman, I, R K Turner and S Bateman (1994) 'Extending Cost Benefit Analysis of UK Highway Proposals: Environmental Evaluation and Equity', *Project Appraisal* Vol 8, No 4, pp, 213–224

Bator, F M (1958) 'The Anatomy of Market Failure', *Quarterly Journal of Economics* Vol 72, pp 351–379

Baumol, W J and W E Oates (1988) *The Theory of Environmental Policy* (Second edition), Cambridge University Press, Cambridge

Bein, P (1994) *Barnet Hastings Benefit Cost Analysis*, BC MoTH, Victoria

Bell, K (1994) *Valuing Emissions from Hermiston Generating Project*, Convergence Research, Seattle

Bergstrom (1982) 'When is a Man's Life Worth More Than His Human Capital?' in M Jones-Lee (ed) *The Value of Life and Safety*, Elsevier, Amsterdam

Beshers, E (1994) *External Costs of Automobile Travel and Appropriate Policy*, Responses Highway Users Federation, Washington DC

Betts, W E, S Floys and F Kvinge (1992) 'The Influence of Diesel Fuel Properties on Particulate Emissions in European Cars', *Society for Automotive Engineers Technical Paper 922190*, The Engineering Society for Advancing Mobility Land Sea Air and

Space, Warrendale, Pennsylvania

Blair, B and F Worsford (1994) *Road Charging in the 90s. An overview and guide to the literature*, The British Library, London

Bleijenberg, A N, W J van den Berg and G de Wit (1994) *Maatschappelijke Kosten van het Verkeer: Literatuuroverzicht*, Centrum voor Energiebesparing en Schone Technologie, Delft

Bonenschansker, E, M G Leijsen and H de Groot (1995) *The Price of Mobility in the Netherlands*, Institute for Research on Public Expenditure (IOO), The Hague

Bonnafous (1994) *Internalising the Social Costs of Transport*, OECD, Paris

Bown, W (1994) 'Dying From Too Much Dust', *New Scientist*, 12 March, pp 12–13

British Road Federation (1994) in Royal Commission on Environmental Pollution report, *Transport and the Environment*, op cit

Buchanan, J M and W C Stubblebine (1962) 'Externality', *Economica* Vol 29, pp 371–384

Button, K (1993) *Transport Economics* (Second edition), Edward Elgar, Cheltenham

California Energy Commission (CEC) (1994) *1993–1994 California Transportation Energy Analysis Report*, CEC, Sacramento

Calthrop, E J (1995) 'The External Costs of Road Transport Fuel: Should the fiscal stance towards diesel be altered?', unpublished MSc dissertation, University College London

Cameron, M (1991) *Transportation Efficiency*, Environmental Defense Fund, Oakland

Cedervall M and U Persson (1988) *Vägtrafikens personskadekostnader. En samhällsekonomisk beräkning an 1985 ars personskadekostnader totalt och fördelat pa aldersgrupper*, Institutionen för trafikteknik, Lunds Universitet, Bulletin 79, Lund

Centraal Bureau voor Statistiek (CBS) (1995) *Kwartaalbericht Milieustatistieken 1995–1*, Sdu, The Hague

Central Statistical Office (CSO) (1995) *Annual Abstract of Statistics*, HMSO, London

Cline W (1992) *Economics of Global Warming*, Institute for International Economics, Washington DC

Coase, R H (1960) 'The Problem of Social Cost', *Journal of Law and Economics* Vol 3, pp 1–44

Confederation of British Industry (1988) cited in McWilliams (1994), op cit

Cox W and J Love (1994) 'Drivers Pay Their Own Way – and Then Some', *Governing Magazine*, April

Crawack, S (1993) 'Traffic Management and Emissions', *The Science of the Total Environment* 134, pp 305–314

Crawford I and S Smith (1995) 'Fiscal Instruments for Air Pollution Abatement in Road Transport', *Journal of Transport Economics and Policy*, January, University of Bath, Bath

Cropper M and F Sussman (1990) 'Valuing Future Risks to Life', *Journal of Environmental Economics and Management* 19, pp 160–174

Crowhurst Lennard, S and H Lennard (1995) *Livable Cities Observed*, Gondolier Press, Carmel

CSERGE/EFTEC (1994) 'A Survey of Noise Cost Estimates', CSERGE, University College London and University of East Anglia

Danish Road Directorate (1992) *Evaluation of Highway Investment Projects* (Undersogelse af storre hovedlandeveejsarbejder. Metode for effektberegninger og okonimisk verdering), Copenhagen

Department of the Environment (DoE) (1990) *UK Blood Lead Monitoring Programme, 1984–1987: Results for 1987*, Pollution Report No 28, HMSO, London

Department of the Environment (DoE) (1994) *Digest of Environmental Protection and Water Statistics* No 16, HMSO, London

Department of Health and Social Security (DHSS) (1980) *Lead and Health: The Report of a DHSS Working Party on Lead in the Environment*, HMSO, London

Department of Trade and Industry (DTI) (1993) *Digest of United Kingdom Energy Statistics 1993*, HMSO, London

Department of Transport (DTp) (1987) *Values for Journey Time Savings and Accident Prevention*, Department of Transport, London

Department of Transport (DTp) (1992) *Road Accidents Great Britain 1992: The Casualty Report*, HMSO, London

Department of Transport (DTp) (1993/4) 'Transport Statistics of Great Britain', *Government Statistical Service Publication*, HMSO, London

Department of Transport (DTp) (1993) *Paying for Better Motorways*, HMSO, London

Department of Transport (DTp) (1994) *Design Manual for Roads and Bridges* Vol 11, section 3, part 1, chapter 7: Air Quality, HMSO, London

Department of Transport, (1994), *National Travel Survey: 1991/93*, HMSO, London

Desvouges, W et al (1993) *Review of the Health Effects Resulting From Exposure to Air Pollution*, Research Triangle Institute, Task Force on Externality Costing, Working paper 1 (revised), November, North Carolina

Diekman, A (1991) 'Kosten en Baten van de Auto: Poging tot en Juiste Afweging', *Mobiliteitschrift* Vol 91/7, 8 pp 3–11, Stichting Weg

Digest of Environmental Statistics (1995) No 17, HMSO, London

Dimitriou, H (1993) *Urban Transport Planning*, Routledge, New York

Dockery, D W, C A Pope III, X Xiping, J D Spengler, J H Ware, M Fay, B G Ferris, F E Speizer (1993) 'An Association Between Air Pollution and Mortality in Six US Cities', *The New England Journal of Medicine* 329(4), pp 1753–1808

Dogs et al (1991) 'Externe Kosten des Verkehrs', *Die Bundesbahn*, No 1

Downs, A (1992) *Stuck in Traffic*, Brookings Institute, Washington DC

Dunne, J (1990) *A Comparison of Various Emission Control Technology Cars and their Influence on Exhaust Emissions and Fuel Efficiency*, LR 770 AP, Warren Spring Laboratory, Stevenage

ECOPLAN (1992) *Damage Costs of Air Pollution: A Survey of Existing Estimates*, ECOPLAN, Bern

El–Gasseir, M (1990) *The Potential Benefits and Workability of Pay-As-You-Drive Automobile Insurance*, California Energy Resources and Conservation Commission

Elvik, R (1995) 'The External Costs of Traffic Injury: Definition, Estimation, and Possibilities for Internalization', *Accident Analysis and Prevention* Vol 26 No 6, pp 719–732

Entranco (1992) *Stormwater Runoff Management Report*, Washington State Department of Transportation, Seattle

Eriksson, G (1994) *I stället för biltullar. Trafikavgifter för bättre framkomlighet och renare miljö i Stockholms innerstad*, Naturskyddsföreningen, Stockholm

Evans, A (1992) 'Road Congestion Pricing: When is it a Good Policy?', *Journal of Transport Economics*, September, pp 213–243

Eyre, N J, E Ozdemiroglu, D W Pearce, P Steele (1995) 'Damage Costs of Transport Emissions – Geographical and Fuel Dependence', CSERGE (draft WP) University College London and University of East Anglia

Fankhauser, S (1995) *Valuing Climate Change, The Economics of the Greenhouse*, Earthscan, London

Faucett, J Associates (1992) *The Costs of Owning and Operating Automobiles, Vans and Light Trucks*, FHWA, Washington DC

Frank, J (1989) *The Costs of Alternative Development Patterns*, Urban Land Institute, Washington DC

Freeman, A (1992) *The Measurement of Environmental and Resource Values*, Resources for the Future, Washington DC

Friedrich, R (1995) *External Costs of Road and Rail Transport in West Germany*, Institute for Energiewirshaft, University of Stuttgart

Fwa, T F and B W Ang (1992) 'Estimating Automobile Fuel Consumption in Urban Traffic', *Transportation Research Record 1366*, pp 3–10, Transportation Research Board, National Academy Press

Ghosh, D D Lees and W Seal (1975) 'Optimal Motorway Speed and Some Valuations of Time and Life', *The Manchester School*, Vol 1, March

Glazer, A, D Klein and C Lave (1995) 'Clean on Paper, Dirty on the Road: Troubles with California's South Coast Air Basin', *Journal of Transport Economics and Policy* Vol 29 No 1, pp 85–92

Glickman, T and R Hersh (1995) 'Evaluating Environmental Equity: The Impact of Industrial Hazards on Selected Social Groups in Allegheny County, Pennsylvania', Resources for the Future Discussion Paper 95–13, RFF, Washington DC

Goddard, H (1994) 'Sustainability, Tradeable Permits and the World's Large Cities', mimeo, University of Cincinnati

Goodwin, P B (1992) 'A Review of New Demand Elasticities with Special Reference to Short and Long Run Effects of Price Changes', *Journal of Transport Economics and Policy* Vol 25 No 2, pp 155–169

Göteborgsregionen (1993) *Luftmiljöanalys för Göteborgsregionen*, Göteborgs Regionens Kommunalförbund, Göteborg

Grosclaude, P and N Soguel (1993) 'Valuing Damages to Historic Buildings Using A Contingent Market: A Case Study of Road Traffic Externalities' mimeo, CSERGE, University College London and University of East Anglia

GVF (1993) 'Dienst für Gesamtverkehrsfragen, Die Soziale Kosten des Verkehrs in the Schweiz', GVF–Auftrag 174, Bern

Haight, F (1994) 'Problems in Estimating Comparative Costs of Safety and Mobility', *Journal of Transport Economics and Policy*, January, pp 14–17

Hamburg, J, L Blair and D Albright (1995) 'Mobility as a Right', paper presented at Transportation Research Board 1995 Annual Meeting, Washington DC

Hammarström, U (1992) 'Bransle– och emissionsfaktorer för kallstart och varmkörda motorer' VTI–Notat T119–1992, Väg– och transportforsknings-institutet, Linkotring

Hammar, T (1974) 'Trafikimmissionaers inverkan pa villapriser', unpublished handout, December, Swedish Road Administration

Handy, S (1995) 'Understanding the Link Between Urban Form and Travel Behavior, Transportation Research Board, Annual Meeting' Paper #950691, Washington DC

Hansen, M, D Gillen, A Dobbins, Y Huang and M Puvathingal (1993) *The Air Quality Impacts of Urban Highway Capacity Expansion: Traffic Generation and Land Use Changes*, Institute of Transportation Studies, University of California, Berkeley

Hansson, L (1993) *Vägtrafiken och det trafikpolitiska kostnadsansvaret*, The International Institute for Industrial Environmental Economics, Lund University, Lund

Hansson, L (1995) 'Värdering av trafikbuller', mimeo, The International Institute for Industrial Environmental Economics, Lund University, Lund

Hansson, L and J Markham (1992) *Internalization of External Effects in Transportation*, Project Report C6Z5 External Effects, UIC–C6, Strategic Planning Committee, Paris

Hardin, G (1969) 'The Tragedy of the Commons', *Science*, November

Harrington, W and P Portney (1987) 'Valuing the Benefits of Health and Safety Regulations', *Journal Of Urban Economics* Vol 22, pp 101–112

Hassel, D and F–J Weber (1993) 'Mean emissions and fuel consumption of vehicles in use with different emission reduction concepts' *The Science of the Total Environment* 134, pp 189–95

Hatzakis, A, K Katsouyanni, A Kalandidi, N Day, D Trichopoulos (1986) 'Short–term Effects of Air Pollution on Mortality in Athens', *International Journal of Epidemiology* Vol 15 No 1, International Epidemiological Association, London

Hau, T (1990) 'Electronic Road Pricing Developments in Hong Kong 1983–1989', *Journal of Transport Economics*, May

Hillman, H (1988) 'Foul Play for Children: A Price of Mobility', *Town And Country Planning*, October, pp 331–332

Hillman, H, J Adams and J Whitelegg (1990) 'One False Move: A Study of Childrens' Independent Mobility', Policy Studies Institute, London

HMSO (1994) *Climate Change: The UK Programme*, HMSO, London

Holden, D (1989) 'Wardrop's Third Principal', *Journal of Transport Economics and*

Policy, 9/89

Holman, C, J Wade and M Fergusson (1993) *Future Emissions from Cars 1990 to 2025: The importance of the cold start emission penalty*, World Wide Fund for Nature UK, Godalming

Homburger, Kell and Perkins (1992) *Fundamentals of Traffic Engineering*, Institute of Transportation Studies, University of California, Berkeley

Hook, W (1993) 'Are Bicycles Making Japan More Competitive?', *Sustainable Transport*, Summer

Hort, K and U Persson (1985) 'Vad kostade 1982 ars vägtrafikolyckor?, IHE meddelande 1982:4', Institutet för hälso– och sjukvardsekonomi, Stockholm

House of Commons Environmental Committee Report (1995), House of Commons, London

House of Commons Transport Committee (1994) 'Transport–Related Air Pollution in London', Session 1993/94, 6th Report, Vol 1, HMSO, London

Hubbard, H (1991) 'The Real Cost of Energy', *Scientific American* Vol 264 No 4

Hughes, P (1993) *Personal Transport and the Greenhouse Effect*, Earthscan, London

Infraconsult AG (1992) 'Soziale Kosten des Verkehrslärms in der Schweiz, Schlussbericht' GVF–Auftrag 191, Bern

Institute of Petroleum (1994) *UK Petroleum Industry Statistics: Consumption and Refinery Production 1990–1993*, Insitute of Petroleum, London

Intergovernmental Panel on Climate Change (IPCC) (1990) *Climate Change 1992: The IPCC Scientific Assessment*, Cambridge University Press, Cambridge

Intergovernmental Panel on Climate Change (IPCC) (1992) *Climate Change 1992: The Supplementary Report to the IPCC Scientific Assessment*, Cambridge University Press, Cambridge

Iten and Maggi (1995) cited in Pearce (1995), op cit

James, H (no date) 'Under Reporting of Road Traffic Accidents', Transport and Road Research Laboratory, Department of Transport, London

Jansson, J O (1994) 'Accident Externality Charges', *Journal of Transport Economics and Policy*, Vol 28 pp 31–43

Jeanrenaud (1992) 'Monetary Valuation of Social Costs of Urban Transport: A Case Study of Neuchatel', Insitute of Economic and Regional Research WP 92-08, University of Neuchatel

Johansson, B and L–G Mattsson (eds) (1995) *Road Pricing: Theory, Empirical Assessment and Policy*, Kluwer Academic Publishers, Amsterdam

Johansson, O (1995) 'Optimal road pricing with respect to accidents in a 2nd–best perspective', mimeo, Department of Economics, University of Göteborg, Göteborg

Johansson, P–O (1987) *The Economic Theory and Measurement of Environmental Benefits*, Cambridge University Press, Cambridge

Johnson, E (1993) *Avoiding the Collision of Cities and Cars*, National Academy of Arts and Sciences, Chicago

Johnson, P, S Mackay and S Smith (1990) 'The Distributional Consequences of Environmental Taxes', *Institute for Fiscal Studies Commentary*, No 23 p 55

Johnston, R and R Ceerla (1994) 'A Comparison of Modelling Travel Demand and Emissions With and Without Assigned Travel Times Fed Back to Trip Distribution', Institute of Transportation Studies, University of California at Davis. Submitted to the Journal of Transportation Engineering

Jones–Lee, M W (1985) 'The Value of Safety: Results from a National Sample Survey', *Economic Journal* 95, pp 49–72

Jones–Lee, M W (1989) *The Economics of Safety and Physical Risk*, Basil Blackwell, Oxford

Jones–Lee, M W (1990) 'The Value of Transport Safety', *Oxford Review of Economic Policy* Vol 6 No 2, pp 39–58

Jones–Lee, M W (1992) 'The Value of Transport Safety', *Oxford Review of Economic Policy* Vol 6, No 2, pp 39–59

Jones–Lee, M W, G Loomes, D O'Reilly and P Philips (1993) 'The Value of Preventing Non–fatal Road Injuries: Findings of a Willingness to Pay National

Sample Survey', Working Paper SRC/2, Transport and Road Research Laboratory, Crowthorne

Jones–Lee, M W and G Loomes (1994) 'The Transferability of Willingness–to–Pay Based Values of Life and Safety,' paper for the GECB meeting, 5 December, London

Kågeson, P (1992) 'External Costs of Air Pollution. The Case for European Transports', *Transport and Environment* 92/7, Stockholm

Kågeson, P (1993) 'Getting the Prices Right. A European Scheme for Making Transport Pay its True Cost', *Transport and Environment* 93/6, Stockholm

Keeler, T et al (1975) *The Full Costs of Urban Transport; Intermodal Comparisons*, Institute of Urban and Regional Development, University of California, Berkeley

Kinney, P L and H Ozkaynak (1991) 'Associations of Daily Mortality and Air Pollution in Los Angeles County', *Environmental Research* Vol 54 pp 99–120

Kinney, P L and H Ozkaynak (1992) 'Associations Between Ozone and Daily Mortality in Los Angeles and New York City', *American Review of Respiratory Disease* Vol 145 (4:2):A95

Kirkby, A (1972), 'Perception of Air Pollution as a Hazard and Individual Adjustment to it in Exeter, Sheffield and London', unpublished paper prepared for the Man-Environment Commission Symposium of the International Geographical Union (Calgary, 23–31 July, 1972), cited in J Taylor (1974), 'Climatic Resources and Economic Activity', David and Charles: Newton Abbot, Devon

Komanoff, C (1995) 'Pollution Taxes for Roadway Transportation', *Pace Environmental Law Review*

Krause, F, W Bach and J Kooney (1989) *Energy Policy in the Greenhouse, International Policy for Sustainable Energy Paths*, El Cerito, California

Krupnick, A J (1986) 'A Preliminary Benefits Analysis of the Control of Photochemical Oxidants', report prepared for the US Environmental Protection Agency, Washington DC

Krupnick, A J and M L Cropper (1989) 'Valuing Chronic Morbidity Damages: Medical Costs, Labor Market Effects, and Individual Valuations', Final report to the US Environmental Protection Agency, Office of Policy Analysis, Washington DC

Lambert et al (1986), cited in Barde and Button (1990) op cit

Lamure (1990) cited in Mayeres (1993) op cit

Laurikko, J, L Erlandsson and R Abrahamsson (1995) 'Exhaust Emission in Cold Ambient Conditions; Considerations for a European Test Procedure', SAE–paper, VTT, MTC, SNV

Layard, R (1977) 'The Distributional Effects of Congestion Taxes', *Economica* Vol 44 pp 297–304

Lee, D (1995) *Full–Cost Pricing of Highways*, Velope National Transportation Centre, Cambridge, Mass

Leitch, G (1977) Report to the Advisory Committee on Trunk Road Assessment, HMSO, London

Leksell, I and L Löfgren (1995) 'Valuation of the local effects of air pollution'/'Värdering av lokala luftföroreningseffekter' How to place monetary values on health effects of exhaust emissions in urban areas, Swedish Communication Research Board, in Swedish but with a six-page English summary, KFB–rapport 1995:5, Stockholm

Levinson, H (1995) 'Freeway Congestion Pricing: Another Look', *Transportation Research Record* No 1450, pp 8–12

Lewis, D (1993) *Road Pricing: Theory and Practise*, Thomas Telford, London

Lindberg, G (1995) 'Road Pricing: Policy and options for the future' in B Johansson and L–G Mattson (eds) *Road Pricing: Theory, Empirical assessment and Policy*, pp 205–221, Kluwer, Amsterdam

Litman, T (1995a) *Transportation Cost Analysis; Techniques, Estimates and Implications*, Victoria Transport Policy Institute, Victoria, BC

Litman, T (1995b) *Housing Requirement Impacts on Housing Affordability*, Victoria Transport Policy Institute, Victoria, BC

Litman, T (1995c) *Calculating Generated Traffic External Costs*, Victoria Transport Policy Institute, Victoria, BC

Loehman, E T, S V Berg, A A Arroyo, R A Hedinger, J M Schwartz, M E Shaw, R W Fahien, V H De, R P Fishe, D E Rio, W F Rossley and A E S Green (1979) 'Distributional Analysis of Regional Benefits and Costs of Air Quality Control', *Journal of Environmental Economics and Management* Vol 6 pp 222–243

MacKenzie, J J, R C Dower and D D T Chen (1992) *The Going Rate: What It Really Costs To Drive*, World Resources Institute, Washinton DC

Mackintosh, I (1994) *Implications of Information Technology* delivered at a seminar entitled Hard Choices in Transport Policy, University College London

McCarthy, P and R Tay (1993) 'Economic Efficiency vs Traffic Restraint; A Note on Singapore's Area Licence Scheme', *Journal of Urban Economics* 34, pp 96–100

McWilliams, D (1994) cited by P Goodwin in 'Traffic Growth and the Dynamics of Sustainable Transport Policies', Linacre Lectures 1994–95, Oxford

Maddison, D (1993) 'The Shadow Price of Greenhouse Gases and Aerosols', CSERGE, University College London and University of East Anglia

Maddison, D (1996) 'Avertive Behaviour, Air Pollution and the Economics of the Barrier Effect', mimeo, Centre for Social and Economic Research into the Global Environment, University College London and University of East Anglia

Mayeres, I (1993) 'The Marginal External Cost of Car Use – With an Application to Belgium', *Tijdschrift voor Economie en management* Vol 38, No 3, pp 225–258

Metz, R (1993) 'Emission Characteristics of Different Combustion Engines in the City, on Rural Roads and on Highways', *The Science of the Total Environment* 134, pp 225–235

Michaelis, L (1993) 'Global Warming Impacts of Transport', *The Science of the Total Environment* 134, pp 117–124

Miller, P and J Moffet (1993) *The Price of Mobility*, National Resources Defense Council, Washington DC

Miller, T (1991) *The Costs of Highway Crashes*, publication No FHWA–RD–055, FHWA, Washington DC

Miller, T (1994) presentation at the FHWA Social Costs of Transport Colloquium, December, mimeo, Washington DC

Miller, T and Li (1994) 'An Investigation of the Costs of Roadway Traffic Congestion', California PATH, University of California, Berkeley

Mishan, E J (1971) 'The Postwar Literature on Externalities: An Interpretative Essay', *Journal of Economic Literature* Vol 9, pp 1–28

Mitchell, R C and R T Carson (1989) *Using Surveys to Value Public Goods: The Contingent Valuation Method*, Resources for the Future, Washington DC

Moore, M R, B C Campbell and A Goldberg (1990) 'Lead' in J Lenihan and W F Fletcher (eds) *The Chemical Environment*, Blackie, Glasgow, pp 64–92

Moore, T and P Thorsnes (1993) 'The Transporation/Land Use Connection: A Framework for Practical Policy Report' No 448/449, American Planning Association, Chicago

MVA Consultancy (1995) *The London Congestion Charging Research Programme: Principal Findings*, HMSO, London

National Economic Development Office (NEDO) (1991) 'A Road User Charge? Londoners' Views', Harris Research Centre, London

National Personal Transportation Survey (NPTS) (1992) *Summary of Travel Trends*, USDOT, Washington DC

Nelson, A (1982) 'Highway, Noise and Property Values', *Journal of Transport Economics and Policy* May, pp 117–138

Newbery, D (1988) 'Road Damage Externalities and Road User Charges', *Econometrica* 56(2), pp 295–316

Newbery, D (1992) 'Economic Principles Relevent to Pricing Roads', *Oxford Review of Economic Policy* 6(2)

Newbery, D (1995) 'Royal Commission Report on Transport and the Environment – An Economic Critique', mimeo, University of Cambridge, Cambridge

Office of Population Censuses and Surveys (1990) *The Dietary and Nutritional Survey of British Adults: A survey of the dietary behaviour, nutritional status and blood pressure of adults aged 16 to 64 living in Great Britain*, HMSO, London

Office of Population Censuses and Surveys (1992) *Key Population and Vital Statistics Series* VS No 19

Office of Technology Assessment (OTA) (1994) 'Saving Energy in US Transportation', US Congress, July 1994, Washington DC

Ohtoshi, T et al (1994) Allergy and Clinical Immunology, *News Supplement 2*, p 264

Organization for Economic Cooperation and Development (OECD) (1991) *Fighting Noise in the 1990s*, OECD, Paris

Organization for Economic Cooperation and Development (OECD) (1993) *Environmental Data Compendium 1993*, OECD, Paris

Organization for Economic Cooperation and Development (OECD) (1994) *Project and Policy Appraisal: Integrating Economics and the Environment*, OECD, Paris

Ostro, B (1994) 'Estimating the Health Effects of Air Pollution: A Methodology with an Application to Jakarta Policy' WP 1301, World Bank, Washington DC

Otterström, T (1995) 'Valuation of the Impacts from Road Traffic Fuel Emissions', *Ekono Energy Limited*, Espoo, Finland

Parliamentary Office of Science and Technology (POST) (1994) *Breathing in Our Cities – Urban Air Pollution and Respiratory Health*, POST, London

Pearce, D W (1993) *Blueprint 3: Towards Sustainable Development*, Earthscan, London

Pearce, D W (1995) 'Social Costs of Road Transport', mimeo, CSERGE, University College London and University of East Anglia

Pearce, D W and A Markandya (1989) *Environmental Policy Benefits: Monetary Valuation*, OECD, Paris

Pearce, D W and I Knight (1992) 'Valuing Non–Fatal Injury Costs', paper prepared for UK Department of Transport seminar on non–fatal injuries, mimeo, London

Pearce, D W and T Cowards (1995) 'Assessing the Health Costs of Particulate Air Pollution in the UK', CSERGE, University College London and University of East Anglia

Pearce et al (1994) *Blueprint 3: Measuring Sustainable Development*, Earthscan, London

Peat Marwick Stevenson & Kellogg (PMSK) (1993) 'The Cost of Transporting People in the British Columbia Lower Mainland, Greater Vancouver Regional District', Vancouver, March

Peirson, J and R Vickerman (1994) 'The MicroEconomic Analysis of the External Costs of Road Accidents', Discussions Paper No 9416, Centre for European, Regional and Transport Economics, University of Kent

Persson, U (1992) *Three Economic Approaches to Valuing Benefits of Traffic Safety Measures*, Institutet för hälso– och sjukvårdsekonomi (IHE), Stockholm

Persson, U and K Odegaard (1993) 'Estimates of external costs of road traffic accidents in Denmark, Finland, Sweden, Switzerland, the UK and West Germany 1990/91' WP 1993:8, Swedish Institute for Health Economics, Lund

Pickrell, D (1993) 'Eliminating Employer–Subsidized Parking' in *Climate Change Mitigation: Transport Options*, National Transportation Research Centre, Cambridge, Mass

Pirkel, J L, J Schwartz, J R Landis and W R Harlan (1985) 'The Relationship between Blood Lead Levels and Blood Pressure and its Cardiovascular Risk Implications', *American Journal of Epidemiology* 21, pp 246–258

Pommerehne (1988) in Pearce (1995), op cit

Pooling Project Research Group (1978) 'Relationship of blood pressure, serum cholesterol, smoking habit, relative weight and ECGT abnormalities to incidence of major coronary events: final report of the pooling project', *Journal of Chronic Disease* 31, pp 201–306

Quality of Urban Air Review Group (QUARG) (1993) 'Diesel Vehicle Emissions and Urban Air Quality', Second Report, December, prepared for the Department of the Environment

Quinet, E (1989) 'Evaluations du coût social des transports' in Proceedings of the Fifth World Conference on Transport Research, Yokohama

Quinet, E (1990) ' The Social Costs of Land Transport' mimeo, OECD, Paris

Quinet, E (1994) in OECD (1994), op cit

RAC (1994) Information Pack, Royal Automobile Association, London

Ratcliffe, J M (1981) *Lead in Man and the Environment*, Ellis Horwood, Chichester

Rietveld, P (1989) 'Infrastructure and Regional Development: A Study of Multiregional Economic Models', *Annals of Regional Science* Vol 23, pp 255–274

Rijksinstituut voor Volksgezondheid en Milieuhygiëne (RIVM) (1993) *Nationale Milieuverkenning 3 1993–2015*, Samsom H D Tjeenk Willink, Alphen aan den Rijn

Rothengatter, W (1994) 'Do External Benefits Compensate for External Costs of Transport?', *Transportation Research* 28A(4), pp 321–328

Rothengatter, W and S Mauch (1994) 'External Effects of Transport', Union Internationale des Chemin de Fers, Paris

Rowe, R D, L Chestnut, C Lang, S Bernow, D White (1995) 'The New York Environmental Externalities Cost Study: Summary of the Approach and Results', paper presented to EC, IEA and OECD Workshop on External Costs of Energy, Brussels, 30–31 January

Royal Commission on Environmental Pollution (1994) Eighteenth Report: Transport and the Environment Cm 2674, HMSO, London

Sælensminde, K (1992) *Environmental Costs Caused by Road Traffic in Urban Areas*, Institute for Transport Economics, Oslo

Sælensminde, K and F Hammer (1994) 'Verdsetting av miljøgoder ved bruk av samvalgsanalyse', Rapport 251/1994, Institute for Transport Economics, Oslo

Sainsbury's Retail Group (1995) 'New Sainsbury's Fuel Will Reduce Traffic Pollution', Sainsbury's City Diesel Press Release, January 1995

Sandmo, A (1975) 'Optimal taxation in the presence of externalities', *Swedish Journal of Economics* Vol 77, pp 86–98

Sandmo, A (1976) 'Optimal Taxation: An Introduction to the Literature', *Journal of Public Economics* Vol 6, pp 37–54

Schwartz J (1994) 'Air Pollution and Daily Mortality: A Review and Meta Analysis', Environmental Research 64, pp 36–52

Schwartz, J and S Zeger (1990) 'Passive Smoking, Air Pollution, and Acute Respiratory Symptoms in a Diary Study of Student Nurses', *American Review of Respiratory Disease* Vol 141, pp 62–67

Schwartz, J, D Wypij, D Dockery, J Ware, S Zeger, J Splenger, B Ferris Jr (1991) 'Daily Diaries of Respiratory Symptoms and Air Pollution: Methodological Issues and Results', *Environmental Health Perspectives* Vol 90, pp 181–187

Schwartz, J and D Dockery (1992) 'Increased Mortality in Philadelphia Associated with Daily Air Pollution Concentrations', *American Review of Respiratory Disease* Vol 145, pp 600–604

Scitovsky, T (1954) 'Two Concepts of External Economies', *Journal of Political Economy* Vol 17, pp 143–151

Seaton A, W Macnee, K Donaldson and D Godden (1995) 'Particulate Air Pollution and Acute Health Effects', *The Lancet* Vol 345, 21 January, pp 176–178

Shell UK (1995) 'Unleaded Petrol – Who should use it and why', media briefing, 6 January

Shoup, D (1994) Cashing Out Employer–Paid Parking: A Precedent for Congestion Pricing, Curbing Gridlock, National Academy Press, Washington DC pp 153–199

Shurtleff, D (1974) 'Some Characteristics Related to the Incidence of Cardiovascular Disease and Death: the Framingham Study, 18 year follow up, Section 30' DHEW

Publication No. (NIH) 74–599, Department of Health Education and Welfare, Washington DC

Small, K (1983) 'Bus Priority and Congestion Pricing on Urban Expressways', Research in Transport Economics Vol 1, pp 27–74

Small, K (1992) Urban Transportation Economics, Harwood, Chur

Small, K and Camilla Kazimi (1995) 'On the Costs of Air Pollution from Motor Vehicles', Journal of Transport Economics and Policy, January, pp 7–32

Smith, S (1992) 'The Distributional Consequences of Taxes on Energy and the Carbon Content of Fuels', European Economy Special Edition No 1, pp 241–269

Snyder, M (1994) 'The Social Costs of Traffic Congestion', unpublished disseration, University College London

Soguel, N (1991) 'Evaluation du coût social du bruit Genève par le traffique routier en ville de Neuchatel', Insitute of Economic and Regional Research, WP 91-05, University of Neuchatel

Soguel, N (1994) 'Measuring Benefits from Traffic Noise Reduction Using a Contingent Market', CSERGE WP GEC 94–03, University College London and University of East Anglia

Soguel, N, (1994), 'Costing The Traffic Barrier Effect: A Contingent Valuation Survey', mimeo, Institute de recherches economique et regionales (IRER), Université de Neuchatel

South East Institute of Public Health (1995) Air Quality in London 1994, London

Standing Advisory Committee on Trunk Road Assessment (SACTRA) (1994) Trunk Roads and the Generation of Traffic, HMSO, London

Statistics Sweden (1993) Trafikskador 1992, Stockholm

Sterner, T (1994) 'Environmental Tax Reform: The Swedish Experience', European Environment, 4(6) pp 20–25

Swedish Car Industry Association (1994) Bilismen i Sverige 1994, Bilindustriföreningen, AB Bilstatistik, Stockholm

Swedish Department of Communication (1987) DsK 1987: Den tunga vägtrafikens kostnader, Stockholm

Swedish Department of Communication (1994a) SOU 1994:91 Trafiken och koldioxiden. Principer för att minska trafikens koldioxidutsläpp. Delbetänkande av trafik– och klimatlommittén, Stockholm

Swedish Department of Communication (1994b) SOU 1994:142 Vägtullar i Stockholmsregionen, Stockholm

Swedish Department of the Environment (1993) SOU 1993:65 Handlingsplan mot buller, Betänkande av utredningen för en handlingsplan mot buller, Stockholm

Swedish Department of the Environment (1994) SOU 1994:111 Bilars miljöklassning och EU, Delbetänkande av miljöklassutredningen, Stockholm

Swedish Department of the Environment (1995) SOU 1995:31 Ett vidareutvecklat miljöklassystem i EU, Delbetänkande av miljöklassutredningen, Stockholm

Swedish Department of Finance (1992) SOU 1992:53 Skatt på dieselolja, Betänkande an utredningen om beskattningen av dieseldrivna fordon, Stockholm

Swedish Environmental Protection Agency (1993a) Trafik och Miljö Underlagsrapport till aktionsprogram, Stockholm

Swedish Environmental Protection Agency (1993b) Utsläpp till luft av försurande ämnen 1992, Naturvårdsverket rapport 4272, Stockholm

Swedish Road Administration (1986) Investment in Roads and Streets, Borlange

Swedish Road Administration (1992) Reviderade värderingar 1993–2004, PM, Borlange

Swedish Road Administration (1993) EVA, Effektberäkning vid Väganalyser, version 1.1, Borlänge

Tolley, G S et al (1986) 'Valuations of Reductions in Human Health Symptoms and Risks' prepared at the University of Chicago, Final Report for the US Environmental Protection Agency, January

Transek (1990) Avgifter i trafiksystemen, Transek Consultancy Inc, Stockholm

Transek (1993) Värdering av miljöfaktorer, Transek Consultancy Inc, Stockholm

Trivector (1992) Användarmanual för AIG/S, VTI Linköping and Trivektor Lund

United States Environmental Protection Agency (USEPA) (1986) 'Air Quality Criteria for Lead EPA 600/8–83–028 a–f, Environmental Criteria and Assessment Office', Office of Research and Development, Research Triangle Park, North Carolina

United States Environmental Protection Agency (USEPA) (1994) PART-5 (software for calculating vehicle particulate emissions), Washington DC

van Gent, H A and P Rietveld (1993) 'Road Transport and the Environment in Europe', The Science of the Total Environment 129, pp 205–218

van Kooten, C (1993) Land Resource Economics and Sustainable Development, University of British Columbia Press, Vancouver

Verhoef, E T (1994a) 'External Effects and Social Costs of Road Transport', Transportation Research Vol 28A, No 4

Verhoef, E T (1994b) 'Efficiency and Equity in Externalities: A Partial Equilibrium Analysis', Environment and Planning A Vol 26, pp 361–382

Verhoef, E T, P Nijkamp and P Rietveld (1995) 'The Trade–Off between Efficiency, Effectiveness and Social Feasibility of Regulating Road Transport Externalities', TRACE discussion paper TI 95–11, Tinbergen Institute, Amsterdam–Rotterdam. Forthcoming in Transportation Planning and Technology

Vickrey, W (1968) 'Automobile Accidents, Tort Law, Externalities and Insurance: An Economist's Critique', Journal of Contemporary Law and Problems, pp 464–84

Viner, J (1931) 'Cost Curves and Supply Curves', Zeitschrift für Nationalökonomie Vol 3, pp 23–46

Virley (1993) 'The Effect of Fuel Price Increases on Road Transport', Transport Policy Vol 1 No 1, pp 43–84

Viscusi, W K, W A Magat, J Huber (1991) 'Pricing Environmental Health Risks: Survey Assessments of Risk–Risk and Risk–Dollar Trade–offs for Chronic Bronchitis', Journal of Environmental Economics and Management Vol 21(1), pp 32–51

VitaliaNo, D F and J Held (1991) 'Road Accident External Effects: An empirical assessment', Applied Economics Vol 23, pp 373–378

Walters, A (1961) 'The Theory and Management of Private and Social Costs of Highway Congestion', Econometrica Vol 29, pp 676–699

Waters, W (1992) 'The Value of Time Savings for the Economic Evaluation of Highways Investments in British Columbia', Ministry of Transportation and Highways, Victoria, BC

Whitelegg, J (1993) 'Transport For A Sustainable Future', Belhaven Press, London

Willson, R (1995) 'Suburban Parking Requirements: A Tacit Policy for Automobile Use and Sprawl', Journal of the American Planning Association Vol 61 No 1, Winter, pp 29–42

Wolff, S P (1993) 'Does Environmental Benzene Exposure Cause Childhood Leukaemia?', paper to Conference on Volatile Organic Compounds in the Environment, 491–501, 27–28 October, London

Wooton, J and M Poulton (1993) 'Reducing carbon dioxide emissions from passenger cars to 1990 levels: a discussion paper', Transport Research Laboratory, September 1993

World Resources Institute (1992) World Resources 1992–3, Oxford University Press, Oxford

Index